COMICS AND CATHARSIS

COMICS AND CATHARSIS

EXPLORING GRAPHIC NARRATIVES OF TRAUMA AND HEALING

EDITED BY JORDAN TRONSGARD

UNIVERSITY PRESS OF MISSISSIPPI / JACKSON

The University Press of Mississippi is the scholarly publishing agency of the Mississippi Institutions of Higher Learning: Alcorn State University, Delta State University, Jackson State University, Mississippi State University, Mississippi University for Women, Mississippi Valley State University, University of Mississippi, and University of Southern Mississippi.

www.upress.state.ms.us

The University Press of Mississippi is a member of the Association of University Presses.

Publication of this book was supported in part by funding from Bishop's University.

Copyright © 2025 by University Press of Mississippi
All rights reserved
Manufactured in the United States of America

∞

Publisher: University Press of Mississippi, Jackson, USA
Authorised GPSR Safety Representative: Easy Access System Europe – Mustamäe tee 50, 10621 Tallinn, Estonia, gpsr.requests@easproject.com

Library of Congress Cataloging-in-Publication Data

Names: Tronsgard, Jordan editor
Title: Comics and catharsis : exploring graphic narratives of trauma and healing / edited by Jordan Tronsgard.
Description: Jackson : University Press of Mississippi, 2025. | Includes bibliographical references and index.
Identifiers: LCCN 2025018673 (print) | LCCN 2025018674 (ebook) | ISBN 9781496858931 hardback | ISBN 9781496858948 trade paperback | ISBN 9781496858955 epub | ISBN 9781496858962 epub | ISBN 9781496858979 pdf | ISBN 9781496858986 pdf
Subjects: LCSH: Psychic trauma in comics | LCGFT: Comics criticism | Essays Classification: LCC PN6714 .C6475 2025 (print) | LCC PN6714 (ebook) | DDC 741.5/9—dc23/eng/20250416
LC record available at https://lccn.loc.gov/2025018673
LC ebook record available at https://lccn.loc.gov/2025018674

British Library Cataloging-in-Publication Data available

TO XAVIER AND MAËLLE.
Keep drawing and writing and reading.

CONTENTS

ACKNOWLEDGMENTS ix

I. INTRODUCTION 3
    JORDAN TRONSGARD

II. DRAWING APART: PHYSICAL AND GENERATIONAL SEPARATION AND BELONGING

· **CHAPTER 1.** From Confinement to Catharsis:
Reading the Comics Aesthetic in Manuel H. Martín's Documentary
30 años de oscuridad/30 Years of Darkness 21
    JENNIFER NAGTEGAAL

· **CHAPTER 2.** Graphic Representations of Violence in
La herencia del coronel by Carlos Trillo and Lucas Varela 48
    DIANA PIFANO

· **CHAPTER 3.** On the Threshold of Being and Belonging:
Refiguring History in Autobiographical Comics 69
    KAY SOHINI

III. DRAWING TOGETHER: NATION AND NARRATIVE

· **Chapter 4.** The Burden of Translating History in Li Kunwu's
A Chinese Life 97
    ANGIE CHAU

· **Chapter 5.** "American God" to a Soviet Superman:
Exploring the Cathartic Function of Counterfactual Narratives 121
    AANCHAL VIJ

- Chapter 6. Re-Framing (Post-)Soviet Ukrainian History: Walter Duranty, Igort's *The Ukrainian Notebooks*, and the Ethics of Graphic Reportage 142
    ANASTASIA ULANOWICZ

IV. DRAWING CLOSE: INDIVIDUAL, INTIMATE, AND TRAUMATIC

- Chapter 7. Alison Bechdel's *Fun Home* and the Impossibility of Testimony 165
    KELLY BARON

- Chapter 8. Graphic Novels and Sexual Trauma: Processing Sexual Trauma Through Creative Expression 185
    LEE OKAN

- Chapter 9. The Good Empty: Trauma, Displacement, and Catharsis in *Sabrina* 211
    RUSSELL SAMOLSKY

V. CONCLUSION 230
    JORDAN TRONSGARD

LIST OF CONTRIBUTORS 233

INDEX 237

ACKNOWLEDGMENTS

This edited volume has been shaped from conception to completion by the COVID-19 global pandemic. From health concerns to lockdowns and quarantines, there were delays and delays and delays at every step of the writing, editing, and peer review process. There were moments when I wanted to quit the project. There were moments when I wanted to quit academia. But I also believed, and still do, in the power of comics. And I believed that we had something valuable to contribute to how we think and talk about comics. At turns, this was the most rewarding and the most frustrating project of my career. I would like to thank the following people for helping the former overcome the latter and for being lights in what was often a dark time.

Above all, I would like to thank the excellent contributors to the volume: Kelly Baron, Angie Chau, Jennifer Nagtegaal, Lee Okan, Diana Pifano, Russell Samolsky, Kay Sohini, Anastasia Ulanowicz, and Aanchal Vij. This work is your work. Its value is the value of your contributions. In addition to recognizing the excellent quality of your work, I would also like to thank you for your patience and understanding throughout. Thank you for sticking with the volume. And thank you for writing about comics.

Thank you to Katie Keene and your team at the University Press of Mississippi. Thank you for believing that this volume matters; I am grateful for the support and encouragement that you have shown to this project. Despite all the COVID-related obstacles along the way, I appreciate how easy and stress-free you made the publication process. I would also like to thank the anonymous peer-reviewers. Your insights and suggestions helped shape and improve the volume in ways I would not have otherwise considered. I do not know who you are, but this volume is better because of you.

I live in a small college town. I am not from here; most of us are not from here. I would like to thank my people for making this place home. To my colleague in Hispanic Studies, Gilberto. We are a team! To Leigh, Anthony, Rob, Jessica, François, Melanie, Steve, and Amber, thanks for community, for being a family away from family. Anthony DiMascio, one positive of the COVID lockdowns was getting to know you better as our kids played together outside when there was nothing else to do. Thank you for listening, sharing, commiserating, and generally just making it a more bearable time. Finally, I would like to thank Steve Cole and Jenn Cianca. I love that we can have erudite discussions one moment and then laugh at a Daffy Duck gif the next. I love you two; your friendship is a sustaining energy in my life.

In closing, I would like to thank my family. Maëlle and Xavier, thank you for being you, you kind, funny, smart, creative, beautiful weirdos. This book is dedicated to you. And to my wife, Kristen, the most difficult acknowledgment of all. There is so much for which I am thankful that it is hard to find the right words. This was a challenging project during a challenging time. You supported me, made me laugh, and listened when I was frustrated or sad. I hope I have done the same for you, as we are partners. You are a force for good in my life. You are a force for good in this world.

COMICS AND CATHARSIS

I.

INTRODUCTION

JORDAN TRONSGARD

This volume seeks to better understand the relationship between comics and pain/healing. Many well-known comics feature pain. Art Spiegelman's *Maus* (1980–1991), Marjane Satrapi's *Persepolis* (2000, 2004), Alison Bechdel's *Fun Home* (2006), to cite a few well-known examples, are marked by individual and collective traumas. But it is not just the canonical texts; many writers and illustrators and readers come to trauma through comics. In my case, I came to comics through trauma. My work focuses on twentieth-century Spain's national traumas: the Spanish Civil War (1936–1939), the subsequent dictatorship of Francisco Franco, and the transition to democracy following Franco's death in 1975. This collective wound is a matrix of individual stories of suffering, memories, and attempts from the present to understand a past not personally lived but inherent to how younger generations view themselves and their nation. And this engagement is taking place in comics. While the subject of "historical memory," the term commonly used in Spain in reference to the war/dictatorship eras, became less present in novels and films at the end of the first decade of the 2000s after a period of proliferation, comics has become more and more the medium for confronting the nation's painful past. Writers have told their stories, their family's stories, and fictional stories set during the periods in question through frames, text bubbles, silence, and all the other possibilities afforded by the multifaceted visual/textual nature of the medium.

Of course, depictions of trauma through comics are not unique to Spain. Indeed, references to 2009's *El arte de volar* (*The art of flying*) by Antonio Altarriba and illustrated by Kim,[1] a graphic memoir of Altarriba's father's life and suicide as a ninety-year-old man, tend to include some reference to *Maus* and how both works exemplify a creator using comics to explore their fathers' traumatic experiences. Researching trauma in Spanish comics often means finding references to *Maus* but also to *Persepolis*, *Fun home*, and many others. These are texts from different cultures, written in different languages, about different manifestations of trauma. But they are all comics. In the introduction to his edited volume *Trauma and Literature* (2008) J. Roger Kurtz begins with the succinct statement: "We live in an age of trauma" (1). To that, I would add that we also live in an age of comics. Not only is there "the unparalleled productivity of comics publishing," (591) as mentioned by Ramzi Fawaz in his contribution to a discussion on Hillary Chute's *Why Comics?* (2017) in a 2019 edition of the prestigious literary journal *PMLA*, there is the fact itself that *PMLA* is giving visibility to comics and comics scholarship.[2] I am not suggesting that *PMLA* validates comics studies—as Fawaz also states, "the demand that scholars must ceaselessly prove or legitimize comics's literary merit is an intellectually bankrupt project, reflecting a self-destructive cynicism in literary studies" (593)—but rather that if we do live in an age of trauma, comics has emerged as a significant voice in discussions about it.

Trauma is a word of Greek origin, meaning wound. While traumatic experiences may include literal, physical wounds, our understanding of the concept here also includes the psychological pain and devastation that arises during and, crucially for the question of trauma narratives, following the events as the resulting physical and psychological wounds are processed. The primary question addressed by this volume is how comics engage with the processing of trauma through its depictions and receptions. Specifically, what is the role of catharsis in the writing, illustrating, and reader-response of trauma in comics? Like trauma, catharsis is also a word of Greek origin, meaning purification or cleansing. Together, the implication is that a wound, unclean, festers; while a wound that has been made pure can heal. Returning to the examples of *El arte de volar* and *Maus*, Ana Merino and Brittany Tullis assert that the authors/sons of these works view their research and writing practices "as a form of therapy" that helps in "overcoming [their] personal traumas" (221–22). In other words, are these graphic memoirs of inherited trauma narratives of catharsis as well as pain? Are comics drawing and cleaning wounds at the same time? While I will go into catharsis in more detail toward the end of the introduction, in the service of framing these questions, it is helpful to consider Richard Kearney's description of the concept: "In short, catharsis invites us a) beyond a pathology of pity to compassion and b) beyond a pathology of fear to serenity. It literally *purges* two of our most basic affects—*pathos* and *eleos*—until they are distilled and sublimated into a healing brew" (italics in the original; 52). For whom is the healing brew? The creator? The reader? Both? Neither? If it is for the reader, is the catharsis of their own personal trauma, whether shared by the content of the work or not, or is the catharsis vicarious?[3] And finally, if we assert that comics do constitute a space for cathartic engagement, what is it about the medium that makes it well-suited for confronting trauma—be it collective and/or personal, relational and/or political, etc.? Why and how? These are the questions with which the essays in this volume engage.

In his groundbreaking comics essay on comics, Scott McCloud states that "the world of comics is a huge and varied one" (4). The chapters in this collection bear out this fact as each examines texts with different characteristics in different genres from different cultural and linguistic origins. All deal with trauma and all are comics; beyond that, the diversity of representation within the medium is on display. While many of the primary works here would be categorized as "graphic novels,"[4] I prefer to avoid the pitfalls and controversy behind any discussion of the medium's taxonomy and use the term "comics" as a cover-all.[5]

If comics as a medium is vast and diverse, so too is the experience of trauma. And yet trauma studies is largely the field of white, Western texts. "Instead of promoting solidarity between different cultures," notes Stef Craps and Gert Buelens:

> trauma studies risks producing the very opposite effect as a result of this one-sided focus: by ignoring or marginalizing non-Western traumatic events and histories and non-Western theoretical work, trauma studies may actually assist in the perpetuation of Eurocentric views and structures that maintain or widen the gap between the West and the rest of the world. (2)

Of course, trauma is universal in the sense that experiencing pain—physical, psychological, emotional, etc.—is not unique to any one group. However, its manifestations and the narratives crafted around it are individual and may depend on cultural context. And yet, while comics and trauma are vast and diverse, in comics studies and trauma studies, many voices are marginalized and silenced. Alongside the research questions above, one of the objectives of this collection is to address such an imbalance by presenting chapters on trauma from different cultural and linguistic backgrounds, and on works outside the canonical few that dominate comics scholarship. In a round-table discussion on the future of trauma studies, Craps maintains that expansion and diversification of the framework is needed:

I think it's important to study how the cultural production of particular non-western or minority groups bears witness to painful histories. This requires specialized knowledge of these other cultures and languages, of the different media and forms of expression they use, and of local beliefs about suffering and healing. So I think that's where we're headed. (909)

In this collection, there are new and comparative approaches to *Fun Home* and *Persepolis*, but most of the works are by comics writers who are little-known or unknown outside their communities or niche audiences. And while some of the works are Western in their origin and focus, there are chapters here on comics from and about many regions around the world, including Russia, China, India, Vietnam, Ukraine, Spain, and Argentina. There are chapters on graphic depictions of trauma with political roots (war, dictatorship, exile, imprisonment), but also of crime and interpersonal trauma, including a chapter on the use of comics to deal with the aftermath of sexual violence. Regardless, all the chapters in this collection situate their analysis at the intersection of trauma studies and comics studies, engaging with the debates and dialogues of these fields as the framework for addressing the question of catharsis in the works discussed.

Our interest in trauma and comics as its medium of expression reflects how the former has shed its scientific roots to become more broadly present in culture. As Katalin Orbán notes, "The rise of trauma as a prominent cultural discourse for the representation of individual and collective injuries and catastrophic events in the twentieth century has transformed trauma from a specialized medical and psychoanalytical term into a household concept that permeates our culture" (29).[6] It is necessary to recognize this shift in order to approach literary expressions of painful and damaging ordeals, including in comics. "Literary trauma theory," specifies Kurtz, "also claims that narrative processes share important features with traumatic processes, that there is a special connection between words and wounds" (8). This "special connection" marks the conventional understanding of trauma in the humanities, which is associated with the influential, but challenged, studies of Cathy Caruth. According to Caruth, the primary psychological mechanisms by which one processes and communicates (or not) trauma are repetition, incomprehensibility, and belatedness. And these reactions may be paradoxical: the intimacy and immediacy of a traumatic event lead to belatedness in its confrontation; incomprehension of what happened leads to repetition of the inaccessible moment (92–93). From this framework, Jean-Michel Ganteau and Susan Onega articulate one of the central tenets of such trauma theory—the incomprehensibility of the event and the impossibility of its representation: "The repression of affects that lies at the heart of trauma is manifested in the impossibility of knowing and communicating the traumatic event or experience in cause-and-effect, rational terms" (2). Adding to the dialogue, Laurie Vickroy notes that the aesthetic response in trauma narratives echoes the incomprehensibility of the wound through fragmentary, experimental forms: "Its narrative styles reproduce aspects of that experience, including fragmentation of thoughts, a dissociative outlook, and decontextualized visualizations" (20). This understanding of how trauma is conceptualized and communicated is widespread and is present, at least in part, in the theoretical base of several of the chapters in this collection.

Nevertheless, as Dominick LaCapra points out, how trauma should be approached "in a given genre or discipline is an essentially contested question" (*Writing* 204–5). That this is a contested question does not deny the influence of Caruth's work, however. To that end, Susannah Radstone suggests that there is both a dominant approach to trauma studies and a need to question such an approach: "the rise of what is becoming almost a new theoretical orthodoxy invites—requires, even, perhaps—some reflection on and reflexivity concerning its implications and contexts" (10). For Harriet E. H. Earle, the problem with this orthodoxy is that it advocates for a totalizing narrative of how trauma is experienced/communicated, denying space for a diversity of manifestations: "in addition to eradicating all traces of difference and personal variance in traumatic experiences, the suggestion that all trauma resists interpretation and representation removes the trauma from the individual" (32). Responding to the notion that trauma resists representation, for example, Earle goes on to state:

> This is not to say that there is not an inherent crisis of representation at the core of trauma, but it does suggest that this crisis is not entirely insurmountable, as the classic trauma model seems to insist. More accurately, the crisis of representation may be said to ask how individuals represent to others an event that affected them in deeply personal and complex ways, a suggestion that is subtly different than the belief that the crisis is of all representation. (33)

In a similar line of thought, Alan Gibbs is explicit in his criticism of Caruth and her theory by stating that it is "far too rigid, partial, and exclusionary" (12). "Trauma is, evidently, difficult to narrate," he adds, "but it is also difficult to transmit through the literary text, and so conflated ethical-aesthetic value judgements should not be unthinkingly deployed as a means to dismiss realist trauma narratives out of hand" (32). Such challenges to trauma studies orthodoxy also have a place in this collection, as certain chapters question the Caruthian understanding of trauma in art. In other words, while the works analyzed in this volume do not constitute a homogenous monolith, so too is there a diversity of approaches to their study. Even the notion of words and wounds having a special relationship has been challenged—by the critic who articulated the very notion in question. "While classical trauma theory has tended to focus on literature and literary forms," explains Kurtz, "the influence of memory studies has shifted that focus to image-based genres such as photography, cinema, and experiential museums. Rather than being represented through language, perhaps it is the case that trauma is most effectively represented through images" (14). To sum up, trauma can defy representation and thus favor an experimental, fragmentary aesthetic. It can also embrace representation through realism. It is intimately connected with words but also images. Far from being irreconcilably different, these varied and even paradoxical characteristics all find a home in comics, a medium that combines visual and textual elements and whose aesthetic possibilities are almost unlimited—anyhow and anything one can draw is conceivable.

Indeed, many comics scholars have underlined the privileged space that comics provide for dealing with traumatic moments while acknowledging the complexity of this relationship. "[I]t is important for us to get the form (comics) and the concept (trauma) the right way around here," explains Dominic Davies, "understanding the latter as not somehow begetting the former, but itself taking shape through its interaction with comics' cultural work" (9). One point of connection between form and concept is the issue of fragmentation. For Chute, the inherently fragmentary nature of comics meets the Caruthian notion of fragmentary memory: "Images in comics appear in fragments, just as they do in actual recollection; this fragmentation, in particular, is a prominent feature of traumatic memory" (4). This coming together of narrative fragments and memory fragments is unique to the composition of the visual/spatial organization in comics. As Sara McNicol clarifies, "A crucial aspect of comics is the notion of 'gaps' or 'gutters' between the frames, spaces the reader must fill in imaginatively so as to make sense of the narrative fragments" (86).[7] Gutters, fragments, and imaginative reconstruction point to comics being an active medium—that is, a medium that demands an active reader. By actively taking part in processing the comic's content, the reader is simultaneously immersed in the created world and conscious of the world's creation. The artifice is on full display even as the content is real.[8]

Sara Lightman states that the conspicuous construction of comics makes the medium apt for confronting the hidden and silent, giving visibility to what is often unarticulated due to its uncomfortability: "Comics, in their constructed and constrained world of panel and borders, offer a space both closed and open to the public. These everyday stories that previously had been silenced, or kept hidden in cultures of silence, find a voice and a space on the comics' page" (203). For Stephanie Burt, such potential for engaging with difficult subject matter stems from the medium's relationship between the creation and how it is consumed: "a person put those lines there; you decide how closely you want to engage with them—[this] makes comics good at showing us what's hard to see: internal states like depression and OCD; taboo scenes and body parts; complex urban planning and architecture, as experienced by a city's inhabitants; historical catastrophe such as ongoing civil wars and even genocide" (574). While Burt focusses more on the reader side of this dynamic, one cannot forget that the "person [who] put those lines there" is also using those visual lines (lines that makes up the frames, lines of text, lines in a drawing) to express themselves and explore their own confrontations of such difficult issues. For example, in his study of comics memoirist Miriam Katin, Diederik Oostdijk explains that in addition to Katin's need to "draw herself out" of her trauma in the sense of "extracting" or "letting go," "On a literal level, especially in the context of Miriam's profession as a graphic artist, drawing out, however, brings in a third meaning, namely that she cannot only speak and write about her trauma, but that she needs to visualize it to herself" (86). In other words, comics provides a space, a literal space, for both artist and public to visualize what is hard to see.

The question of "seeing" is not just a matter of form but also content when one considers that comics often function as the drawn memory of witnessing and testimony. Indeed, Maheen Ahmed and Benoît Crucifix explain that the varied intersections of memory theory are present in comics due to the medium's visual nature (both in terms of images on a page and testimony upon recollection):

> This oscillation between individual and collective memories in early twentieth-century theories of memory is reflected in comics, where different kinds of memories are in constant interaction, for instance, through the confluence of an individual reader's memory, historical context, and the collective memories of comics, including the intertwined memories of the genres, styles, and series populating them. (1–2)

On a related note, Ahmed and Crucifix also underline the potential for comics to be a tangible marker of memory on a collective level by stating that

> comics can be understood as opening up a space marked out by the graphic trace that is not only intersubjective, but also memorializing. In this way, comics too can be seen as the famous lieux de mémoire described by Pierre Nora as the recourse of an era that found itself without memory, since memory had been replaced by the compulsive re-organization of the past or history. (281)

For example, *Maus* articulates Spiegelman's memory of his father and the second-hand testimony of his father's memory, but it also serves as a site of memory for the Holocaust in general.

Given that many graphic depictions of traumatic events and graphic depictions of living with and confronting (or not) traumatic events are first-hand or even second-hand memoirs, it is logical that self-reflexivity be necessary for the insight required to explore them.[9] For this point, I again return to the issue of the explicit artifice of comics, obliging consciousness and self-consciousness. The creator confronts their creation and demands an active reader. According to Ahmed, "the potential for self-reflexivity in visual narratives is manifested through the self-conscious employment of visual elements on pages drawing attention to the conventions of art and image production" (165). To tie this and the previous point together, the readers' active self-reflections make them witnesses, too, allowing for the comic to be a witness for traumatic events and for the readers to be witnesses to that depiction, involving them directly in the communication of a possible pain/healing dynamic. As Davies states, "With their tendency to self-reflexivity and their interpellation of the reader-as-witness, comics are drawn (sometimes compulsively) to the documentation of the processes by which trauma is socially constructed, publicly circulated, and retrospectively experienced—whether by firsthand survivors, second hand witnesses, or postmemory generations" (21). For a specific example of self-reflexivity, Randy Duncan et al. have pointed to the confessional nature of comics, citing the Catholic background of many such memoirists as a medium through which one may seek peace and healing for their wounds. "The act of telling others about their pain or shame," they note, "seems to have a therapeutic effect for some memoirists" (247). Of course, the power of confession is not unique to Catholicism, and indeed, this point has already been raised regarding *Maus*. For this volume, the issue of the medium's capacity to "have a therapeutic effect" brings us to the question of catharsis in comics.

As mentioned, catharsis is a term of Greek origin that refers to cleansing or healing through purgation. According to Stanley W. Jackson, catharsis in the ancient world "might entail a literal cleansing in the narrowest sense or involve a therapeutic cleansing in a medical sense or be a spiritual or moral cleansing with magical import or, often enough, constitute a complex combination of all three" (119). Contemporary usage of the term, regarding literary affect in particular, traces its origins to this period and to Aristotle's ideas of tragic theater providing relief by facilitating the purging of negative emotions. "This was a psychic catharsis," explains Jackson, "or psychological purgation, of troubling passions from the soul, and it involved a psychosomatic process of relieving and calming that led to a healing result" (120). However, as Jonathan Lear notes, cathartic relief is not merely the product of "'releasing pent-up emotions' per se; it is the relief of 'releasing' these emotions in a safe environment" (205). For Aristotle, it was the theater, for this volume, the question is, can it be comics? To consider this question requires us to go beyond Aristotle, not just because comics did not exist then as they do now, but also because conceptualizations of catharsis have evolved over time. "Aristotle is somewhat vague about the exact nature of catharsis in the Poetics and elsewhere," explains Carl Plantinga, "leaving literary theorists, philosophers, and psychologists to mull over the problem for hundreds of years" (177).

In service of arriving at an understanding of catharsis that suits the diversity of this volume but that is not so permissive as to lose all meaning, I suggest that catharsis here involves the notion of release as it relates to "working through" trauma. This is the approach taken by Plantinga in his study of catharsis in film: "What is missing from many catharsis theories is the cognitive component of purgation. It is not the mere expression of negative emotions that purges them from the self, but a 'working through' and resolution that must occur, in part, on the level of cognition" (178).[10] Plantinga equates "working through" with "dealing with" or a "reconceptualization" of the trauma leading to comparatively positive developments, whatever form that might take. "Working through" is also a key concept in LaCapra's work on trauma theory, and although neither Plantinga nor Jackson (see note 10) cite LaCapra in their approaches to catharsis, nor does LaCapra mention catharsis in his understanding of working through, I argue that LaCapra's conceptualization is helpful for approaching comics as a site for engaging with and releasing the bad in service of moving toward the good.

Understanding catharsis in this way recognizes that the purging of emotions, so to speak, may refer to an ongoing confrontation of their power to stress and overwhelm the individual or community more than to a cure. "Working on and through," explains LaCapra, "does not imply the achievement of closure and full identity or autonomy. It points instead to a self-implicating process in the attempt to reconstruct the past in ways that may raise questions for the present and create openings to often unpredictable but to some extent shapable futures" (*Understanding Others* 39). In other words, catharsis by this understanding does not require transcendence of the burden of trauma as closure but rather sees release as an aspirational and varied process:

> The open-ended, recurrent process of working through does not point to the achievement of a total cure or an effort to forget the past and achieve normalization by "turning the page of history." Nor does it mean that everything that has happened, everyone who has been lost, may be laid to rest or transcended. . . . Working through the past is a process that may never reach closure or entirely transcend acting out and compulsive repetition but may allow for a reinvestment in the present with openings to the future. (LaCapra *Understanding Others* 57–59)

Regarding this point, LaCapra cites giving testimony as evidence of one being free from the paralysis caused by trauma without being evidence of absolute closure, as if such a thing were possible: "giving testimony is an indication that one is not simply bearing witness to trauma by reliving the past and being consumed by its aftereffects. It is also performative in that it helps to provide some space in which one may gather oneself, engage the present, and attempt to open viable possibilities" (*History and its Limits* 75–76). As such, comics that depict testimonies of trauma, or are themselves testimonies of trauma, are textual/visual sites of engagement with these "open viable possibilities." If catharsis requires purgation, then comparing it to "working through" allows us to acknowledge that purging is always somewhat incomplete, but that this incompleteness is not incompatible with healing as a process. To use LaCapra's words when describing "working through," catharsis here is not a "panacea" but "implies the possibility of agency that does not disavow vulnerability but rather affirms it" (*History and its Limits* 84).

To bring the discussion back to comics as I conclude this introduction, it is clear that the "working through" required for catharsis has an intimate relationship with narrative: "it is important to understand working through as both a narrative and other-than-narrative psychosocial and political practice of articulation" (LaCapra *History, literature* 162). Of course, catharsis has been linked to narrative since Aristotle and the theater. Comics are visual and textual narratives: narrative fiction, memoir, documentary—they all tell stories and, as such, involve a complex communicative exchange between creator and audience. On the creator side, the act of writing (and in the case of comics, drawing) may be itself an act of purgation, of working through distress. As Miriam K. Harris explains regarding trauma narratives: "Writing functions not only as catharsis of the soul but as a record of the heroic enterprise of regaining self-power. Transcendence becomes possible when, having told the story as it occurred, we begin to imagine a shift into a story of new possibilities" (XXII). For the audience, catharsis involves identification with the content of the narrative, either from having experienced similar trauma and thus they can relate from a position of empathy or from the implication that what is being depicted could happen to them or to those they care about (Lear 207). Catharsis, then, is not a peripheral consideration to approaching the stories we tell but rather a fundamental part of understanding the power that these stories have. As Plantinga summarizes: "To explore the role of catharsis in narrative fiction is central because . . . the discussion will touch on the deeper issues of affect elicitation in the movies and in art generally, including its possible therapeutic, cultural, quasireligious, and ideological effects" (177). In the case of comics, the potential for catharsis is not limited to narrative fiction but to narrative in general. The chapters in this volume explore such potential toward individual and collective traumas, in words and images, in the silent spaces, in the frames, in the gutters, in memoirs, in documentaries, and in fiction. Every chapter has a different approach to different works. But they are all about comics, they are all about trauma, and they all explore the potential for catharsis in comics.

CONTENT AND ORGANIZATION

This volume will be an original contribution to the fields of comics studies and trauma studies while at the same time engaging in dialogue with related scholarship. The nine chapters are divided into three sections under the following headings: "Drawing Apart: Physical and Generational Separation and Belonging"; "Drawing Together: Nation and Narrative"; and "Drawing Close: Individual, Intimate, and Traumatic."

"Drawing Apart" begins with two chapters that deal with the separation of time and experience between generations and bring together two commonalities among Spanish-speaking countries: Military (or military-adjacent) dictatorships in the twentieth century and a proliferation of comics in the twenty-first. In Jennifer Nagtegaal's "From Confinement to Catharsis: Reading the Comics Aesthetic in Manuel H. Martín's Documentary *30 años de oscuridad/30 Years of Darkness* (Spain, 2012)" the focus is on the Franco regime in Spain. This chapter is distinct in that its primary work is not a comic book but rather a documentary film made with a comics aesthetic. Nagtegaal employs theories of haunting by Jacques Derrida and others to demonstrate how the comic film builds to catharsis in confrontation with Spain's collective trauma of the Civil War and dictatorship. In the second chapter of this section, we cross the Atlantic to Argentina and the military junta of the late 1970s and early 1980s. In her essay "Graphic Representations of Violence in *La herencia del coronel* by Carlos Trillo and Lucas Varela," Diana Pifano inserts comics into the dialogue about other cultural representations of this period in Argentina and explores how the medium here is utilized to communicate the difficult subject matter of torture and sexual violence in the titular *La herencia del coronel* (*The Coronel's Inheritance*), a serialized publication from 2007–2008 by Carlos Trillo and Lucas Varela. The final chapter in this section is Kay Sohini's "On the Threshold of Being and Belonging: Refiguring History in Autobiographical Comics." Here, Sohini explores feelings of what she calls "unbelonging" for migrant characters who find themselves between two or more cultures in three long-form comics from three memoirists of different backgrounds: Vietnamese author Thi Bui's *The Best We Could Do* (2017), Indian author Malik Sajad's *Munnu: A Boy from Kashmir* (2015), and the Iranian Satrapi's *Persepolis* (2000).

"Drawing Together" contains chapters on national traumas and national narratives, with special attention paid to who is writing the comics and for whom. In the first chapter of this section, "The Burden of Translating History in Li Kunwu's *A Chinese Life*," Angie Chau focuses on the comics memoir *A Chinese Life* (2009), a collaboration between Chinese cartoonist Li Kunwu and French writer Philippe Ôtié, with regard to how the work depicts Chinese history, and how Chinese, Anglophone, and French audiences receive the text, criticizing and celebrating its content in accordance with their preexisting political leanings. In "'American God' to a Soviet Superman: Exploring the Cathartic Function of Counterfactual Narratives," Aanchal Vij considers the cathartic potential of alternate reality fiction comics, with a specific focus on Alan Moore's *Watchmen* (1986) and Mark Millar's *Superman Red Son* (2014). She maintains that these "what if" stories may be viewed as starting a cathartic dialogue for wounded national narratives (American exceptionalism and the Vietnam War, for example) but that such catharsis is futile in these terms in these works. In the final chapter of this section, "Re-Framing (Post-)Soviet Ukrainian History: Walter Duranty, Igort's *The Ukrainian Notebooks*, and the Ethics of Graphic Reportage," Anastasia Ulanowicz compares Italian comics artist Igort's graphic depiction of

Ukrainian history—in particular the Holodomor, the deadly famine with ties to Stalinist policy—with previous Western coverage, notably by the Pulitzer Prize-winning journalist Walter Duranty and his dismissal of the famine in his reporting during the 1930s.

With Drawing Close, the volume, to use a homonym, draws to a close. These three chapters engage with more intimate manifestations and depictions of trauma and catharsis in their primary texts: a memoir, a comparison of six distinct narratives, and a crime-drama work of fiction. In "Alison Bechdel's *Fun Home* and the Impossibility of Testimony," Kelly Baron articulates a theoretical base around the idea of testimony resisting representation and uses this approach to examine issues of fidelity of representation and catharsis in Bechdel's canonical work. In "Graphic Novels and Sexual Trauma: Processing Sexual Trauma Through Creative Expression," Lee Okan engages with Graphic Medicine, comparing how three different creators employ comics for confronting memories of sexual violence: *Ghost Stories* by Whit Taylor (2018), *Lighter Than My Shadow* by Katie Green (2013), and *Becoming Unbecoming* by Una (2016). In addition to analyzing these memoirs of individual trauma, Okan also studies reader reception and the potential for catharsis on a collective level in two other works that speak to community healing for victims of sexual violence: *Take It as a Compliment* by Maria Stoian (2016) and *The Courage to Be Me* by Dr. Nina Burrowes (2018). Finally, in "The Good Empty: Trauma, Displacement, and Catharsis in *Sabrina*" Russell Samolsky takes on a rarity in this volume—a work of fiction. In this study of Nick Drnaso's *Sabrina* (2018), a long-form comic centered on the grisly murder of a young woman, Samolsky explores the performative nature of trauma in the text, considers how comics—and this text in particular—oblige an active reader, and how the readers become part of the trauma/catharsis dynamic as they identify with, and distance themselves from, the violent and disquieting content of the work.

NOTES

1. Kim is the artistic name for Joaquim Aubert Puigarnau.
2. It should be mentioned that in his article, Fawaz points to the disconnect between the proliferation of works and the academy that studies only a small emerging canon.
3. Roger Luckhurst considers a related question on the ethics of trauma narratives: "Transmissibility has become a central ethical concern about the representation and response to traumatic narratives and images. Can or should the right to speak of trauma be limited to its primary victims? Who can claim 'secondary' status without risking appropriation?" (3).

4. The decision to avoid the term graphic novel in the introduction to this volume is due in part to the fact that not all the works in question here would be considered "graphic novels," but also because this phrase is a) a marketing term, and b) implies fiction through its designation as "novel" (Chute 18, 19). Individual contributors are free to use terminology as they see fit in their chapters. The term "graphic narrative" is also used at times in this introduction and throughout the volume, simply as a descriptive term for comics that tell stories.

5. Matt Silady explains, "The linguistic taxonomy of comics is a convoluted mess best dealt with by simply saying that anyone who draws a quick doodle on a napkin makes comics" (621). For his part, McCloud defines comics by recreating the look of a dictionary entry to state that comics are "Juxtaposed pictorial and other images in deliberate sequence, intended to convey information and/or to produce an aesthetic response in the viewer" (9).

6. Orbán also notes that in response to trauma becoming a "prominent cultural discourse," its narratives and how we talk/write about them are often limited in scope and circular: "These aesthetic tropes correspond to a specific view of trauma that fosters particular expectations, such as absence and inexpressibility, and the production and reception of trauma narratives have become mutually reinforcing in this respect" (30). Craps, too, is critical of this narrow view and the absence of psychology therein: "Trauma theory for the most part continues to adhere to the traditional, event-based model of trauma, according to which trauma results from a single, extraordinary, catastrophic event, and recovery takes the form of the talking cure. So, in a sense, the situation in the field of cultural trauma research is even more dire than that in the field of psychological trauma research, because recent insights from the latter field—in which there is a growing awareness, at least, of the need to move beyond psychic universalism—aren't even taken up in the former field. Or, that is, they weren't until very recently" ("Decolonizing" 907–8). In the same round-table discussion, Alan Gibbs adds: "One of the things that I have been arguing is that this set of cultural trauma theories that have become so dominant are not only inadequate for the postcolonial experience but even for many representations in fairly mainstream American writing as well" ("Decolonizing" 910). In this paragraph, I will summarize this traditional view, and in the following, highlight some of its criticisms and suggested new directions.

7. According to McNicol, fragmentation and imaginative reconstruction serve the medium's capacity to "haunt:" "This resonates with the way in which becoming aware of normally invisible social ghosts can help is make sense of the more visible, yet fragmented, present. Furthermore, the complex way in which comics deal with the representation of past, present, and future, and the passing of time more generally, has parallels with ideas of social haunting. Just as a comic demands the active participation of those living in the present to make sense of social ghosts" (86–87). There is a clear metaphorical connection between ghosts of the past and trauma. To that end, a community's collective trauma is an example of McNichol's "social ghosts," though the metaphor is maintained in individual cases too with the individual "haunted" by their own unique experiences. As the focus of this collection is catharsis in comics, it is worth mentioning the possible relationship in these terms between "exorcism" and healing.

8. To be clear, "real" here does not refer to nonfiction as if our focus was on a binary between fiction and documentary/memoir. "Real" refers to societal issues, individual suffering, emotional responses, etc., that are present in fictional and nonfictional representations alike.

9. Marianne Hirsch coined the term "Postmemory" to describe the active and creative "memory" processes of the descendants of survivors of traumatic events. These are "memories" of those who did not experience the trauma but for whom the trauma is still an essential part of their identity. In particular, Hirsch studies the articulations of the memory of children and grandchildren of those who were victims of the Holocaust.

10. Jackson also uses this term, stating that "it could be argued that many patterns of repetition and working-through were very gradual, attenuated forms of catharsis" (130).

WORKS CITED

Ahmed, Maaheen. *Openness of Comics. Generating Meaning within Flexible Structures*. Jackson: University Press of Mississippi, 2016.

Ahmed, Maaheen, and Crucifix, Benoît, eds. *Comics Memory. Archives and Styles*. Cham, Switzerland: Palgrave Macmillan, 2018.

Burt, Stephanie. "Why Not More Comics?" *PMLA* 134, no. 3 (2019): 572–78.

Caruth, Cathy. *Unclaimed Experience: Trauma, Narrative, and History*. Baltimore: Johns Hopkins University Press, 1996.

Chute, Hillary. *Why Comics? From Underground to Everywhere*. New York: Harper, 2017.

Craps, Stef, and Gert Buelens. "Introduction: Postcolonial Trauma Novels." *Studies in the Novel* 40, nos.1–2 (2008): 1–12.

Craps, Stef, and Gert Buelens et al. "Decolonizing Trauma Studies Round Table Discussion." *Humanities* 4 (2015): 905–23.

Davies, Dominic. "Introduction: Documenting Trauma in Comics." In *Documenting Trauma in Comics. Traumatic Pasts, Embodied Histories, and Graphic Reportage*, ed. Dominic Davies and Candida Rifkind, 1–26. Cham, Switzerland: Palgrave Macmillan, 2020.

Duncan, Randy, Matthew J. Smith, and Paul Levitz. *The Power of Comics. History, Form, and Culture*. 2nd ed. London: Bloomsbury, 2014.

Earle, Harriet E. H. *Comics, Trauma, and the New Art of War*. Jackson: University Press of Mississippi, 2017.

Fawaz, Ramzi. "A Queer Sequence: Comics as a Disruptive Medium." *PMLA* 134, no. 3 (2019): 588–94.

Ganteau, Jean-Michel, and Susan Onega. "Introduction: Performing the Void: Liminality and the Ethics of Form in Contemporary Trauma Narratives." In *Contemporary Trauma Narratives. Liminality and the Ethics of Form*, ed. Susana Onega and Jean-Michel Ganteau, 1–18. New York: Routledge, 2014.

Gibbs, Alan. *Contemporary American Trauma Narratives*. Edinburgh: Edinburgh University Press, 2014.

Harris, Miriam K. *Rape, Incest, Battery!: Women Writing Out the Pain*. Fort Worth: TCU Press, 2000.

Jackson, Stanley W. *Care of the Psyche: A History of Psychological Healing*. New Haven: Yale University Press, 1999.

Kearney, Richard. "Narrating Pain: The Power of Catharsis." *Paragraph* 30, no. 1 (2007): 51–66.

Kurtz, Roger J. "Introduction." In *Trauma and Literature*, ed. J. Roger Kurtz, 1–17. Cambridge: Cambridge University Press, 2018.

LaCapra, Dominick. *Writing History, Writing Trauma*. Baltimore: Johns Hopkins University Press, 2001.

LaCapra, Dominick. *History and its Limits: Human, Animal, Violence*. Ithaca: Cornell University Press, 2009.

LaCapra, Dominick. *History, Literature, Critical Theory*. Ithaca, Cornell University Press, 2013.

LaCapra, Dominick. *Understanding Others: Peoples, Animals, Pasts*. Ithaca: Cornell University Press, 2018.

Lear, Jonathan. "Catharsis." *A Companion to the Philosophy of Literature*, ed. Garry L. Hagberg and Walter Jost, 193–217. Malden, MA: Wiley-Blackwell, 2010.

Lightman, Sarah. "Metamorphosing Difficulties: The Portrayal of Trauma in Autobiographical Comics." In *The Unspeakable: Narratives of Trauma*, ed. Magda Stroińska, Vikki Cecchetto, and Kate Szymanski, 201–27. Frankfurt: Peter Lang, 2014.

Luckhurst, Roger. *The Trauma Question*. New York: Routledge, 2008.

McCloud, Scott. *Understanding Comics*. New York: William Morrow, 1994.

McNicol, Sarah. "Exploring Trauma and Social Haunting Through Community Comics Creation." In *Documenting Trauma in Comics. Traumatic Pasts, Embodied Histories, and Graphic Reportage*, ed. Dominic Davies and Candida Rifkind, 85–102. Cham, Switzerland: Palgrave Macmillan, 2020.

Merino, Ana, and Brittany Tulis. "The Sequential Art of Memory: The Testimonial Struggle of Comics in Spain." In *Memory and Its Discontents: Spanish Culture in the Early Twenty-First Century*, ed. Luis Martín-Estudillo and Nicholas Spadaccini. *Hispanic Issues on Line* 11 (Fall 2012): 211–25.

Oostdijk, Diederik. "'Draw yourself out of it': Miriam Katin's Graphic Metamorphosis of Trauma." *Journal of Modern Jewish Studies* 17, no. 1 (2018): 79–92.

Orbán, Katalin. "Hierarchies of Pain: Trauma Tropes Today and Tomorrow." In *Documenting Trauma in Comics: Traumatic Pasts, Embodied Histories, and Graphic Reportage*, ed. Dominic Davies and Candida Rifkind, 29–48. Cham, Switzerland: Palgrave Macmillan, 2020.

Plantinga, Carl. *Moving Viewers: American Film and the Spectator's Experience*. Berkeley: University of California Press, 2009.

Radstone, Susannah. "Trauma Theory: Contexts, Politics, Ethics." *Paragraph* 30, no. 1 (2007): 9–29.

Silady, Matt. "Three Wishes for *Why Comics?*." *PMLA* 134, no. 3 (2019): 620–24.

Vickroy, Laurie. *Reading Trauma Narratives: The Contemporary Novel and the Psychology of Oppression*. Charlottesville: University of Virginia Press, 2015.

II. DRAWING APART:

PHYSICAL AND GENERATIONAL SEPARATION AND BELONGING

CHAPTER 1

FROM CONFINEMENT TO CATHARSIS

Reading the Comics Aesthetic in Manuel H. Martín's Documentary
30 Años de Oscuridad/30 Years of Darkness

JENNIFER NAGTEGAAL

The present chapter[1] seeks to critically engage with the comics aesthetic that characterizes the documentary film *30 años de oscuridad/30 Years of Darkness* (Spain, 2012). The Goya-nominated film by Andalusian director Manuel H. Martín interchanges a largely static, print-comics aesthetic with archival materials and talking-head interviews to recount the story of some of Spain's so-called post-war "moles." The term, coined by journalists Manuel Leguineche and Jesús Torbado in their work of investigative journalism, *Los topos/The Moles* (1977), appositely refers to a group of Republican and other anti-Nationalist men that, fearing capital punishment or incarceration at the close of the Spanish Civil War (1936–9), were forced into hiding during the decades-long Franco dictatorship that ensued (1939–75).[2] By foregrounding the traumatic experience of self-imposed imprisonment—sometimes, and for long periods of time, in cramped quarters and with limited access to basic necessities and human interaction—*30 Years of Darkness* questions the very term "post-war" for such men who hid in the shadows for up to three long decades, as the film's title suggests.

Although free to emerge from hiding following the Franco regime's official pardon in 1969, the testimonies of the men who endured such were silenced for decades more with the enactment of the Amnesty Law in 1977, implicit to which was the aim of forgetting the civil war and moving forward towards democracy with a clean slate. Finally, a few years after the turn of the millennium, Spain's citizens saw the ratification of a subsequent law that directly opposed the Amnesty Law's narrative of disremembering the past. Spain's Historical Memory Law, enacted under José Luis Rodríguez Zapatero's socialist government in 2007, did not seek to point the finger of guilt at either side but rather encourage open dialogue at long last about historical memory.[3] This changing political atmosphere, together with a growing social movement aimed at recuperating historical memory, meant both a metaphorical digging up of testimony as well as a literal excavation of mass graves containing thousands of unidentified war victims, with the first scientific exhumation taking place in the year 2000.[4]

It is in this context that *30 Years of Darkness* appeared as one of many articulate testimonial artifacts belonging to Spain's contemporary visual culture. Martín's hybrid comics-documentary project is evidence of what Frederick Luis Aldama notes to be "the exciting ways that comics have permeated other media forms such as literature and film" (3). But beyond being seen as exciting from a purely aesthetic standpoint, Martín's assimilation of the comics medium and documentary film into what the director himself refers to as a "novela gráfica documental" ['graphic novel documentary'] should also be understood as strategic from a socio-cultural standpoint. After all, it is in this same backward-looking context that graphic novels have come to be seen as "formidable ground" for the historical memory debates taking place in contemporary Spain (Tahmassian 29).[5] Samuel Amago, in his contributing chapter to *Consequential Art: Comics Culture in Contemporary Spain*, writes that "[a]longside other art forms—photography, fiction, documentary and fiction film, theatre, poetry—comics have taken up the call to contribute to the project of building and expanding the vernacular archive of historical memory of Francoist repression in Spain" (32).

This is not to say that the events of the Spanish Civil War did not influence comics creation prior to the twenty-first century. The contrary is true. Images of war have, in fact, been filling frames of Spanish comics since the very outbreak of the bloody battle between Nationalist rebels and anti-Nationalist forces. The conflict quickly shaped the content of inaugural children's magazines that developed in parallel to the war. In the weekly publications produced by the Nationalist side, for example, the ideological treatment of the war's opposing players ranged from ridicule of the Republican "adversary" and a hailing of the young Falangist hero in *Flechas*, to hatred and even hysteria building in *Pelayos* (see Matly).[6] Conversely, it was Francisco Franco, Spain's soon-to-be dictator, and his generals who were often the subject of derision in the pages of the Republican-backed *Pionero Rojo*.[7]

Now, bordering on one century later, we can see that the representation of Spain's civil war in comics form has migrated across genres and geographical borders, from America's mainstream comics scene in the 1940s to the European graphic novel movement that took off in the early 2000s. No doubt, however, the creative impetus with which so many comics artists and script writers have drawn (on) the Spanish Civil War varies across contexts. For example, in the iconic tale *Un miliciano rojo/A Red Militiaman* (*Pelayos* no. 25, June 13, 1937), we see a propagandistic depiction of the republican armed fighter as dehumanized and a cold-blooded killer. Meanwhile, we have come to understand that a few years later, and a few thousand miles across the Atlantic, when Marvel's Captain Terror took up the fight against fascism, first battling Franco's Nationalists and then Nazi agents in the Second World War, young readers were largely witnessing an unnuanced glorification of war common to mainstream comics that, during their Golden Age, worked under the formula of "fascist-inspired superpowers employed against greater fascist threats" (Gavaler 112).

Conversely, the vigilantism carried out by the group of elderly anti-fascist ex-comrades in Enki Bilal and Pierre Christin's *Les Phalanges de l'Ordre Noir/The Black Order Brigade* (France, 1979), serialized in Spain under the title *Los comrades del orden negro* in the first four issues of the underground comix magazine *Vértigo* (1982–3), can be read as both a testament to the international character of the Spanish Civil War, as well as to the critical function that fiction narratives played during a time when Spain itself was transitioning to democracy under the societal pact of forgetting. Finally, we should not find it happenstance that the Trump era is the sociopolitical context in which ¡*Brigadistas! An American Anti-Fascist in the Spanish Civil War* (2022) was conceptualized. Especially so, given that the legacy of the Lincolns—thousands of volunteer soldiers, pilots, and medical personnel fighting alongside republican forces under the banner of the Abraham Lincoln Brigade—was simultaneously being invoked by progressive activists in their defense of democracy.

Back on Spanish soil, twenty-first-century comics creation that revolves around the Spanish Civil War has largely occurred, as mentioned, through the vehicle of the graphic novel with the recuperation of historical memory in mind. Be they works of fiction protagonized by a composite character inspired by true testimonies, or the image/text inscription of private memories and family histories onto the comics page, a progression of themes in these graphic narratives—although not completely clear cut—can be detected. What began with a focalization on the soldier's testimony and the male perspective (for example, Antonio Altarriba and Kim's *El arte de volar/The Art of Flying* from 2007 or Paco Roca's *Los surcos del azar/Twists of Fate* in 2013) shifted to meaningful attempts to account for women's private lives and wartime experiences (here Altarriba and Kim's *El ala rota/The Broken Wing* in 2016, or, to name another from the same year, Jaime Martín's *Jamás tendré 20 años/I'll Never be 20*). Shortly following this, comics artists began working on narratives that center on political processes rather than private memory (Penyas and Alberto Haller's *En Transición/In Transition* in 2017, for example).

Yet a surprising lacuna in Spain's contemporary comics creation is the recounting of the trauma suffered by the nation's post-war moles. This lack of image/text testimony causes one to pause and consider for at least two reasons. The first is that accounts of notorious moles have for decades now inspired works of cinema and literature on Spanish soil, beginning with Leguineche and Torbado's *The Moles* and culminating recently in the Goya award-winning historical drama also inspired by Cortés' story, *La Trinchera Infinita/The Endless Trench* (2019), codirected by Jon Garaño, Aitor Arregi and José Mari Goenaga.[8] The second reason is that the comics medium—especially when transferred to and transformed within the context of cinema—is actually the ideal narrative form for communicating the subjective experience of Spain's post-war moles that is characterized by a fear of discovery and even death, enduring extreme confinement, and surviving a ghost-like existence. That is, as I will suggest in my analysis of *30 Years of Darkness*, the "architecture" of comics, as it is now commonly referred to, becomes an effective vehicle for building aesthetics of terror, confinement, and even haunting no doubt on its own, but especially when assimilated to the documentary film genre.

Nevertheless, it can be said that in a roundabout way, and one deserving of sustained critical attention where any has yet to be given,[9] Martín's graphic novel documentary brings the testimonies of Spain's post-war moles into contact with the larger comics memory project that is unfolding within the nation. In the pages that follow, I explore the ways that *30 Years of Darkness'* graphic novel aesthetic bears on its reconstruction of the past. I also explore the cathartic function of this comics-documentary film project as a whole. Both of these questions bear further meaning when taking into consideration that Martín's project does not simply signify the marrying of Spanish comics and animated documentary, but more importantly, it signifies the divorcing of current cinematic Spanish Civil War representations from a more realistic, documentary or *costumbrista* (meaning realistic, with a particular local or regional look) style that has predominated since the 1990s (Labanyi "Memory and Modernity" 103; Colmeiro 28).

The graphic novel documentary *30 Years of Darkness* strays even further from this familiar realism by re-employing the trope of haunting, a device common in the highly allusive representations of Spain's turbulent past that were released prior to the 1990s, but one that waned with what Spanish cultural studies scholar Jo Labanyi has repeatedly called a "memory boom." A cultural discourse on Spain's twentieth-century war and dictatorship first emerged in the years surrounding the nation's political transition to democracy, largely through the vehicles of cinema, television, and literature during the late 1970s and 1980s. However, towards the end of the following decade, as Labanyi notes, increasing cultural production of the sort resulted in a memory boom that escalated at the turn of the century and continued to intensify during the first decade of the twenty-first century ("Memory and Modernity" 95, "The Language of Silence" 26). Around this same time, however, Labanyi elsewhere speculates that the flood of civil- and post-war texts has abated, above all in the case of the Spanish novel (2008:119).

What occurred just following such speculation, however, is an additional "boom;" the aforementioned explosion of civil war-related graphic novels. From early on in this movement, historical memory in Spanish comics has been said to exhibit a cathartic function for present generations. This was first suggested by Antonio Martín in his invited prologue to Altarriba and Kim's *The Art of Flying*. Martín's assertion echoes the broader understanding of the healing powers of storytelling, a notion expounded by Irish philosopher Richard Kearney, who has continually theorized the ways in which narrative retelling and remembering might provide a cathartic release for sufferers of trauma. Martín's comment can be read as an ushering in of this idea into the realm of Spanish comics and, likewise, an attempt to further the Kearneysian notion of narrative catharsis, which largely recognizes the cathartic power of storytelling "to review *one's own* insufferable pain" (emphasis mine, 61).[10]

What Martín seems to suggest is that, through narrative recounting, catharsis can also occur for later generations who, despite not having lived the traumatic past being depicted, still feel it as their own. Thus, in Martín's assertion can also be found echoes of Marianne Hirsch's concept of Postmemory, a frequently-cited term introduced in the early 1990s that Hirsch herself continues to define and redefine, one that at its core suggests the transgenerational transmission of trauma: "[P]ostmemory most specifically describes the relationship of children of survivors of cultural or collective trauma to the experiences of their parents, experiences that they 'remember' only as the narratives and images with which they grew up, but that are so powerful, so monumental, as to constitute memories in their own right" (2001:9).

Given this definition, and knowing as we do that second- and now third-generation remembrance is a key characteristic of historical memory in Spanish comics, it should not come as a surprise that Postmemory has recently become a key critical lens through which *The Art of Flying* and other recent Spanish Civil War-themed comics have been read.[11] In his prologue, Martín makes specific reference to Altarriba, who published his comic in the wake of his father's suicide at the age of ninety. Yet resonances of the comics historian's notion of the cathartic function of Spanish comics for broader and later generations can be found in recent scholarly work, which asserts that the testimonial value of these graphic narratives transcends personal memory to become representative of collective memory, a painful remembering not only for the sake of generations past but likewise for the sake of the current, collective cultural identity.[12]

Martín's graphic novel documentary fits squarely into the broader, cathartic historical memory project intrinsic to Spanish comics through its emphasis on private memory conveyed by a later generation. The eighty-five-minute film centers on the figure of Manuel Cortés Quero (1906–1991), a barber by trade who, on March 3, 1936, would become the last republican mayor of Málaga in a public appointment that ultimately condemned him to a life of extreme privacy. The film narrates how, unable to escape Spain as the war drew to a close, Cortés made the covert retreat to Málaga. There, with the help of his wife, Juliana, he created a hiding place in a hole in the walls of his adoptive father's home, unaware at the time that he would come to inhabit this and other cramped hiding spaces for the next three decades.

The film moves between first-person and third-person narration as Cortés' testimony is voiced by popular Sevillian actor Juan Diego, while interview segments from expert historians and family witnesses corroborate Cortés' story and likewise provide accounts of other men in hiding. Meanwhile, the comics aesthetic does the work of "animando los hechos" ['animating the facts'] (*Notas sobre la película* 6).[13] Given that the Spanish documentary film relies on animation yet employs a nonconventional animation technique, *30 Years of Darkness* can be seen as a special class of animated documentary. The question at the heart of animated documentary scholarship, stemming from Annabelle Honess Roe's seminal book *Animated Documentary* (2013), is how animation functions as a representational strategy in documentary film.

This question gains further relevancy for Martín's graphic novel documentary, and an analysis of the function of the graphic novel aesthetic in *30 Years of Darkness* must likewise take into account that there has been much recent dialogue in comics studies regarding the documentation of history through drawing. A key issue explored in Hillary Chute's *Disaster Drawn: Visual Witness, Comics, and Documentary Form*, for example, is to what end, aesthetically and politically, the now-numerous comics about world-historical conflict visualize testimony (2). Chute's question echoes an assertion made earlier by Thierry Groensteen, who writes that "[i]n truth, in an image-based story, as in film or comics, each element, whether it is visual, linguistic, or aural, participates fully in the narration" (11).

Taking a cue from these two scholars, we are faced with many factors for consideration in the interpretation of Martín's comics-inspired animated documentary thriller. *30 Years of Darkness* combines a dark color palette of black, grey, and blue tones with a suspenseful soundtrack and uncanny fluctuations between abrupt character movements (the turn of a head, the blink of an eye, and the brusque movement of a limb) and the complete staticity that one would expect from figures within a comics panel. Movement is created by the panning and zooming of the camera in, out, and across the drawn images, much in the same way the reader's eye travels the comics page to construct meaning, thus through its technique mirroring the way in which comics are "at once static and animate" (Chute *Disaster* 16). Martín himself describes his pioneering aesthetic as "una novela gráfica en movimiento" ['a graphic novel in motion'] (*Notas* 8).

While *30 Years of Darkness*' graphic novel veneer explicitly echoes the notion that, during the bleak years of the Franco dictatorship, comics were "el mejor sitio para irse a vivir" ['the best place to go live'] (161), the elements that make up the mise-en-scène fittingly invoke the theme of terror that infiltrated comics in Spain beginning in the post-war period and that proliferated during these so-called thirty years of darkness. The jarring concurrence of movement and staticity that the added motion lends to the comics aesthetic heightens the mood of suspense and terror built within the documentary narrative. We see this from early on in, for example, the scene depicting Manuel's attempt to flee Málaga at the outbreak of the war. En route by foot to the Republican zone in the seaside city of Almería, a medium shot situates the protagonist amongst a crowd of roving exiles. These are collectively drawn in the act of walking yet appear on screen completely immobile save for the sudden turn of Manuel's head as he spots warships approaching. The ships, depicted in the following shot, almost imperceptibly bob in the water as their flashing lights amidst the foggy seascape constitute the majority of the on-screen movement and also serve as a stark sign of warning for Manuel and spectators alike.

This motion should not be perceived as cinematic animation, which, within a comics panel, would result in competing temporalities, but rather can be classified as short animation loops that "can be used within the [comics] panel without overly distorting the temporal map or impeding the reader as they move their attention across space" and, accordingly, do not change the role of the reader to that of a viewer (Gowdy 180). In a study on the communicative potential of animated elements within digital comics, Joshua Gowdy notes that when short animation loops are inserted into a comics' panel, the primary mode of narrative progression remains spatial, as "the loop in isolation does not progress either temporally or through space [...] as it operates at the rate of the reader's attendance" (179–80). A loop, according to Gowdy, "continually plays whether the reader is looking at it or not, it is only an active element of the fictive world while the reader attends to it; through attention to the preceding and subsequent panels, the reader is able to intuit duration in the same way they would with static panels" (183). For Gowdy, these movements have purpose. While they provide the reader with an "immersive experience" of a real-world environment, they should not be seen as a superfluous addition (as Groensteen himself has claimed of motion added to digital comics), but rather as one of many elements of signification, i.e., with communicative potential, cooperating within the comics page (184). Gowdy continues that "[m]otion can also be employed to represent specific acts or emphasize ideas that are latent within the still image" (178) as a means of "provid[ing] additional layers of signification to panels, contributing connotative meaning to mostly denotational images" (186).

We see this in the same scene with a quick jump to a close-up of Manuel that reveals his shocked expression, eyes wide and mouth agape, as Diego's voiceover narrates, "de pronto comenzaron a disparar contra nosotros. Fue terrible" ['suddenly they started shooting at us. It was terrible'] (00:15:35). Emphasizing this, one ship fires a missile into the crowd of again stationary onlookers, their dark, motionless silhouettes lifting unnaturally into the air before being enveloped by a cloud of black smoke and flames. In a subsequent shot, an extreme close-up features the ships' guns as they fire once more, and another quick jump to an extreme long shot of the seaside reveals the guns' target as the camera ever so slightly pans across the crowd of exiles along the escape route. Here, the majority of the motion is reserved for the exploding artillery, billowing smoke, and angry rising flames. On the one hand, these largely atmospheric injections of motion introduce to the film's comics aesthetic "a general sense of liveliness, and arguably a means to achieve immersion" (184). Amidst the carnage, the depiction of the citizens as motionless black dots, together with the restrained movement of the camera, reflects the notion of paralysis from fear and, likewise, the vulnerable and diminutive position the exiles hold facing the attacking warships and large enemy forces.

In a subsequent shot, which features a total juxtaposition of mobility and stasis, the camera rapidly zooms in on Manuel's motionless figure and face, his frozen look of terror rendered even more powerful by animation's creative control, as the sparks and ash that fly around his expressive but static face serve as minute on-screen indications of the full-scale horror that is being taken in by his terror-stricken eyes (figure 1.1).

Figure 1.1. *The Andalusian Guernica*

With a swift shift to a subjective shot, the viewer now watches from Manuel's perspective the massacre of women, children, and dozens of civilians in what has become known, as the film narrates, as "el Guernica andaluz" ['the Andalusian Guernica'] (00:16:50).

And, while in early scenes such as this, the graphic novel aesthetic together with creative control of motion and stasis and soundtrack are an aesthetics of terror that communicates the way Manuel might have felt behind enemy lines during the civil war, the same techniques further along in the film, along with character creation processes, are employed to move beyond suspense and terror to build an aesthetics of haunting that symbolizes Manuel's experience in hiding and likewise the phenomenon described by Patricia Keller in *Ghostly Landscapes* as "feeling the past in the present" (8). Keller's assertion that "[g]hosts are everywhere in contemporary Spain and hold a pervasive and profoundly palpable place in the country's cultural landscape" (*Ghostly Landscapes* 15) reflects a predominant psychological interpretation of historical memory that has prevailed in Spanish cultural studies.[14]

While Labanyi is credited with having inspired the pervasive application of a Derridean hauntology to Spanish cultural texts, asserting by 2007, for example, that habitually silenced testimonies re-emerge in an "aesthetics of haunting" (Labanyi "Memory," 109) many other notable critics of Spanish literary and cultural studies have since alluded to the notion of a haunting within contemporary Spanish society. Amago writes from a very recent standpoint that "the country's authoritarian past still reverberates through its cultural present" (32). Through a slightly more violent metaphor, Ulrich Winter speaks to the "irruption" of the lost past, which rematerializes in the present (19), a notion echoed more than one decade later by Joan Ramon Resina in *The Ghost of the Constitution*, where he states that "the Civil War's and the dictatorship's effects erupt in contemporary Spanish society" (4). And although Resina leaves the question of what the ghost of the constitution may be an open-ended one, Keller, in her review of the book, aptly writes that "[i]t may very well be historical memory itself, operating as the necessary force that keeps the door to that unbearable breach open, relentlessly working to make us—and future generations—aware that the past remains here, with us, always" ("The Ghost" 805).

In accordance with this notion of a ghostly haunting specifically, José Colmeiro cites the "spectral nature" of Spain's past, which contains stories that have been "silenced and erased, leaving only their ghostly traces" (31). Likewise, social anthropologist Francisco Ferrándiz speaks of the "recent rapid emergence of the ghosts of the Spanish Civil War" in his article that documents the exhumation process of mass graves in the first decade of twenty-first-century Spain (10). The second half of this chapter develops the argument that Martín's graphic novel documentary dialogues with the Derridean concept of hauntology to reflect this cited "spectral nature" of Spain's past, and likewise plays with the idea of the ghost through, in the words of sociologist Avery Gordon, "the merging of the visible and the invisible, the dead and the living, the past and the present" (24).

To follow in the footsteps of scholars of Spanish cultural studies who, for two decades now, have found Derrida's concept of hauntology particularly fitting for discussing the spectrality of the nation's repressed past is no doubt a predictable choice. However, in this particular case, it seems that the Derridian concept, which hinges on an idea of the ghost as "the traces of those who were not allowed to leave a trace" (Labanyi "Introduction" 1), is particularly germane to approaching the specters of Spain's post-war moles who were not once but twice forbidden to leave any trace: first, in hiding, and then through testimony as a side effect of the Amnesty Law.

To understand how the trope of haunting that guides the film lends itself to the nature of the moles' post-war experience, one has only to look as far as the live interview segments that direct the narrative. As Torbado, who participates in the narration of the film, states, "aunque físicamente Manuel Cortés estaba vivo, moralmente estaba ya muerto" ['although Manuel Cortés was physically alive, he was already morally dead'] (01:04:56). Torbado's revelation is soon after reiterated by Cortés' granddaughter, María de la Peña, who admits that "lo que percibo ahora es que era una fantasma dentro de su casa" ['what I perceive now is that he was a ghost within his home'] (01:05:26). Torbado's statement coupled with Peña's remark suggests an inversion of the typical ghost, however: these men were physically alive yet morally dead, and their presence in society and family life was reduced to an onlooker lurking and confined in the darkness of their hiding spaces.

30 Years of Darkness becomes an exceptional case, then, for not only employing the trope of haunting but for doing so to directly refer to a traumatic past, and likewise by employing a modern aesthetic that does not reinforce the "pastness of the past," and thus symptomatically create a disconnect between the narrative and the present-day audience (28), but rather does the work, in the words of Chute, of offering the "absorptive intimacy" inherent to comics narratives, while "defamiliarizing received images of history ... to communicate, [and] to circulate in the realms of the popular" (*Disaster* 142). Here I wish to turn to a discussion of how the reconstruction of Cortés's body, carefully constructed from photographs and voiceovers of contemporary actor Juan Diego, results in a ghostly imbrication of past and present. In the pages that follow, I will suggest that *30 Years of Darkness* becomes a filmic space to symbolically, as Derrida says, "speak *to the* specter, to speak with it, therefore, especially *to make or to let* a spirit *speak*" (emphasis in text, 11).

No doubt, there is an irony of recuperating the memory of Spain's postwar moles through the documentary genre as these citizens attempted to live for decades without a trace. Juliana recounts how she destroyed most photographs of Manuel in the hopes that it would help him avoid recognition from neighbors and authorities (00:23:37). Her confession highlights the scarcity of any archival materials with which to reconstruct this particular story. Luckily, the merits of Martín's graphic-novelesque reconstruction need not be debated, as cultural studies has reached the point where it readily accepts "the power of *drawing to tell*" (emphasis in text, Chute *Disaster* 252) and likewise recognizes that animation is not only a legitimate substitution for the archival but moreover, that its capabilities to represent certain aspects of life can in fact go beyond that of live-action filmmaking (Roe *Animated* 22).

Yet, to the spectator familiarized with Spanish cinema, and likewise with the predominant realism within civil war portrayals and the documentary genre alike, *30 Years of Darkness* raises questions. This is not just for the fact that it lacks any indexical sign that points to the real Manuel Cortés, but, moreover, for the fact that it displays a *double*-indexicality that points to an altogether different person from an altogether different era: contemporary Spain in the voice and face of Juan Diego. In the documentary film, Manuel both sounds and looks like someone other than himself, save for one brief archival clip at the film's conclusion, the implications of which will later be discussed. Yet, the creative element of Diego's vocal and visual inspiration behind Cortés' figure (and that of fellow sevillana actress Ana Fernández

Figure. 1.2. Juan Diego for Manuel Cortés Quero

behind his wife Juliana's character) is one immediate way that produces the trope of haunting. Not only does the color palette and *mise-en-scène* evoke a spectral past, as mentioned, but the specific character animation technique likewise evokes the concept of this past haunting the present.

As Roe has argued, in animated documentary, indexical connections to real subjects can result in an "uncanny sense of reality haunting the animated image" ("Uncanny" 31). This sense becomes heightened in Martín's film, as Manuel's body seems not real enough, or not archival enough, and yet appears too real, and too indicative of the present. The word *behind* is not coincidentally used here, as the actors' likenesses appear to exist just behind the layer of animation (see figure 1.2). Using a process similar to Rotoshop, the production team captured Diego and Fernández's emotions over four hundred times in photographic form to assure the final drawing of their protagonists were conceivably life-like.

Although, as noted above, comics narratives that document war and trauma have the purposeful effect of "defamiliarizing received images of history" (Chute *Disaster* 142), Diego, being a very recognizable face in Spanish cinema, gives Manuel an uncanny aspect of familiarity and reality. He is at once graphic and photographic, present and absent, himself and yet Other. Likewise, it renders the real Cortés virtually invisible in the documentation of his own testimony, tacitly reemphasizing the invisibility he faced during the decades of hiding.

Fittingly, Derrida's notion of hauntology directly relates to what Freud calls "the most striking" example of something uncanny: the return of the dead and spirits and ghosts (241). In depicting Manuel's narrative through

Diego's likeness, the dichotomies of past/present, presence/absence, and history/story become uncannily blurred. The animated aesthetic of Manuel's testimony acts as a border, but one that is permeable, between Cortés' memory and Diego as the communicating body, and likewise as Cortés' uncanny double in the Freudian sense. The psychoanalyst mentions the *interchanging of the self* that gives rise to the double. This occurs when "the subject identifies himself with someone else, so that he is in doubt as to which his self is, or substitutes the extraneous self for his own" (234). This first appearance of Diego on the documentary screen, as he identifies as Manuel, likewise suggests the apparitional debut of the latter's ghost as he speaks: "Mi nombre es Manuel Cortés Quero, y fui uno de esos hombres que pasarontoda una vida entre las sombras" ['My name is Manuel Cortés Quero, and I was one of those men who spent an entire lifetime within the shadows'] (00:03:24). The shot mimics that of a traditional talking-head interview, and the result is that the Spanish actor appears not to be re-enacting, but rather transmitting a testimony, apparently possessing the knowledge, feelings and experiences of the historical figure known as the "mole of Mijas (Málaga)." In this sense, the fact that Diego is never actually portrayed as speaking (his mouth remains closed as Manuel's voice reverberates from off-screen) can be read as an additional suggestion that the action on screen is not an objective re-enactment but rather a subjective remembering.

Photorealism in animated documentary has largely been said to function as what Roe has called "mimetic substitution," in the absence of archival footage striving to "create a visual link with reality" by closely resembling it, or, one step further, to "create an illusion of a filmed image" (*Animated* 24). For Martín's film, however, the double-indexical link to Diego suggests that, rather, the animation serves an "evocative" function: the portrayal of certain concepts, feelings, emotions, and states of mind that live-action imagery has difficulty representing—regardless of whether or not live-action footage exists (Roe *Animated* 25). The graphic novel aesthetic in *30 Years of Darkness*, then, can be said to exhibit Roe's function of evocation, ironically through a style that is highly mimetic rather than the more common abstract or symbolic style that usually characterizes evocative animation (Roe *Animated* 25). The distinctive animation technique stands out as even more remarkable considering that, by "[a]ctivating the past on the page, comics materializes the physically absent. It inscribes and concretizes, through the embodied labor of drawing, 'the spatial charge of a presence,' the tactile presence of a line, the body of the medium. The desire is to make the absent appear" (Chute *Disaster* 27).

Rather than capitalizing on the medium's ability to make the absent appear, the photorealism of Martín's comics aesthetic renders Manuel as absent, or only spectrally present, while likewise sketching Diego's contemporary figure into the historical past. And rather than concretizing either presence, the animated-yet-highly-realistic anachronism becomes an apt means of evoking the spectral quality of ghosts which, in the words of Colmeiro, are "nor here nor there" (25). Or, as Keller has pointed out following Derrida, the understanding "that ghosts exemplify not only a non-presence (the presence of an absence) but also the condition of non-contemporaneity" (*Ghostly* 5). In short, the graphic novel aesthetic should not be seen as a means of suggesting fiction but rather of suggesting friction, precisely the *merging* of the visible and the invisible, the dead and the living, and the past and the present of which Gordon writes.

It does not seem casual that Martín employed Diego to act as the communicating body for the Franco-era specter, as the actor's previous work in notable cinematic productions portraying the Franco dictatorship makes the conflation of his figure with the post-war specter an easy one in the spectators' mind. Diego has both symbolically and directly embodied Franco through his role as señorito Iván in Mario Camus' film adaptation of *Los Santos Inocentes* (1984) and his portrayal of the former dictator in Jaime Camillo's *Dragon Rapide* (1986), a career-defining performance that led to the first of his nine Goya award nominations. Throughout his career, the Sevillian actor has also participated in other Spanish productions that allude in various ways to Francoist Spain, such as José Luis García Sánchez's *La Corte del Faraón* (1985). However, his more recent participation in Azucena Rodríguez's nameless short documentary is notable, as the film, published in 2010 on Spanish media sites such as RTEV.es and ElPais.com, among global sites such as YouTube, similarly appears to dialogue with a Derridean model of hauntology. Rodríguez's film, part of the larger project *Cultura contra la impunidad del franquismo*, features fifteen personalities from the Spanish art scene who embody Civil War victims who were summarily executed.

In less than ten minutes, the recognizable faces of nine men and six women alternate on screen to deliver brief but compelling first-person testimonies that similarly conclude with the words "mi familia sigue buscándome. ¿Hasta cuándo?" ['my family continues searching for me. Until when?'] after which the sound of gunshots rings out as the subject fades from view in a phantasmagorical fashion; the dimly lit backdrop remains on screen throughout while each talking head, in turn, fades out, dissolving as the next subject fades in directly in its place.[15] The direct and (often unblinking) identification of the artist as victim unquestionably evokes the paradoxical "return" and the apparitional debut of a ghost theorized by Derrida, while the repetition of the closing statement, 'Until when?,' emphasizes the lingering of the past in the present that is currently alluded to by Spanish literary and cultural studies.

It is, to an even greater extent, however, that *30 Years of Darkness* plays with the return/apparition of the post-war specter. Derrida reasons that the apparition of the ghost cannot be controlled: "Each time is the event itself, a first time is the last time. Altogether other. Staging for the end of history. Let us call it *hauntology*" (emphasis in text, 10). Unlike Rodríguez's documentary, which solely relies on the concept of a communicating body, Martín's own film evokes a first apparition as a purely auditory phenomenon. Manuel's first line delivered in the film, set against a black screen, appears as "an echo without a communicating body" (Ribas-Casasayas and Petersen 2). Manuel recounts, "recuerdo como si fuera ayer, la boda de mi hija" ['I remember my daughter's wedding as if it were yesterday'] (00:01:30). Following this statement, shots of the festivities materialize on screen as the off-camera voice—seemingly everywhere and yet nowhere—carries on speaking, describing how, at his daughter's wedding, for the first time in a long time the house was filled with music, dancing and laughter, save for his wife and daughter who remain on high alert for the danger that he might be discovered. Not ironically, then, the first apparition as a purely auditory event mimics Cortés' experience as a mere haunting presence at his daughter's wedding, his memory limited to the sounds of the festivities.

As the scene unfolds, the suggestion is that, as Manuel's ghost is given the opportunity to narrate this memory—to speak—his presence becomes more tangible. The second apparition provides a partial view of Manuel as the camera follows a curious young guest into the house and up the stairs. The change of music as the girl enters the house to a soundtrack of chilling string instruments and pluckish piano notes, together with the creaking floorboards and the echo of footsteps, suggests the magnitude of the discovery that is about to take place as she reaches the door behind which Manuel hides until the tension and eerie silence are shattered with Juliana's sharp command: "¡No entrés ahí!" ['Don't go in there!'] (00:02:39). Following this, an extreme close-up features an eye center screen, captured in the act of peering through a brass keyhole belonging to this door. As the camera holds still, the eye momentarily wavers in the keyhole before vanishing from sight. In contrast to the jovial celebration taking place outside on the patio, this early scene works to introduce the Cortés home as a haunted house, a metaphor that the film continues to employ from these opening moments onwards. After establishing this motif in the opening scenes, the narrative introduces a third apparition of the ghost, this time by means of the communicating body pictured in figure 1.2.

From this third apparition onwards, Diego seemingly becomes the vehicle through which the specter communicates, although many subsequent shots similarly restrict the view to a single eye, symbolically reflecting the way in which the moles' identity was reduced during their confinement. In many scenes, the camera becomes the eye, capturing the scene through a small hole in a wall or foundation, attributing to these men the quality of haunting observer. The eye becomes a synecdoche *pars par toto* for the figure of the mole, accurately rendering them nothing more than a watchful eye.[16] This cinematic tactic reflects how the moles' other human senses diminished, sometimes purposefully, as the role of sight increased. Manuel recounts how he tried not to move, became accustomed to not speaking, and even willed himself not to fall ill (00:29:03). Limited to this subsistence, Manuel's own home becomes what Freud calls an *unheimliche haus* (Freud 219).

Rather than a place of security, Manuel's house and his relationship with it becomes characterized by surveillance. This control tactic has historically been employed in many regimes, and Franco's was no exception. The largely inanimate representation of Manuel's character also speaks to the limits of his experience within his own home under the regime's surveillance. In this vein, it does not seem casual that Cortés' animated yet largely inanimate figure juxtaposes Franco's archival figure, depicted in a newsreel clip of his victory parade (00:24:53–00:25:21). The dictator appears very much animate, visible, and present; three attributes emphasized by subsequent long shots that capture him high on his podium as he surveys the parade in the streets of Madrid. While this segment reinforces the mood of surveillance and Franco's omnipresence, the narration of Manuel's testimony in sequential, panel-like shots, rather than fluid animation or newsreels metaphorically speaks to "a fragmentary, discontinuous, spectral past" (Labanyi "History" 69), just as it does his desire to escape notice, or, metaphorically speaking, slip through the cracks. As Chute explains, while "comics is a form about presence, it is also stippled with erasure—in the interruption provided by the ambiguous spaces of the gutter" (*Disaster* 17).

What is more, the use of victory parade footage, which features a wide-angle shot and often maintains a far distance between camera and subject (here, Franco), works to tacitly reiterate the claustrophobic confinement that marks Manuel's existence. This is not so tacitly communicated to us through the graphic novel segments, which effectively create an affective aesthetics of confinement. This begins with the way that, when the camera does not take on the subjective eye/I shot, it keeps a very close proximity to Manuel. The already claustrophobic shots are made even more so by the lack of depth that the 2D comics page affords to the mise-en-scène, as well as by the (un)natural stifling of character movement within the tight comics-cinematic shots. We feel as if we are together thrust into the close quarters of the comics panels

Figure 1.3. The film studio and the Haunted House Motif

with our protagonist. And although the frames that surround these panels are often only implied, as they exist beyond the frame of the shot, we can feel their crushing weight in a way that allows us to imagine the proximity of the four walls that surround the protagonist in his hiding space.

Aside from the animated scenes and the archival segments, the film studio can be read as a third space that substantiates the motif of the haunted house. The live interviews recorded against a solid black backdrop are offset by beige partitions onto which dull beams of light are cast (see figure 1.3). The dim spotlights aimed at these partitions, rather than at the interviewees' bodies, result in the casting of shadows over their figures. In this space, the camera likewise creates the majority of the movement, creeping around the expert and family witnesses. The camera bobs, draws near to, and sways around the subjects, but rarely provides a direct, head-on shot, as if the interviewees are unaware of this looming presence and are, in fact, addressing an unseen audience.

As the haunted house motif from the graphic novel segments crosses into the shots of the film studio, the metaphor extends itself both forward and backward temporally. The spectator understands that, just as Manuel's life was reduced to a haunting presence within the walls of his own home, so too this spectral past lingers within the borders of twenty-first-century Spain. This notion of a multi-temporal haunting emerges through the relationship between the archival, live-action, and animated spaces in yet an additional way. The setting of the film studio is evidently a space of the present, notable in on- and off-screen cues such as language, clothing, and furnishings, as well as the production clarity and techniques. Conversely, the numerous archival scenes clearly indicate a space of the past: grainy shots depict agrarian culture in the western region of Andalusia, battlefield scenes from the Civil War, Franco's troops occupying Málaga, and the 1939 Victory Parade. However, a third temporal space—the comics realm of Cortés' first-person testimony—is not so easily defined. On the surface, the reconstruction of mid-twentieth century Spain in the form of a so-called "graphic novel documentary" also appears to be a space of the past, yet closer attention to this animated level of the story, especially when juxtaposed with the indisputable spaces of past and present depicted through live-action and archival footage, reveals that it is actually a space in which both the past and the present are in flux. The graphic novel aesthetic reveals a spatiotemporal nonsynchronism: the image of the past has been reconstructed using modern tools and has a modern façade, and while the narrative recounts the traumatic happenings of mid-twentieth-century Spain, the voice and face of the story point to the present. Ultimately, the aesthetic mirrors, in the words of Keller, the fact that a haunting occurs "at a disjuncture in time," which is to say that "time can be (and can be *made* to be) out of sync with itself" (emphasis in text, *Ghostly* 4).

In other words, Martín's chosen aesthetic for transmitting Manuel's testimony does the opposite of reinforcing the "pastness of the past," which, as Colmeiro suggests, is the effect of realistic and costumbrista depictions. Instead, it depicts the imbrication of past and present, a defamiliar gray area emphasized by the gray tones on screen. In short, the comics realm is the medium through which the specter of the past is reanimated: cinematically drawing them on screen and likewise drawing on the notion of its return. In this regard, there is an important juxtaposition between the animated sphere and the film studio, one that has to do with the notion of letting the ghost speak. Derrida theorizes that when it comes to letting the ghost speak, a scholar "believes that looking is sufficient," and is, therefore, "not always in the most competent position to do what is necessary: speak to the specter" (11). While the film studio is a place in which the ghost is *spoken of* by intellectuals and scholars, the animated narrative is a place in which, as the film suggests, the ghost *speaks*. Cortés' testimony is voiced by popular culture, aptly through a popular culture medium.

Derrida suggests that we talk to ghosts out of a need "to exorcize not in order to chase away the ghosts, but this time to grant them the right ... to a hospitable memory ... out of a concern for justice" (175). Derrida's proposition is that ghosts of the past feel anything but hospitable memory, which is something Manuel remarks early on in the film: "a veces lo único que nos quedaen la vida son los recuerdos, aunque para nosotros estos no son más que pesadillas" [sometimes the only thing we have left in life are our memories, although for us these are nothing more than nightmares'] (00:02:45).

Following Derrida, in order to move from nightmare to hospitable memory, Manuel's ghost must speak. Performing this, Martín's film becomes what Ferrándiz calls the "resonating chambers" that voices like Manuel Cortés lacked for over sixty years (10). Moreover, the conclusion of the film suggests that through recounting its testimony, Manuel's ghost becomes exorcized.

The final scene visually suggests a separation of Manuel's ghost from its communicating body. This scene can be said to contain the first appearance of Manuel's archival body and likewise the last apparition of his ghost. The tone of the accompanying music changes from the eerie tune dominant throughout the film to a peaceful piano melody that parallels the calm that Manuel, now an old man, feels as he experiences his first few steps as a free man in his home. A brighter turn in the color palette, at times iridescent white, also suggests that his home has returned to a *heimliche* place once again and likewise accentuates the cathartic moment being depicted. As Manuel makes his way slowly through his house and towards the front door, the camera adopts his view. This time, however, the subjective lens is not restricted to a hole-in-the-wall perspective but rather offers a full view of his surroundings. The mood is no longer one of threatening surveillance, but rather the bright color palette and wide angle shot suggest both the freedom to see and be seen. Through the subjective lens, the spectator experiences the walk towards freedom, descending together with Manuel the staircase from his second-story hiding place, pausing with the old man to consider the family portraits on the living room wall, as Manuel's reflection in the glass frames emphasizes his spectral presence within his family and likewise his absence within the photos, and finally approaching the front door through which he is about to traverse. As Manuel opens the door, the subjective shot abruptly changes to an objective one. The camera draws backward as the spectator is left gazing at the back of the animated Diego-figure standing at the threshold. The scene suggests an exorcism of Cortés' ghost, and the audible and prolonged exhale emphasizes this moment of release.

The following scene reiterates the notion of a separation of the afterlife of the past from the present. Now, outside the Cortés home in the streets of Málaga, the camera rests in front of Manuel and Juliana. Though there is a moment in which the duo is depicted in their animated bodies, the camera again draws backward as the animated bodies simultaneously shift into the archival figures of Manuel and Juliana. The distancing of the camera from the archival bodies communicates a distancing of the past, and, with the turn to veracity in the film's final moments, there is a positive connotation to the pastness of the past. The film's singular archival photograph of Cortés confirms what the scene at the threshold suggested: a moment of catharsis in which there is a release of a specter of the past from the present (social) body. The trope of haunting ceases to exist in the narrative at the moment this archival scene appears, as it is at this point that the exhumation has apparently taken place, and the imbrication of the past and present ceases.

The turn to the archival at the film's conclusion is a characteristic that *30 Years of Darkness* shares with the acclaimed animated documentary, Ari Folman's *Waltz with Bashir* (Israel, 2008). Roe has noted of Folman's documentary that "concluding the film with live-action footage suggests narrative resolution" (*Animated* 167). Roe ponders, however, whether or not the sudden switch from a consistent animation style throughout to live-action material undermines the potential of the animation that came before, especially at this moment of narrative resolution. This is also an appropriate question for Martín's film, but one to which there is a definitive answer. Here, the turn to archival in the conclusion of a film that employs the trope of haunting is a reinforcement of the exhumation of the ghost, of the departure of the past from the present, and of the perceived end of the haunting through the long-awaited speaking to the past. This cinematic move at the film's end accurately reflects the nature of the ghost, which, as Gordon writes, are "haunting reminders of lingering troubles." However, as Gordon continues, "once the conditions that call them up and keep them alive have been removed, their reason for being and their power to haunt are severely restricted" (xix). Moreover, Gordon elaborates on the photograph's relationship to haunting and to the ghost story, noting that "[w]hen photographs appear in contexts of haunting, they become part of the contest between familiarity and strangeness, between hurting and healing, that the ghost is registering" (102–3).

In this case, the spectator understands upon viewing the archival image that it is familiarity and healing that wins out. With the archival turn, Cortés' story is relegated firmly to the past, or better yet, to the realm of historical memory. This visually communicates the same notion echoed by Torbado in the final minutes of the film. As Torbado narrates, in all the uproar that has risen about historical memory, no one has remembered these people who were the most victimized of all (1:19:24–1:19:34). What is more, Juliana's wide smile and Manuel's slight grin in the archival image communicate Derrida's notion of the past becoming a "hospitable memory." In this sense, *30 years of Darkness* performs the work of unsuturing the past from the present.

Nicole Mombal, who takes a pedagogical approach to Martín's documentary film, concludes that by inserting the story of Spain's post-war moles into historical memory debates, the film offers catharsis to these men and their families by "restor[ing] moral, political, and legal personhood to the topos" (179). While I am in complete agreement with Mombal's evaluation of the cathartic function of the film, I would add that it is in the turn to the archival where we can precisely witness this symbolic *restoration* of personhood, or catharsis. It is fair to say that this was felt by Cortés, who testifies in Torbado and Leguineche in *The Moles* that the initial euphoria he felt, as well as the general satisfaction of being able to go wherever he pleased, toasting his freedom in the company of others, including town officials and local members of law enforcement. The then-sexagenarian admits, however, the disillusionment that he felt towards societal corruption, rampant urbanization, a transformation of customs, and, notably, a changing and politically disinterested youth. Meanwhile, we know that, in the decade or more following the publication of his testimony and his passing, Cortés himself, an apparently steadfast and resolute man, reintegrated himself into politics, founding a municipal group for the Socialist Workers' Party in his municipality of Mijas, and serving as chairperson until his death in 1991.

It is worth mentioning that Chute, taking her lead from Art Spiegelman, who talks of the creative process behind his Pulitzer Prize-winning *Maus* (1991), might actually disagree with the suggestion that comics narratives dealing with personal traumatic stories are cathartic. For this comics scholar, they are not about an emotional recuperation, "but a textual, material one" (*Graphic* 3). And while Chute may have a point for the group of women comics authors whose autobiographical narratives of personal traumas she analyzes, it is undeniable that a traumatic history tied to material and textual disappearances (first of one's physical trace in life and then a later stifling of testimonies) might mean both a textual and material recuperation as well as a cathartic emotional recuperation (or what Mombal calls a recovery of personhood). In other words, in the case of the repression suffered by Spain's post-war moles, it is not easy to distinguish where the emotional recuperation begins and the material or textual recuperation ends, as the two are interconnected in the visual representation of their trauma.

I would be remiss, however, to not return to the idea that the film holds an additional cathartic function. This would be particularly problematic after having outlined the close ties between Martín's graphic novel documentary and the cathartic recuperation of historical memory unfolding in Spain's graphic novel movement by a (mostly) new generation of Spanish artists that take it upon themselves to represent the trauma of generations past. Here, it was mentioned the painful remembering of the past is being carried out because young Spaniards still feel it as its own due to a phenomenon that Hirsch calls postmemory. In this way, the turn to the archival symbolizes a cathartic release of the past from the present. Although this was just mentioned, what remains to be said is how *30 Years of Darkness* plays a part in what Hirsch very recently called the "connective arts of postmemory." For Hirsch, postmemory, which is not only intergenerational—between generations—but also intra-generational—between populations ("Connective Arts" 173), offers a responsibility that hinges on an ability to *respond* and "can become a practice of repair and transformation" (my emphasis, 173, 5). What Hirsch finds particularly exciting is that "[a]cross the globe, contemporary writers, filmmakers, visual artists, memorial artists and museologists have forged an aesthetic of postmemory in relation to past and geographically distant catastrophic histories" (174). In this way, for its "aesthetic continuities" (175)—with one foot in the realm of comics and the other in animated documentary, and meanwhile employing various haunting-related tropes to visualize traumas of repression, the testimonial ties and transformative potential that *30 Years of Darkness* holds goes further than national borders with Spain's historical memory comics project, to a global connectivity that instead "reminds of multiple pasts while facing potential futures" (175).

NOTES

1. This essay contains content from the chapter "Animating Autobiography: Historical Memory and Catharsis in Manuel H. Martín's Graphic Novel Documentary *30 años de oscuridad / 30 Years of Darkness* (2012)" in *Politically Animated: Nonfiction Animation from the Hispanic World* by Jennifer Nagtegaal © University of Toronto Press 2023 (pp. 89–111). It has been adapted and reprinted with permission of the publisher.

2. As the text on the book jacket of Torbado and Leguineche's *The Moles* describes, while many of these "forgotten men" were Republican soldiers who fought against Franco's Nationalist forces, others were prominent Socialist leaders and activists whose prewar authority was seen as a threat to the new regime, while others were peasants and artisans who were recruited against their will to what would end up being the losing side.

3. Although the Law's full title is "Ley por la que se reconocen y amplían derechos y se establecen medidas en favor de quienes padecieron persecución o violencia durante la guerra civil y la dictadura" ['Law to Recognise and Broaden Rights and to Establish Measures in Favour of Those Who Suffered Persecution or Violence during the Civil War'], it quickly became coined as the *Ley de Memoria Histórica* ['Historical Memory Law'] by the Spanish media. Jo Labanyi succinctly outlines the law's pathway to enactment when she states that it was "proposed by the PSOE government initially in 2004; first published in July 2006 to outcries from the Partido Popular and the right-wing media; finally approved by Congress on 31 October 2007 after last-minute revisions to secure the support of Izquierda Unida; and implemented on 26 December 2007" (2008:119).

4. The effort, led by journalist Emilio Silva, founder of the Association for the Recovery of Historical Memory, started as an attempt to identify the remains of his grandfather, who was executed during the war. Guided by historical records, a team of biologists, anthropologists, and researchers located and excavated a mass grave, finding thirteen skeletons. The following year, a DNA match was established between Silva and some of the remains, the first DNA-aided identification of Spanish Civil War remains.

5. It should be noted from the outset that the widely-used but not un-problematic nor un-controversial term "historical memory" makes exclusive reference to the determined period of twentieth-century history of the Spanish Civil War and immediate post-war period, becoming, as Labanyi notes, synonymous with the civic duty of recalling the repression carried out during these four decades, largely, although not exclusively, by addressing the repression of *republican memory*, and ultimately with the goal of *national* reconciliation (emphasis in text, 2006: 87–90)

6. In 1938, *Pelayos*, a propagandistic by-product of the Carlist traditionalist movement, was fused with the Falangist *Flechas* under the title *Flechas y Pelayos*, mirroring the unification by Franco of the two political movements that backed them. As Michel Matly makes clear, although the children's magazines remained propagandistic, from this moment on, their pages and comics panels were no longer employed as vehicles for warlike and political messages.

7. Although there are too many to name, these appear to be three of the most popular and successful children's magazines produced within and because of the war, though others of note include *Chicos* (1938–1955) on the side of the Nationalists and for the Republicans we can name the two-issue *El Soldado Canuto* in 1937 as well as the already established commercial children's magazine, *Pocholo*, born at the start of the 1930s which evolved as the events of the second half of the tumultuous decade unfolded.

8. The trio of directors was nominated to the category of Best Director at the 2020 Goya Awards, only one of fifteen nominations tied to *The Endless Trench*. The film's cast and crew did succeed in taking home a pair of these: Best Actress (awarded to Sevillana actress Belén Cuesta) and Best Sound.

9. To date, two studies exist that briefly analyze the animated aesthetic in Martín's documentary. In 2019, Sonia García López examined how *30 Years of Darkness*, along with a handful of other animated documentaries from Spain and Latin America, participates in a global trend in digital culture in which documentary filmmakers are repeatedly turning to animation for the representation of cognitive realities, as well as political and historical processes lacking audiovisual records. In a study from 2013, Inmaculada Sánchez Alarcón and Alejandro Jerez Zambrana likewise briefly analyze the form of Martín's film while also examining more than a dozen other recent Spanish historical documentaries of a fictional or subjective nature, concluding that a shift is occurring in conventional thought, which holds the visual index as the mark of authenticity is the documentary genre. A third study by Nicole Mombell approaches *30 Years of Darkness* from a pedagogical standpoint, offering advice on how this and other popular Spanish films from the current century can be employed to teach representations of resistance and repression and what these portrayals "can teach us about how contemporary filmmakers have reacted to the historical period and recreated it" (180).

10. Although Kearney initially draws his examples from psychotherapy, ancient myth, and historical and fictional narratives (largely from Irish literature), it is subsequently through global narratives of genocide that he seeks to explore "how the cathartic function applies to the most controversial limit cases of trauma" (59). While one could argue, as Kearney points out, for the utter inadequacy of the cathartic narrative in these testimonies of genocide, "it is important to go on telling the story and seeking some sort of purgative release, however minimal or provisional. Otherwise, melancholy wins out over mourning,

paralysis over pathos and oblivion over remembrance" (59). The latter is particularly relevant to the case of historical memory in Spain, although remembrance is being fostered by later generations, as evidenced by the recent boom of Spanish comics that depict the Spanish Civil War.

11. Tronsgard, for example, critically applies the concept of Postmemory to not only Altarriba and Kim's comic but likewise to Sento Llobell's *Un medico novato* (2013), which conceptually mirrors *The Art of Flying* and *A Long Silence* for the fact that the graphic narrative protagonizes a father figure to narrate the memories of Sento's father-in-law, Dr. Uriel, whose life was altered by the civil war. These two works, as Tronsgard notes, "are not merely historical but are also self-reflexive about the inherited nature of their memory . . . these works act out postmemory by playing with the question of biography/autobiography, silent and fantastic imagery, and political engagement" (268).

12. Sarah Harris, for example, concludes that personal narratives like *A Long Silence*, *Paracuellos*, *The Art of Flying* and *The Furrows of Chance* "retrieve and mourn shared community violence in a manner unlike any other medium" (np). Similarly, Javier Sánchez Zapatero notes of *A Long Silence* and *The Art of Flying* that their testimonial value transcends the personal story of struggle and despair to become chronicles of twentieth-century Spain (1093–4). Additionally, Carla Suárez-Vega's study of *The Art of Flying* and *Un medico novato* leads her to conclude that these narratives "showcase the need for a dialogue and a space where to renegotiate a trauma that is still present and that has an effect in the later generations, who haven't lived this traumatic past but who still feel it as its own" (287–8).

13. All translations throughout this essay are my own.

14. While Keller's 2016 seminal study evidences the perpetuation of the hauntological perspective introduced by Labanyi in the early 2000s, I would be remiss not to note that this debate has been met with some criticism. Notably, Ángel G. Loureiro labels figures of speech such as the *return of the repressed* "poor metaphors for extremely complex, multilayered and contentious historical or cultural processes," for, as he argues, "physical and psychical pathologies that pertain to individuals . . . cannot be easily translated to social bodies or processes," see Ángel G. Loureiro, "Pathetic Arguments," *Journal of Spanish Cultural Studies* 9, no. 2 (2008): pp. 225–37, https://doi.org/10.1080/14636200802283746, 225. Meanwhile, others have attempted to dialogue with the hauntological perspective in order to broaden its application: echoing Loureiro, Juan F. Egea, in his reading of Ricardo Franco's 1994 documentary *Después de tantos años / After So Many Years*, calls such metaphors "ruinous" for that fact that they are, in his esteem, more aptly symbolic of "futuros perdidos" ['lost futures'] rather than of repressed pasts, see Juan F. Egea, "Después De Tantos Años: Filme Espectral y Metaforicidad Ruinosa En La España Post-92," *Journal of Spanish Cultural Studies* 17, no. 2 (2016): pp. 163–76, https://doi.org/10.1080/14636204.2016.1 165853, 170.; and, while Santiago Morales Rivera does not object to psychoanalytic readings of traumatic symptoms in Spain's cultural products from the final two decades of the twentieth century, he aims for a re-reading that rather approaches melancholy through lenses such as that of ironic humour, see Santiago Morales Rivera, *Anatomía Del Desencanto: Humor, Ficción y Melancolía En España, 1976–1998* (West Lafayette: Purdue University Press, 2017). Nevertheless, the release of *30 Years of Darkness* in 2012, just following the apex of the swing towards spectrality in the realms of Spanish media and scholarship alike,

no doubt reveals it as a cultural product that reflects and signifies a major ideology in contemporary Spanish society, and accordingly warrants reading in this light.

15. The short documentary, which can be found at http://elpais.com/elpais/2010/06/14/videos/1276503418_870215.html, features personalities such as Pedro Almodóvar, Maribel Verdú, Javier Bardem, Almudena Grandes, Juan Diego Botto, María Galiana, Carmen Machi, Juan José Millás, Aitana Sánchez-Gijón, Paco León, Pilar Bardem, José Manuel Seda, Hugo Silva, and Miguel Ríos.

16. In fact, the 2010 version of Torbado and Leguineche's *The Mole*, published by Capitán Swing, adopts a similar image on their cover: an eye, peering out from its hiding place, is painted over in the colors of the flag of the Second Spanish Republic.

WORKS CITED

Amago, Samuel. "Drawing (On) Spanish History." In *Consequential Art: Comics Culture in Contemporary Spain*, ed. Samuel Amago and Matthew J. Marr, 31–64. Toronto: University of Toronto Press, 2019.

Alarcón, Inmaculada Sánchez, and Alejandro Jerez Zambrana. "¿La memoria encontrada o la memoria inventada? Recursos narrativos y pautas de estilo de índole ficcional o subjetiva en los documentales históricos españoles recientes." *Historia y Comunicación Social* 18 (2013): 299–311.

Aldama, Frederick Luis, ed. *Comics Studies Here and Now*. New York: Routledge, 2018.

Altarriba, Antonio. "Los años que vivimos en viñetas. Breve sociología sentimental del tebeo en tiempos de Franco." *Cuco, Cuadernos de cómic* 2 (2014):160–63.

Ausente, Daniel. "La memoria gráfica y las sombras del pasado." In *Supercómic: Mutaciones de la novela gráfica contemporánea*, coordinated by Santiago García, 107–35. Errata Naturae, 2013.

Bórquez, Néstor. "La épica del exiliado en viñetas: el cómic y los matices de la historia. Entrevista con Paco Roca." *Olivar* 15, no. 22 (2014), n. pag.

Chute, Hillary L. *Disaster drawn: Visual witness, comics, and documentary form*. Cambridge: Harvard University Press, 2016.

Chute, Hillary L. *Graphic Women: Life Narrative and Contemporary Comics*. New York: Columbia University Press, 2010.

Colmeiro, José. "Nation of Ghosts?: Haunting, Historical Memory and Forgetting in Post-Franco Spain." *452ºF. Electronic journal of theory of literature and comparative Literature* 4 (2011): 17–34.

Derrida, Jacques. *Specters of Marx: The State of the Debt, the Work of Mourning, and the New International*, trans. Peggy Kamuf. New York: Routledge, 1994.

Egea, Juan F. "Después de tantos años: Filme espectral y metaforicidad ruinosa en la España post-92." *Journal of Spanish Cultural Studies* 17, no. 2 (2016): 163–17.

Ferrándiz, Francisco. "The Return of Civil War Ghosts: The Ethnography of Exhumations in Contemporary Spain." *Anthropology Today* 22, no. 3 (2006): 7–12.

Ferrándiz, Francisco, and Alejandro Baer. "Digital Memory: The Visual Recording of Mass Grave Exhumations in Contemporary Spain." *Forum Qualitative Sozialforschung*

/ *Forum: Qualitative Social Research* 9, no. 3 (2008): www.qualitative-research.net/index .php/fqs/article/view/1152/2558. Accessed October 21, 2016.

Freud, Sigmund. "The Uncanny (1919)." In *An Infantile Nurosis and Other Works*, trans. James Strachey, 219–52. London: The Hogarth Press, 1955.

Gavaler, Chris. *Superhero Comics*. London: Bloomsbury Publishing, 2017.

Gordon, Avery F. *Ghostly Matters: Haunting and the sociological imagination*. Minneapolis: University of Minnesota Press, 2008.

Gowdy, Joshua. "Meaning from Movement: Blurring the Temporal Border Between Animation and Comics." *Studies in Comics* 9, no. 2 (2018): 177–92.

Groensteen, Thierry. *The System of Comics*, trans. Bart Beaty and Nick Nguyen. Jackson: University Press of Mississippi, 2007.

Harris, Sarah. "'I had not dared to remember': Trauma and Historical Memory in Recent Spanish Comics." *ImageTexT* 9, no. 1 (2017): n. pag.

Hirsch, Marianne. "Surviving Images: Holocaust Photographs and the Work of Postmemory." *The Yale Journal of Criticism* 14, no. 1 (2001): 5–37.

Kearney, Richard. "Narrating Pain: The Power of Catharsis." *Paragraph* 30, no. 1 (2007): 51–66.

Keller, Patricia. *Ghostly Landscapes: Film, Photography, and the Aesthetics of Haunting in Contemporary Spanish Culture*. Toronto: University of Toronto Press, 2016.

Keller, Patricia. "The Ghost in the Constitution: Historical Memory and Denial in Spanish Society by Joan Ramon Resina." *Revista de Estudios Hispánicos* 53, no. 2 (2019): 803–5.

Labanyi, Jo. "Historias de Víctimas: La Memoria Histórica y el Testimonio en la España Contemporánea." *Iberoamericana* 6, no. 24 (2006): 87–98.

Labanyi, Jo. "History and Hauntology; or, What Does One Do with the Ghosts of the Past? Reflections on Spanish Film and Fiction of the Post-Franco Period." In *Disremembering the Dictatorship: The Politics of Memory in the Spanish Transition to Democracy*, ed. Joan Ramón Resina, 65–82. Amsterdam: Rodopi, 2000.

Labanyi, Jo. "Introduction: Engaging with Ghosts; or, Theorizing Culture in Modern Spain." In *Constructing Identity in Contemporary Spain: Theoretical Debates and Cultural Practice*, edited Jo Labanyi, 1–14. Oxford: Oxford University Press, 2002.

Labanyi, Jo. "Memory and Modernity in Democratic Spain: The Difficulty of Coming to Termswith the Spanish Civil War." *Poetics Today* 28.1 (2007): 89–116.

Labanyi, Jo. "The Language of Silence: Historical Memory, Generational Transmission and Witnessing in Contemporary Spain." *Journal of Romance Studies* 9, no. 3 (2009): 23–35.

Labanyi, Jo. "The Politics of Memory in Contemporary Spain." *Journal of Spanish Cultural Studies* 9, no. 2 (2008): 119–25.

López, Sonia García. "El Documental de Animación: Un Género Audiovisual Digital." *ZER: Revista de Estudios de Comunicación/KomunikazioIkasketenAldizkaria*. 24, no. 46 (2019): 129–45.

Loureiro, Ángel G. "Pathetic arguments." *Journal of Spanish Cultural Studies* 9, no. 2 (2008): 225–37.

Martín, Antonio. "Para Iniciar el Despegue." In *El Arte de Volar*, Antonio Altarriba and Kim, creators, 5–10. Edicions de Ponent, 2010.

Martín, Manuel H., director. *30 Años de Oscuridad*. La Claqueta, 2012.

Matly, Michel. "L'image de la Guerre civile espagnole dans la bande dessinée entre 1936 et 1975-II." *Cahiers de Civilisation Espagnole Contemporaine* 15 (2015). https://doi.org/10.4000/ccec.5911.

McCloud, Scott. *Understanding Comics*. New York: William Morrow, 1994.

Mombell, Nicole. "Teaching Representations of Resistance and Repression in Popular Spanish Film." *Periphērica: Journal of Social, Cultural, and Literary History* 1, no. 2 (2020): 163–83.

Morales Rivera, Santiago. *Anatomía Del Desencanto: Humor, Ficción y Melancolía en España, 1976–1998*. Purdue: Purdue University Press, 2017.

"Notas Sobre la Película." *30 Años de Oscuridad*. La Claqueta, 2012.

Resina, Joan Ramon. *The Ghost in the Constitution: Historical Memory and Denial in Spanish Society*. Liverpool: Liverpool University Press, 2017.

Ribas-Casasayas, Alberto, and Amanda L. Petersen, eds. *Espectros: Ghostly Hauntings in Contemporary Transhispanic Narratives*. Lewisburg: Bucknell University Press, 2015.

Roe, Annabelle Honess. *Animated Documentary*. London: Palgrave Macmillan, 2013.

Roe, Annabelle Honess. "Uncanny Indexes: Rotoshopped Interviews as Documentary." *Animation* 7, no. 1 (2012): 25–37.

Tahmassian, Leah. "*Espacios en Blanco*: Historical Memory, Defeat, and the Comics Imaginary." In *Spanish Graphic Narratives: Recent Developments in Sequential Art*, ed. Collin McKinney and David F. Richter, 29–46. London: Palgrave Macmillan, 2020.

Torbado, Jesús, and Manuel Leguineche. *The Moles*, trans. Nancy Festinger. London: Secker & Warburg, 1981.

Tronsgard, Jordan. "Drawing the Past: The Graphic Novel as Postmemory in Spain." *Romance Notes* 57, no. 2 (2017): 267–79.

Vega, Carla Suárez. "Memoria Histórica en Viñetas: Representaciones de la Guerra Civil Española a Través de la Narrativa Gráfica y los Testimonios Familiares." *Caracol* 15 (2018): 286–307.

Winter, Ulrich. "'Localizar a los Muertos' y 'Reconocer al Otro': Lugares de Memoria(s) en la Cultura Española Contemporánea." In *Casa Encantada: Lugares de Memoria en la España Constitucional (1978–2004)*, ed. Joan Ramón Resina and Ulrich Winter, 17–39. Madrid: Iberoamericana, 2005.

Zapatero, Javier Sánchez. "La memoria de la Guerra Civil en Viñetas: *El Arte de Volar* y *Un Largo Silencio*." *Signa: Revista de la Asociación Española de Semiótica* 25 (2016): 1081–1095.

CHAPTER 2

GRAPHIC REPRESENTATIONS OF VIOLENCE IN *LA HERENCIA DEL CORONEL* BY CARLOS TRILLO AND LUCAS VARELA

DIANA PIFANO

In his inaugural address in 2003, former Argentinian President Nestor Kirchner vindicated the memory of the 30,000 people detained and disappeared during the country's last military dictatorship (1976–1983). Throughout his government, he would renew his solidarity with what he called a decimated generation by enacting policies that shifted sociopolitical attitudes, altered public perception, and encouraged the work of human rights groups and the victims' family members, who have sought truth and justice for decades.[1] However, the most enduring aspect of this leader's politics of memory is perhaps his contribution to the revitalization of the cultural dialogue regarding Argentina's tragic past and nurturing the production of novels, plays, films, documentaries, and photographs that explore the enduring damage caused by the regime.

We find the comic *La herencia del coronel*, written by Carlos Trillo and illustrated by Lucas Varela, amongst an impressive corpus that explores the topic once again, three decades after the Military Junta came to power. *La herencia* was initially published in serialized form between 2007 and 2008 in the Argentine comic magazine *Fierro*, and later edited as a graphic novel in Spain (2010). It is the story of Elvio Gustavino, the son of a Colonel tasked with detaining and interrogating militants during the dictatorship. In the narrative present, the protagonist is deranged by the memories of his father's acts, and in particular, the memory of Analía Sylveira, a woman who the Colonel tortured and raped in their home. As the plot begins to unfold, we find that Elvio is possessed by an intense sexual desire toward an antique doll he calls Luisita, which he believes to be related to the doll on which his father practiced his torture techniques. As Elvio's paraphilia grows, his overall mental state deteriorates. He begins to have frequent hallucinations and neglects his invalid mother, who eventually dies of starvation. The reader's initial rejection of him builds throughout the text and is cemented upon learning that he willingly partook in the rape of Analía. After that, not even his frenzied descent into madness and eventual suicide are enough to redeem him. *La herencia* presents a dark and violent narrative universe filled with scenes of explicit brutality that require the reader to face the heinous crimes perpetrated by the apparatus of state terror. Additionally, the characters are entirely amoral, and the authors do nothing to allay the complicity of the Colonel's family.

However, despite being a challenging and uncomfortable read, this text merits close analysis, given that Trillo and Varela explore two topics that have remained on the periphery of the dialogue regarding Argentina's tragic past. The first is the sexual crimes committed by the agents of the military Junta. In 2012, Elizabeth Jelin spoke of the marginalization of these crimes over the last thirty years and reflected hopefully on developments in the way these events are viewed by society and the treatment of victims' testimonies during ongoing trials in Argentina.[2] The second topic of social and political relevance broached by Trillo and Varela is the responsibility of the aggressor's families. Félix Bruzzone and Máximo Badaró have written about the trauma suffered by the children of the repressors, their resistance to discuss their experiences, and the pervasive taboo surrounding the topic. However, in 2017, a small group of family members of the regime's repressors came together to form *Historias desobedientes* [Disobedient Histories], a collective that repudiates and denounces the actions of their relatives. That same year, they sought to have Argentina's Penal Code modified so that they would be able to testify at trials involving accusations of crimes against humanity. Since then, they have begun to form part of the human rights landscape in that country, albeit in small numbers.

While the overwhelming majority of artists demonstrate respect for the Junta's victims by depicting these crimes with solemnity, at the core of *La herencia* we find striking portrayals of violence, which Jordana Blejmar describes as pushing the limit of what can be shown and what is tolerable (n.pag). In this paper, I propose that these graphic representations of torture and sexual violence constitute a narrative recourse that enables Trillo and Varela to construct an unreserved condemnation of the military government and its wrongdoings, which can be considered commensurate to the atrocities they represent. I develop this discussion along three axes, beginning with an examination of the social and political environment that favored the artistic discourse from which *La herencia* emerges. This analysis is underpinned by the theories of W. J. T. Mitchell regarding trauma theory's cult of the unrepresentable and Gabriel Gatti's discussion of the catastrophe that occurs when attempting to represent events as abhorrent as those that took place in Argentina. Secondly, I explore the ways in which these depictions of violence are facilitated by the novel's graphic medium. Looking to Comics Studies, I discuss how the representational aesthetic of this genre is ideally suited to the narrative. Through my exploration of the interplay between form and theme, I describe how the cartoonish nature of the illustrations dehumanizes its subjects, creating distance between the reader and the subject matter and allowing the authors to present a fierce, no-holds-barred critique of an unseen accomplice who has remained on the periphery of this artistic, social, and political discourse. The final point of our study pertains to *La herencia's* open treatment of Elvio and his father's sexual crimes. In this matter, I will turn to Elizabeth Jelin's discussion of sexual abuse as a form of political torture to analyze the reasons why these crimes remain largely undisclosed and why Trillo and Varela's representation of them is unparalleled.

AN EVOLVING SOCIOPOLITICAL LANDSCAPE

It is not surprising that artistic works that examine the dictatorship and its enduring consequences have evolved alongside political events, adapting to censorship, engaging in public discourse, and pushing the boundaries of social acceptance. Argentina has a long tradition of fierce political humor and graphic art that can be traced back to the years preceding the coup d'état that led the Military Junta to power.[3] However, beginning in the early 70s, graphic artists, authors, and filmmakers fought strict censorship to shed light on the country's deteriorating situation. Among them, a publication titled *Humº* (1978–99)—where Trillo published some of his early work—quickly became known for its use of humor and satire in both opinion pieces and comics. Additionally, on a clandestine level, comics, cartoons, and graphic narratives were vital to militant groups. Fernando Reati describes how:

[a]ny Argentine citizen brave enough in the mid-1970s to have in his or her possession one of the underground publications of the left-wing guerrilla organization Montoneros couldn't but have noticed with some surprise that among the communiqués, editorials, messages from the leadership, photos of fallen comrades, and other habitual staples of the revolutionary press, there were numerous comics, cartoons, and visual icons that visually reinforced the ideological message (97).

However, the single most important reference from this period remains the work of Héctor Oesterheld, who was a master of the genre and often considered a pioneer. His masterpieces *El Enternauta* (1957–59) and *El Enternauta 2* (1976) remain some of the country's most beloved comics. Working under intense censorship, artists like Oesterheld had no choice but to articulate their political views around allegories and subterfuge; in the case of *El Enternatua*, a futuristic world where Argentina is under siege by alien invaders.[4] Traditionally, this series has been read as an unambiguous allegory in which the alien invasion constitutes a critique of imperialism in the first installment and the Military Junta in the second. Pablo de Santis explains that at the time of its publication, readers went as far as to search *El Enternauta 2* for coded messages that would reveal Montonero's upcoming plans and strategies (1998, 76–77).[5]

As the regime came to an end and the country transitioned towards democracy, the political landscape was highly unstable. The Junta had relinquished power, but most officers who had held positions of influence continued to serve. Newly elected president Raúl Alfonsín had the delicate task of addressing allegations of widespread crimes against humanity and opening judicial proceedings against the perpetrators while consolidating democracy under the threat of a military uprising.[6] In 1984, Alfonsín commissioned the report of the *Comisión Nacional sobre la Desaparición de Personas* (CONADEP) [National Commission on the Disappearance of People], which brought to light the regime's crimes. However, for a decade after its publication, all branches of the military officially denied their involvement. As the Junta's practices of illegal detentions, torture, disappearances, and death became known; artists began to represent these crimes, forcing Argentines to bear witness to a reality they had ignored.[7] By the late 1980s, many notable texts provided a window into the lives of militants, offered testimonies of the victims' experiences, and illustrated the government's agents' hidden practices. However, despite their desire to reveal the mechanisms of state repression, artists and intellectuals struggled to make sense of the overwhelming atrocity of these acts.[8] While they were once again free to denounce the regime, artists continued to avoid outright representations of traumatic events and instead employed allegories and allusions. The *Perramus* series, written by Juan Sasturain and illustrated by Alberto Breccia, emerges at this time as an important reference in this discussion.[9] *Perramus* depicts daily life during the dictatorship by exalting the omnipresence of the military in an apocalyptical cityscape where concrete structures and darkness overwhelm the reader. Much like *El Enternauta*, the protagonist undertakes secret missions to resist the tyrannical regime, and as the series progresses, the corruption and degradation brought on by the regime is revealed. Pablo de Santis calls it one "of the best comics of the decade," adding that: "[a]t a time of many films, comics, literary, and journalistic texts on the military dictatorship, *Perramus* belongs to the small group of truly significant works produced" (2009, 196).[10] On a technical level, this series can be seen as a precursor to Varela's illustrations of the city of Buenos Aires, given that they both share the same urban backdrop and a preference for darkness and shadows. While the dominant feature in Breccia's illustrations is the large scale and imposing geometrical features of surrounding buildings, Varela depicts a much softer city where, in the initial pages, the reader can still appreciate pleasant skylines and appealing architectural features. In what follows, I will discuss how Varela's depictions of Buenos Aires contribute to the communicative ethos of *La herencia*. Given that the city decays alongside Elvio's mental state, as the protagonist loses control, his environment becomes progressively darker, dirtier, more chaotic, and repulsive, which in turn strengthens the readers' rejection of the character and their condemnation of his actions.

The 1990s were marked by a fierce economic recession that changed the way graphic art was produced and consumed. Laura C. Fernández and Horacio Gago explain that while the industry had traditionally been centered around the publication of serialized magazines, the years of profound economic crisis gave way to rising unemployment figures and decreased the purchasing power of middle-class readers (85). At the same time, foreign comics became more popular, and many experienced graphic artists began to work for American publications that did not embrace local or even regional topics. Pablo de Santis notes that with the closing of the main magazines, *Fierro* and *Skorpio*: "many artists began their own publications. However, lacking the support of a big publishing company, these efforts often ended after a few issues, given financial and distribution difficulties" (2009, 199). Fortunately, the new century brought a measure of economic prosperity and renewed interest in the genre, which led to a resurgence of serialized magazines. Among them, *Fierro* reopened in 2006 with the subtitle "La historieta argentina" [the Argentine comic], focusing once again on the work of local artists, and national themes. A year later, it would publish *La herencia* in its original format.

As Nestor Kirchner's administration began in 2003, Argentina witnessed a brusque departure from previous governmental policy regarding the dictatorship and a proliferation of artistic interpretations of the now historical theme. One of the fundamental differences between these works and their predecessors is that they place themselves at a temporal and ideological distance from the dictatorship and can, therefore, cast a critical eye over the past. Contemporary artists assume that their audience shares their knowledge of the political and cultural evolution of the topic in Argentina and often dialogue with these events: the horror of discovering the crimes, the grief and indignation over a generation lost, and the frustration behind decades of injustice. This emerging group of artists includes an important contribution by the children of the disappeared, many of whom are themselves victims of atrocities and whose works are marked by a struggle to define their identity and reestablish lost family bonds. It is important to remember that these artists (most notably authors, filmmakers, photographers, and comedians) came of age some two decades after the Junta rose to power, at a time when human rights groups were at a stalemate in their search for justice and answers. As such, they shared a growing sense of disappointment and resentment that motivated them to engage in political activism and to create art that represents their trauma and experiences. However, alongside the children of the disappeared, we must also recognize the important contribution of artists who were themselves militants, those who were on the periphery of the regime's cruelty, and those like Trillo and Varela who speak from the perspective of an aggrieved society that grapples with coming to terms with the past. Generally, they present emotional and personal viewpoints that highlight the familial relationships of both the victims and their children and individual participation in left-wing militant groups. However, few among them have explored the intimate spheres of the regime's agents and their families, and those who have done so do not share Trillo and Varela's candid portrayal of violence.[11] This graphic novel stands alone in its unmediated representation of the Junta's violent crimes. Not only do Trillo and Varela reject the solemn approach to the topic shared by its contemporaries, but they also punctuate their sordid storyline with explicit illustrations that are in sharp contrast to the allegory and subterfuge upon which their predecessors in the genre had notably relied.

A COMMENSURATE RESPONSE TO HEINOUS CRIMES

In order to understand the approach to *La herencia* in this chapter, we must consider that it is a product of both favorable social and political circumstances and a climate of collective indignation and frustration that still exists after more than four decades of searching for truth and justice. As in other cases of grave societal trauma, the temporal distance resulting from decades past is essential for this type of dialogue to take place. Trillo and Varela's condemnation of the regime is remarkable not only due to its striking representations of violence but also because it broadens the scope of responsibility for the crimes by addressing the role played by the families of the aggressors. In the case of Elvio, we are presented with a character that is directly complicit yet escaped any kind of prosecution, and in the case of his mother, we encounter an example of complicity by omission. Furthermore, the text portrays sexual assaults as a form of torture, a type of crime that has remained on the periphery of judicial proceedings. As Elizabeth Jelin explains:

> In the cultural climate of the time, rape was part and parcel of torture. It was not seen as a specifically gender-related act. The main focus was on the enforced disappearances as the epitome of state terror. The denunciations and the search for "truth and justice" concentrated on those who had committed this ultimate heinous crime. Compared to this, all the rest seemed of less importance, painful and full of suffering, but not worth the same amount of attention. (344)

By denouncing these acts and symbolically naming both the victims and the perpetrators, the authors forcefully inscribe these events into the cultural discourse, the nation's collective consciousness, and the conscience of the reader. Rewriting those who were erased by the apparatus of state terror (erased from life, from society, and from history) is both a testimonial act and a counter-discourse to the regime's official denial of these events. While the majority of the Junta's crimes and the responsibility of those directly involved were addressed by the social discourse during the years following the return to democracy, Trillo and Varela take up the task of condemning events and groups that have not yet been confronted. They do so without reservation by forcing us to face the families of the aggressors, the victims, and the horrors that remain unspoken, unseen, and are considered too private for public discussion. Doing so vindicates the victims of sexual crimes, symbolized by Analía Sylveira, and yet presenting these events to the reader on both the visual and verbal registers simultaneously has an unpalatable effect that Juan Sasturain, has described as being so strong that he could not, or would not, tolerate it (qtd. in Martín, n. pag). So, a paradigm emerges: while the text is difficult to read, violent, dark, and aggressive, we can appreciate it as a commensurate response to the atrocity of the acts it depicts and the scorn of a society that is still torn apart by state terrorism and decades of failed politics of memory. In the words of Hillary Chute, these texts "do not conceal or cloak trauma, but rather put its elements in view: graphic narratives make the rolling lines of history readable" (233).

GRAPHIC NARRATIVES AND TRAUMA

One of the most striking qualities of the artistic works of the Kirchner era is that, despite their temporal and emotional distance from the subject matter, the vast majority of them continue to employ a series of auxiliary rhetorical devices and prevarications to circumvent direct portrayals of violence and trauma. Gabriel Gatti has attributed the use of these alternative narrative strategies to the catastrophic collapse of language that occurs when attempting to describe events that are as abhorrent as the detentions and disappearances carried out in the Southern Cone during the late twentieth century. Based on Theodor Adorno's celebrated phrase on the impossibility of writing poetry after Auschwitz, Gatti proposes that the figure of the disappeared person is so abhorrent that it is beyond comprehension. Therefore, even for descendants of the victims, and those artists who did not experience these atrocities first-hand, attempting to depict it unhinges traditional representation strategies, and language is simply insufficient to describe such a tragedy.[12] It's worth noting that a victim's inability to put such traumatic experiences into words has been well documented by Bessel Van der Kolk, who, in *The Body Keeps the Score*, explains that while frightful events are remembered intensely and accurately when we are confronted with true horror, the region of the brain necessary to put feelings into words is thought to shut down. He goes on to state that: "As a result, the imprints of traumatic experiences are organized not as coherent logical narratives but in fragmented sensory and emotional traces: images, sounds and physical sensations" (176). Van der Kolk describes how this connection was first identified in the nineteenth century, when Jean-Martin Charcot described hysteria in both men and women, emphasizing "embodied memory and a lack of language" (177), adding that Charcot's studies later led to the first scientific accounts of traumatic stress, which were conducted by his disciple Pierre Janet.

Given the inherent difficulty of representing the ineffable events and figures associated with the horrors of the regime, how, then, does *La herencia* circumvent this limitation? It is my position that graphic narratives are especially adept at depicting traumatic events and engaging history, and while there are very few Argentinian narratives that approach the Junta's crimes as directly as *La herencia*, there is an abundance of examples in the international arena that parallel Trillo and Varela's work.[13] According to Hillary Chute, graphic novels that explore events of profound social crisis: "push on conceptions of the unrepresentable and unimaginable that have become commonplace in the discourse about trauma" (17). Amongst them, Art Spiegelman's *Maus* is undoubtedly the prime reference. Based on his father's accounts of his time at Auschwitz, this Pulitzer-Prize-winning graphic narrative uses animals as a metaphor to depict the harrowing ordeal of life in a concentration camp. Another notable example is the graphic novel *Palestine* by Joe Sacco, which recounts the author's experiences in the West Bank and Gaza in the early 1990s. Finally, it is worth mentioning *The 9/11 Report*, written by Sid Jacobson and illustrated by Ernie Colón, which is based on the report by the National Commission on Terrorist Attacks Upon the United States.

As Chute proposes, graphic narratives have a long tradition of bearing witness and operating on the fringes of testimony, given that they are capable of both giving the reader an eyewitness perspective of the events and rejecting realism and transparency, fully embracing their bias (30). In the case of *La herencia*, the authors cast aside political neutrality in the prologue and state their open disgust for the regime. They highlight this position by drawing a parallel between the Junta's actions and the history of fascist Italy—an unquestioned example of totalitarianism— where General Della Chiesa refused to resort to torture, elevating himself and his nation above such abhorrent actions. This section is made up primarily of prose but also includes illustrations of prominent figures of the time.[14] It presents a complete indictment of the military, speaks of disappearances and the appropriation of children, and exposes the Junta's preposterous justification for the sexual assault of detained women. This is done through the character of Elvio's mother, Georgina Gustavino, who claims that because militant women had no morals and were promiscuous, they would frequently become pregnant and abort in the fifth month, implying that these presumed qualities made them deserving of the sexual abuse they endured.[15] After having appraised the reader of the circumstances, and as if attempting to justify the barbarity of the text ahead, Trillo and Varela end the prologue by stating that after the coup, the power and impunity under which the Argentine armed forces operated was absolute: "allowing them to kidnap, torture and murder thousands of human beings." They go on to say that: "Now the story of Elvio Gustavino can begin" (np).

Figure 2.1 *La herencia del coronel*, page 69.

Figure 2.2 *La herencia del coronel*, page 11.

Let us now turn our attention to the ways in which *La herencia*'s genre allows the reader to better approach this difficult subject matter. Firstly, we note that Varela's illustrations are far from realistic, and his characters are cartoonish. Elvio's face is dominated by thick glasses and a mustache, and the proportion of his chin is exaggerated. Likewise, the doll with which he is obsessed has large eyes and a small nose, which give her face an infantile appearance that stands in contrast to the hypersexualized qualities of her body, which is defined by large breasts and a minute waist (figures 2.1 and 2.2).

This caricaturesque exaggeration of their features casts aside realism and dehumanizes the characters, for they are identified by the reader as cartoons rather than mimetic representations of historical figures. This quality becomes most prominent when they convey a strong emotion. While the actions of both Elvio and Luisita render them unappealing, it's their facial expressions–primarily conveying anger, desperation, and suffering—that are most gruesome and further create emotional distance on the part of the reader. Furthermore, Elvio's hairstyle (deeply parted to one side) and clothing (he prefers business suits, thin ties, and an overcoat) bring to mind a 1950s-era aesthetic, while Luisita is a nineteenth-century antique in period dress, with ringlet curls that protrude from under a flowered bonnet. Together, their attire recalls distant and yet asynchronous times. However, the subject matter of the text refers the reader to Argentina's present, and in this context, the characters contrast their surroundings and ultimately differ from Trillo and Varela's intended reader. By rejecting mimesis and highlighting temporal distance, the images we observe are distinct from our reality as readers, establishing a buffer that is much needed given the qualities of the text.

A second element that insulates the reader from the violent world of the Gustavinos is the narrative's temporal fragmentation, which is achieved by the repeated inclusion of memories and hallucinations. Each time we depart from the linear progression of the action, Varela indicates the break by muting the color palate of the illustrations and overlaying the panels in question onto a blue or grey background. Truly heinous images like those of the rape of Analía appear in panels with a red background, as does the dress worn by Analía in her present-day encounter with Elvio and also the clothing of the prostitute that represents Analía in Elvio's hallucinations. While it is not specifically indicated within the text, red—which often represents blood and rage—becomes associated with Analía and the sexual violence she suffered at the hands of the Gustavinos. The appearance of this vibrant crimson coloring stands in contrast to the grey and muted pallet of the remaining illustrations, punctuating the content around which it appears. These chromatic contrasts highlight the separation between the heinous images of the past and the visions of Elvio's fractured psyche and the narrative present, where we witness Elvio's desperation to fulfill his sexual desire for the antique doll and his growing mental instability. The distinction between past or imagined violence and Elvio's present state is absolute, as it is always indicated in such a way that there can be no confusion between the two. With this in mind, if we set aside the images that correspond to the time of the dictatorship, we note that the violence we witness in the narrative present is minor in comparison, and it corresponds to Elvio's misery, his descent into madness and suicide, as well as his mother's abandonment and death. What is nearest to the reader is a portrayal of their comeuppance. While the plot lacks any cathartic ethos, and there is no recognizable morality among the characters, once we are able to set aside the depictions of the past and the illusions of Elvio's mind, there is an implied sense of justice in our witnessing the suffering and death of such reprehensible characters. As we move forward, it is important to note that Elvio's mental state deteriorates as a result of his growing obsession with Luisita and the frustration that arises from not being able to fulfill his sexual desire for her. Although he eventually realizes that he precipitated his mother's death, the character does not show regret for his actions during the dictatorship, nor can it be said that he develops a sense of morality.

An important point of consideration is that each panel in a graphic novel can be read as a single unit, and their sequence as a series of fragments that is both intrinsically incomplete and related to the others. Chute states that: "Comics makes a reader access the unfolding evidence in the movement of its basic grammar, by aggregating and accumulating frames of information" (2). The author goes on to state that panels are simultaneously still as they contain static images, and fully animated, as the act of reading anticipates the next panel (16). The structure of the genre, which arranges panels into a grid and creates a contrast between the image and the surrounding blank space of the gutter, leads to what Chute calls a special syntax that "offers opportunities to place pressure on traditional notions of chronology, linearity and causality" (4). We can observe this effect in *La herencia* during the portrayal of Elvio's final hours. After finally obtaining the doll, he attempts to fulfill his sexual desires; only Luisita rejects him. Elvio's hallucinations come to life, a struggle ensues, and the lines of reality are blurred. In the end, a vision of the Colonel kills Luisita with an electric prod, an instrument known to be used by the regime's torturers. In this moment of pain and grief, Elvio realizes that he may have caused his mother's demise, and this knowledge, coupled with the loss of Luisita, accelerates his descent into madness. Donning his father's combat uniform, the protagonist sets out to get revenge on all those who wronged him: the antique dealer who sold his beloved Luisita to another person, the family that bought the doll, and Analía, who has previously confronted him. On page 93 we see a large-scale image of Elvio running in army fatigues (figure 2.3).

Figure 2.3. *La herencia del coronel*, page 93.

The illustration is superimposed on a grid of panels that shows his interaction with a prostitute who he has mistaken for Analía. The oversized image of him running toward the reader defies both space and time, signaling his desperation and delusion. The composition signals that Elvio is running away from all the things that torment him: his frustrated desire for the doll, his responsibility for his mother's death, and his inability to escape the memory of his father. In a perverse twist of fate, Elvio is terror-stricken, and he jumps from a window.

The illustrations of the city in these final pages show a polluted and fetid space inundated by trash, decay, and homelessness. Throughout the text, Varela represents Buenos Aires as a crowded and decomposing space; however, as Elvio's thoughts and behavior spiral out of control, the city becomes progressively dirtier and more repulsive. Initial illustrations show Elvio's workplace as a large open room where a vast number of desks are lined up, and employees work close together in silence among large stacks of paper. Although the streets are packed with pedestrians, walls seem to crumble, and storefronts have heavy metal security gates, the reader can still identify esthetically pleasing architectural features that speak to Buenos Aires' neoclassical style. The interior of the Gustavinos apartment is dirty and disorganized, and the overall sense is that the characters' surroundings are in line with the readers' rejection of the Gustavinos and their loathsome amorality. However, as the plot progresses, Elvio's surroundings worsen. The interior of his apartment is now full of garbage; spiders and insects walk across the floor, and the walls are covered in vomit. Illustrations of city streets show sidewalks full of litter and empty bottles; there are homeless people sleeping in archways and graffiti covering cement block walls. In the final pages, the panels are crowded with symbols of the abject, and the environment decomposes alongside the protagonist's sanity. As the plot reaches its denouement, the protagonist's chaotic surroundings become oppressive and contribute to the sense of urgency and desperation that Elvio experiences as he approaches his final moments.

Furthermore, the final pages present tense actions that take place at night, so the color palate is muted, dark, and many panels have a blue background, which facilitates the confusion between reality and hallucination. In these pages, the formal qualities of the medium work in conjunction with the previously discussed technique for altering the linear progression of the narrative. Together, they depict Elvio's mental state and his traumatic memories, which are disorganized, nonlinear, and shatter time and space. Christophe Doly and Caroline Van Linthout discuss the relationship between the layout of comics and the breakdown of traumatic memory, explaining the parallel between form and theme by stating that within the "collapse of the notions of time and space, the memory of the traumatic events can only be fragmentary, given that the act of remembering itself implies fragmentation" (181). The layout of the graphic novel, with its innate temporal fractures and visual indicators of alternate timelines and realities, makes it an ideal genre for representing tragedy and trauma. What is unique to *La herencia* is that the trauma being represented is not that of Analía but rather of Elvio, for whom we have no sympathy.

SEXUAL VIOLENCE

It is clear by now that *La herencia* does not seek to extol the memory of the regime's victims but rather condemn Elvio and those he represents: the family members of the aggressors who were complicit and remain unpunished. This is not a historiographical text, nor does it pay reverence to the victims and their suffering. *La herencia* is an unrelenting condemnation of a modern and ongoing societal crisis. It follows in the footsteps of the artistic discourse that precedes it but distinguished itself for approaching delicate topics in a most indelicate way. In *Realms of Memory*, Pierre Nora proposes that anything that contains the memory of a community—be it a person, object, or place—is an object of memory (15), and that these objects are referential given that, rather than belonging to a specific historical moment, their content refers to history in such a way that they only reference themselves. Within that context, we can consider *La herencia* as an object of memory that references historical events in order to bring attention to a social circumstance that far postdates the dictatorship. That is to say, that is a social artifact that leverages history, building on more than thirty years of the hard-fought search for truth and justice, to draw attention to the sexual crimes that remain concealed and condemn the perpetrators and their accomplices, who have evaded justice.

The children and family members of the regime's aggressors have largely remained on the periphery of the cultural dialogue regarding Argentina's troubled past. The social consensus regarding this group is well expressed by author Felix Bruzzone and Dr. Pablo Campos, a psychologist who treats the now-adult children of the agents of the regime. They echo the commonly held belief that the only way for the children of the aggressors to reclaim their subjectivity and personal history is to distance themselves from their parents, participate in judicial proceedings against them, and assist in determining the fate of people who disappeared. Anything else, they state, would imply complicity (n. p.). In *La herencia*, Trillo and Varela quash any ambiguity surrounding Elvio's role in his father's crimes when they reveal that he willingly raped Analía and that, at that time, he wasn't quite as young and helpless as the reader initially thought. Throughout the text, the reader does not only witness Elvio's perverse enjoyment in abusing Analía, but they also witness an encounter between the two that takes place in the narrative present of the text. During this meeting, Analía confronts the protagonist at gunpoint and shatters the illusion that he was a young boy at the time she was held prisoner in his home. She accuses him of being as guilty as his father and hiding behind the disguise of an innocent paper-pushing public servant, and in the face of Elvio's excuses and denial of his guilt, Analía reveals that he was, in fact, two years older than her at the time he raped her. This knowledge cements the readers' judgment of Elvio and places him firmly in the category of accomplice and active participant. In this narrative universe, Trillo and Varela leave no room for the reader to consider Elvio a victim of his father's actions, for he is clearly the Colonel's accomplice.

In a text that focuses on terrorism in the twenty-first century, W. J. T. Mitchell refers to the difficulty involved in speaking of trauma by referring to "the frontiers of the unimaginable and the unspeakable, the place where words and images fail, where they are refused, prohibited as obscenities that violate a law of silence and invisibility, muteness and blindness." His interest lies in the ineffable quality of horror and its effect on the reproduction of terror. In Mitchell's view, speaking of trauma, both overcomes the limits of words and language and invokes the violence to which they refer. There is no doubt that by speaking of and depicting such horrors, the authors of *La herencia* reproduce violence. Let us be clear that despite acknowledging the skill and talent of Trillo and Valera, the public and critical reception of *La herencia* has often been negative because many have felt that these explicit representations of brutality have no value other than shock and awe. Trillo and Varela have often been accused of disrespecting the victims and their families.[16] However, in this discussion, our attention is drawn to the social norms surrounding the limitations of describing such events, in particular as they apply to the representation of sexual crimes like those of Elvio and his father, around which there is an unspoken cone of silence both in art and the sociopolitical sphere.

In "Sexual Abuse as a Crime against Humanity and the Right to Privacy," Elizabeth Jelin speaks of the privatization of sexual violence and how the body is central to memories of torture. In her view, disclosing these memories creates a paradox for the victims as:

> the act of repression violated their privacy and intimacy, destroying the cultural division between public space and private experience. To overcome the void created by repression implies the possibility of elaborating a narrative memory of the experience, which is necessarily public in the sense that it must be shared and communicated to others. (346–7)

She goes on to speak of the alterity of those with whom these memories would be shared and the need for spaces of trust and understanding that would allow victims to come forward. We must recognize that due to its outright portrayals of violence, *La herencia* adds no benefit to the preservation and furtherance of victim's rights. In fact, the depiction of Elvio and his father's crimes against Analía Sylveira further strips victims of their intimacy by sensationalizing the horror. However, the text does contribute to the social discourse surrounding the topic by denouncing the existence of these crimes and inscribing them in both the conscience of the reader and the cultural dialogue. The inclusion of these crimes into the public domain and the denunciation of the regime's preposterous justification for systematically raping militant women—which we have discussed as part of the graphic novel's introduction—is a step towards normalizing the discussion of sexual abuse in the public spheres. It echoes the work done by authors and filmmakers in the years following the return to democracy when the regime's crimes were generally unknown and art had a testimonial ethos. Within the historical context of the search for truth and justice, Trillo and Valera's forthright approach to revealing these sexual crimes can be interpreted as testimonial. If the aim of the evolving discourse surrounding the Junta's practices of rape as a form of torture is the just prosecution of these crimes, then we must acknowledge there is value in their portrayal and discussion in art, for until now, they have remained in the shadows, cloaked by societal taboo and therefore beyond reproach.

A FURTHER CONDEMNATION

Artistic representations of Argentina's last military dictatorship and its devastating effects abound, with the last fifteen years being especially fruitful across all genres. Yet these texts (prose, plays, blogs, films, photography, and others) share an invariant solemnity in their portrayal of the victim's suffering. Children of the disappeared, for whom mirth is a rhetorical device in the construction of their identity, have achieved humor by directing laughter at themselves and their own suffering, but artists have avoided the representation of acts of torture and the sexual abuses perpetrated by the military and their agents.[17] It is, therefore, surprising to encounter a text like *La herencia* where unreserved portrayals of state terror are central to the denouement of the plot. However, once we have contextualized this graphic novel, tracing the path of its predecessors, and considering the social and political circumstances that influenced its production, we can begin to understand that the scorn that Trillo and Varela direct towards Elvio Gustavino is, in fact, a representation of the collective outrage for the crimes of the Junta, and in particular those that have not been brought to justice. Such is this anger that spurred the creation of a character as vile and despicable as Elvio and portrayals of violence that stretch the limitations of language.

It is thanks to the nature of the genre, which allows the reader to establish distance between him or herself and the subject matter, that Trillo and Varela can address these difficult yet social, significant topics; and yet the text remains overwhelmingly violent and difficult, causing many readers to feel alienated by it. Nevertheless, the authors' direct approach to the topic is perhaps their most valuable contribution, for without prevarications, they have been able to rewrite and make visible the victims of a crime that has been considered too private to be discussed and extend responsibility to a group that has been able to remain concealed. While it seems unlikely that artists working in other genres will soon embrace the forthright ethos of graphic art, Elizabeth Jelin reveals that in recent years, there have begun to be testimonies of sexual abuses at the trials of Argentina's former military agents, so we remain hopeful that we will witness a change in social and judicial practices (343). With that in mind, perhaps *La herencia* has contributed to speaking out and further condemning the regime's heinous crimes.

NOTES

1. Upon taking office, Kirchner removed the portraits of the Military Junta's leaders that still hung in government buildings. He later created a memorial space and cultural center at the site of the former *ESMA - Escuela Superior de Mecánica de la Armada*: an educational facility for the Argentine Navy that housed one of the country's most prolific detention and torture centers. At a more profound level, the former president abolished the laws of *Punto final* [Full Stop] (1986) and *Obediencia debida* [Due Obedience] (1987), which respectively prevented new criminal charges from being brought forth after December 10th, 1983, and protected officers of lower rank from prosecution by establishing that they were simply following orders. Finally, he made financial reparations to the children of the regime's victims.

2. Jelin also references an emerging international interpretative framework for sexual crimes that are committed as part of armed conflicts, that would lead to them being classified as crimes against humanity.

3. At this time two important magazines, *Satiricón* and *Chaupinela*, voiced their opposition to Isabel Perón's government through serialized comics and editorial cartoons. Censors closed the former on three occasions between 1973 and 1976, while the latter was only published for a few months between 1974 and 75. Though short-lived, these publications were instrumental to the careers of many writers and illustrators, including Carlos Trillo.

4. Oesterheld, who belonged to the militant group Montoneros, went as far as to create an alter ego for himself in the *Enternauta* series: a character that gives up his work writing comics to join the battle against the invaders. The series ended in 1976 when the author, his four daughters, and their partners were disappeared by the regime.

5. More recently, Joanna Page has interpreted the text within the context of the cultural debates that took place at the time of the publication of each instalment, leading her to

view them as the self-critiques of an author haunted by the possibility of a bloody civil war (46). Other notable readings include David William Foster's discussion of the central role of masculinity in this narrative, and the male figure as an agent of social change.

6. A further discussion of this topic can be found in *Radical Evil on Trial* by Carlos Nino.

7. In particular, the film *La historia oficial* directed by Luis Puenzo, introduces a protagonist who discovers that her adopted daughter was born in captivity to a woman detained by the regime. Her reaction upon learning this information, and willing search for the child's biological family, stands in contrast to the complicity of the average citizen who chose to look the other way.

8. Critics like Beatriz Sarlo note that in the late 1980s and early 90s, artists avoided mimetic representations and singular depictions of reality, and instead favored a discourse where both subjectivity and facts were fragmented.

9. It was originally published in France to avoid the Junta's censorship, with the first three of four instalments reaching Argentina in 1987.

10. While the vast majority of this series predates the transition to democracy, and public knowledge of the regime's crimes, certain elements speak of its horrors. For example, in the texts the military dispose of the bodies of their enemies in the river, just as the Junta did in the now infamous "vuelos de la muerte" [death flights] during which they sedated their prisoners and threw them from airplanes into the Rio de la Plata.

11. It's worth mentioning the novels *Dos veces junio* by Martín Kohan, and *Una misma noche* by Leopoldo Brizuela as examples of texts that portray the regime's aggressors, however they do so in a manner much less aggressive than *La herencia*.

12. A memorable example of the strategies Gatti describes appears Albertina Carri's film *Los rubios*, where the author-filmmaker depicts her parent's kidnapping by way of Playmobile figurines. While her work was celebrated for being an innovative representation of the victims of state terror, it has also been criticized for infantilizing those events through her use of children's toys. Further discussions can be found in Beatriz Sarlo's *Tiempo presente*, Martín Kohan's "La apariencia celebrada" and Gonzalo Aguilar's *Otros mundos. Un ensayo sobre el nuevo cine argentino*. In literature a significant example is ¿Quién te crees que sos? By Ángela Urondo Raboy, who describes the emotional toll of discovering the circumstances of her father's death and her mothers' disappearance when she was a teenager; attending and testifying at the trial of the government agents involved; and the process of dissolving the legal bonds between her and the family members who adopted her and withheld her true identity. Urondo Raboy's is exceptionally direct and detailed but even she employs allusions to describe the experience of being held in a detention centre as a toddler. When narrating the horror suffered by herself and other children in those centres she merely says: "The starting point for horror is high, and it only increases. Everything you imagine and more. There's no refuge, nowhere to hide, no way to keep denying or skirting that reality that reaches me and swallows me whole" (93). All translations are mine.

13. Aarnoud Rommens compiled a series of comics, produced between 2002 and 2005, that depict the military dictatorship. They were brought together as part of a project titled "Camouflage Comics: Dirty War Images." Unfortunately, the webpage that contained this archive no longer exists. However, the author's published works remain. By way of a brief conclusion, Rommens states there is a strange continuity between these comics and the

handful of what one could call "critical avant-garde" comics published during or around the time of the military regime, by such pioneers as Alberto Breccia, Carlos Trillo, Hector Oesterheld, and others. Indeed, the two parallel timelines cannot be clearly separated. On the contrary, they continuously intersect, urging us to interpret the 'new' in light of the 'old'—and vice versa.

14. The illustrations are of Christian Von Wenich, a clergyman sentenced to life for colluding with torture squads by urging detained persons to make confessions to him; Gen. Jorge Rafael Videla; and two French nuns, Alice Domon and Léonie Duquet, who were detained, tortured and murdered during a death flight for their involvement with the Mothers of the Plaza de Mayo. A final illustration shows a grid containing many faces, presumably of persons who were disappeared. This arrangement is reminiscent of the photographs printed onto the glass windows of the Cuatro Columnas hall at the former ESMA.

15. Georgina's speech reproduces the words of the wife of Genero Díaz Besone, an ideologue of the regime.

16. One need not look further than the previously quoted words of Jordana Blejmar and Juan Sasturain.

17. Primary examples are Mariana Eva Perez's novel *Diario de una princesa montonera—110% verdad*—and Victoria Grigera's comedy show: *Montonerísima*.

WORKS CITED

Aguilar, Gonzalo. *Otros mundos: Un ensayo sobre el nuevo cine argentino*. Buenos Aires: Santiago Arcos Editor, 2010.

Arfuch, Leonor. "Debates Críticos: Los Tuturos de la Memoria. Actores, Demandas, Intersecciones." Paper presented at the *Simposio de la Sección de Estudios del Cono Sur LASA*, Santiago, Chile, August 4, 2015.

Blejmar, Jordana. "La Vida Puerca. Sobre El Síndrome Guastavino, de Carlos Trillo y Lucas Varela." *Afuera: Estudios de Crítica Cultural*. 16 (2016): n pag.

Bruzzone, Felix, and Máximo Badaró. "La Herencia de la Dictadura. Hijos de Represores: 30,000 quilombos." *Anfibia*. https://www.revistaanfibia.com.

Chute, Hillary. *Disaster Drawn. Visual Witness, Comics, and Documentary Form*. Cambridge: Harvard University Press, 2016.

Dalmaroni, Miguel. "La Moral de la Historia: Novelas Argentinas Sobre La Dictadura (1995-2002)." *Hispamérica* 32, no. 96 (2003): 29–47.

de Santis, Pablo. *La Historieta en la Edad de la Razón*. Buenos Aires: Paidos, 1998.

de Santis, Pablo. "The Fierro Years: An Exercise in Melancholy." In *Redrawing the Nation: National Identity in Latin/o American Comics*, ed. Héctor D. Fernández l'Hoeste and Juan Poblete. Palgrave Macmillan, 2009.

Fernández, Laura Cristina, and Sebastián Horacio Gago. "Nuevos Soportes y Formatos: Los Cambios Editoriales en el Campo de la Historieta Argentina." *Cultura, Lenguaje y Representación. Revista De Estudios Culturales De La Universitat Jaume I* 10 (2012): n. pag.

Foster, David William. *El Eternauta, Daytripper, and Beyond: Graphic Narrative in Argentina and Brazil*. First ed. Austin: University of Texas Press, 2016.

Jelin, Elizabeth. "Sexual Abuse as a Crime against Humanity and the Right to Privacy." *Journal of Latin American Cultural Studies* 21, no. 2 (2012): 343–50.

Kohan, Martín. "La Apariencia Celebrada." *Punto de Vista* 78 (2004): 24–30.

Martín, Lucas. "Lo Tolerable: Política, Sexo y Humor en *El Síndrome Guastavino*." *Soretes Azules: Blog sobre Carlos Trillo*, Blogspot, October 27, 2012, http://soretesazules.blogspot.co.uk/2012/10/lo-tolerable-politica-sexo-y-humor-en.html. Accessed June 16, 2019.

Nino, Carlos Santiago. *Radical Evil on Trial*. New Haven: Yale University Press, 1996.

Nora, Pierre. *Realms of Memory: Rethinking the French Past. Volume 1, Conflicts and Divisions*. New York: Columbia University Press, 1996.

Page, Joanna. "Intellectuals, Revolution, and Popular Culture: A New Reading of El Eternauta." *Journal of Latin American Cultural Studies* 19, no. 1 (2010): 45–62.

Pérez, Mariana Eva. *Diario de una Princesa Montonera: 110% Verdad*. 1st ed. Buenos Aires: Capital Intelectual, 2012.

Pifano, Diana, and María Soledad Paz-Mackay. "Suturas al Pasado: Ausencias, Fotografía y Legado Familiar en *Lengua Madre* y *Diario de una Princesa Montonera 110% Verdad*." Submitted to the *Canadian Journal of Latin American and Caribbean Studies*.

Piñeyro, Marcelo, et al. La Historia Oficial. Koch Lorber Films, 2004.

Reati, Fernando. "Argentina's Montoneros: Comics, Cartoons, and Images as Political Propaganda in the Underground Guerrilla Press of the 1970s." In *Redrawing the Nation: National Identity in Latin/o American Comics*, ed. Héctor D. Fernández l'Hoeste and Juan Poblete. Palgrave Macmillan, 2009.

Sarlo, Beatriz. *Tiempo Presente. Notas Sobre el Cambio de una Cultura*. Buenos Aires: Siglo XXI, 2010.

Trillo, Carlos. *La Herencia del Coronel*. Illustrated by Lucas Varela. Buenos Aires: Dibuks, 2010.

Urondo Raboy, Angela. ¿*Quién te Creés que Soy?* Buenos Aires: Capital Intellectual, 2013.

Van der Kolk, Bessel. *The Body Keeps the Score: Brain, Mind, and Body in the Healing of Trauma*. New York: Penguin, 2014.

CHAPTER 3

ON THE THRESHOLD OF BEING AND BELONGING

Refiguring History in Autobiographical Comics

KAY SOHINI

The graphic memoir genre or 'autographics' (Gillian Whitlock) combines sociohistorical accounts with lived experience by juxtaposing words and pictures in seamless narratives, which traverse cultural, ethnoracial, and generational borders. By using a host of universally recognizable imagery, comics find a way to articulate complex identities that lie at the intersection of multiple marginalities and to "represent the invisible" (McCloud 129), which renders the comic creators and its readers "partners in the invisible creating something out of nothing time and again" (205). In comics, both the content in the panels as well as the spaces in between them create meaning. To transition from one panel to the next, the gutter space prompts readers to imagine the action between the panels and to use their own imagination and/or experiences to fill in the gaps. Put another way, since comics is an additive medium, it "actively solicits through its constitutive grammar the participant's role in generating meaning" (Chute, *Comics and Media* 21). The reader witnesses the conflict of the narrative unfold in a temporal sequence—deriving "movement from stillness," instead of simply "observ[ing] motion" (Chute, "Critical Inquiry" 25). Moreover, through the process of "synecdoche" or "metonymy," an "associated detail [is used] to represent the whole," which the reader is expected to make sense of based on convention (Duncan 134). Consequently, in the process of being an active participant in data synthesis, the creator and the reader form a space of shared sensibilities. As scholars such as Hillary Chute (in *Disaster Drawn*) and Gillian Whitlock (in "Autographics") have noted, comics make space for witnessing. In that vein, I contend that the participatory nature of comics, its place in witnessing disasters, makes it function as literatures of resistance, as it prompts readers "to question the relationship between identity, belonging and home" (Ahmed 78) and to consider the question of who belongs and who does not.

In this article, I use the term 'unbelonging' to refer to the sense of *homelessness* that individuals and collectives experience due to extreme sociopolitical, cultural, or geographical shifts. Unbelonging is when a person does not belong either here or there; when they are bereft of a place to call home, owing to ideological and/or sociocultural displacements that lead to "vexed questions of identity, memory and home" (Ashcroft et al. 217–18); when "clearly demarcated parameters of geography, national identity and belonging" (Braziel and Munnur) are interrupted. Through a close reading of how different artists make use of the formal affordances of the medium, I consider the question of unbelonging as visually embodied in contemporary graphic memoirs situated against the backdrop of three different sociopolitical crises across Vietnam, Iran, and Kashmir. In the first section, I look at Thi Bui's autoethnographic exploration of migration and multi-generational trauma in *The Best We Could Do* (2017). In the second section, I look at Malik Sajad's incisive criticism of the (lack of) autonomy of Kashmir, told in tandem with his lived experience of being othered in his own country in *Munnu: A Boy from Kashmir* (2015). I conclude with Marjane Satrapi's *Persepolis* (2000), an affective account of how she is twice othered: first by the Islamic fundamentalist regime in Iran and then as a racial minority and immigrant in Austria.

BIRTHING AS A METAPHOR FOR BORDER-CROSSING

Thi Bui's *The Best We Could Do*, despite being an account of displacement, war, and refugeeism, does not begin with an origin story or even at the site of conflict, as is common with the genre. Instead, it begins in the delivery room of Methodist Hospital, New York, where Thi, the author-protagonist, is undergoing a long, arduous labor. On the second page of the narrative, Bui paints the absence of her mother in the room conspicuously with an abandoned chair by the bed, closely followed by the discomfited figure of her mother on the next page, standing right outside the delivery room. Thi writes that her mother flew all the way from California to New York to be with her daughter, yet could not stand to be in the same room. In addition

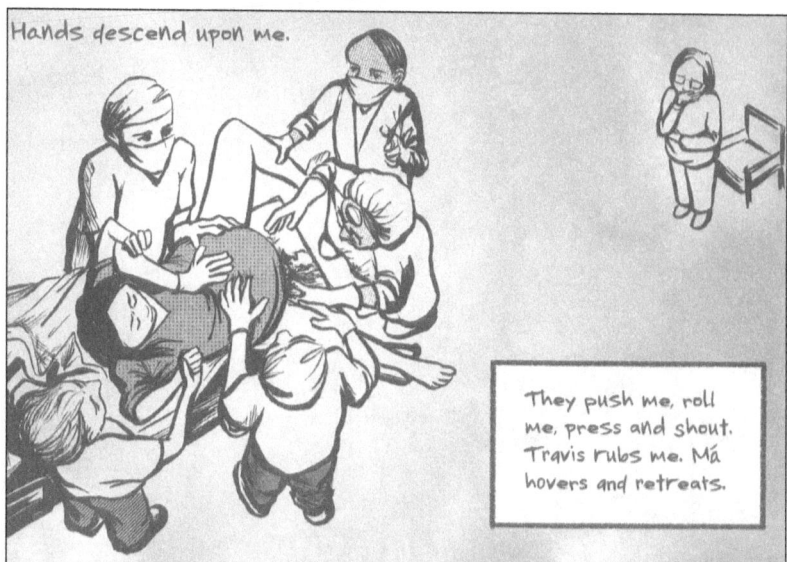

Figure 3.1. *The Best We Could Do*, page 10. Use of innovative perspective to create the illusion of distance within a single panel.

to the generational gap, Thi—having been raised in the US in a society distinctly different from Vietnam's—shares a considerable cultural gap with her parents. In figure 3.1, Bui judiciously uses the space within the panel to represent the emotional distance between them. In comics, artists can avail of at least three visual layers in any given frame: the foreground, the midground, and the background. Strategic positioning of objects in each of these layers aids in creating an illusion of distance between them, as well as between the objects and the reader.

In figure 3.1, Bui is situated squarely in the foreground, while her mother is in the background; the empty midground signifies an emotional distance between the two characters. The absence of any extraneous objects in the panel in conjunction with the semi-isometric point of view further serves to underscore this forced perspective. Moreover, the distance between the two is also insinuated by the framing of her mother's character, who is drawn much smaller in scale compared to the narrator's figure in the foreground. Bui's keen awareness of the spatio-temporality of the medium and the perceptive placement of characters within the scope of her panels create a visual tension that mirrors the emotional tension between the protagonist and her mother. Lastly, the panel above, being decidedly borderless, has "a timeless quality" (McCloud 102) that not only advances the relational dynamics in this scene but also sets the tone for the rest of the narrative.

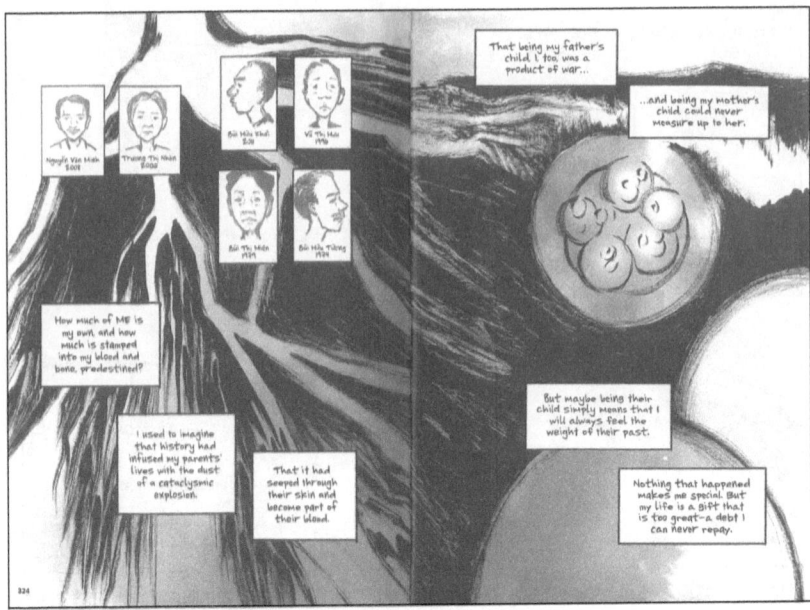

Figure 3.2. *The Best We Could Do*, pages 324–325.

When Thi is through the birthing ordeal, her mother explains that she could not stand to be in the delivery room with her and had to leave because "it all came back to [her]" (Bui 20), referring to the traumatic memory of giving birth several times (two were stillbirths) in refugee camps and war-torn South Vietnam. The comic medium's ability to accommodate multiple, simultaneous narratives through the technique of 'braiding' enables Bui to narrate her own experience of giving birth while recounting her mother's trauma. Braiding links unrelated or tangentially related images in panels "through non-narrative correspondence, be it iconic or other means" (Beaty and Nguyen in Groensteen 8). In Groensteen's words, it "overdetermines the panel by equipping coordinates that we can qualify as hyper-topical, indicating their belonging to one or several notable series, and the place that it occupies" (124). Via narrative braiding, Thi reveals how her parents' trauma of migration resulted in her life always being suffused by a darkness that she does not entirely understand but "can always feel" (Bui 59–60). When Bui learned that she was pregnant, she was particularly apprehensive about passing her trauma down to her son as her parents did to her, albeit unintentionally— a phenomenon that Marianne Hirsch notably theorizes as "post-memory," an act of intergenerational transfer of trauma (155).

In figure 3.2, in the form of a double-page spread, she gives shape to her unceasing fear—the weight of history seeping into her being from her parents through intertwined vein-like structures, like roots of old trees sinking deep into the ground in search of sustenance. In an interview with NPR, the author revealed that her pregnancy was one of the motivations for drawing this graphic memoir and that she relied on the medium to "filter stuff out so that [she] could pass on something cleaner" (Mallory) to her son. In the text, when her newborn son is handed to her by the nurse, Thi whispers, partially to herself—"Don't let him fall" (12). This moment, and especially Bui's stylistic rendering of it that emphasizes her vulnerable facial expression, gives the reader a palpable glimpse into her deep-seated anxiety of lacking something concrete to hold on to, which she bore all her life both as an immigrant and as a racial Other. As a product of war and migration, she finds herself "culturally, nationally, and genealogically disinherited from [her] country of birth," as well as "ambivalent toward [her] country of adoption" (Munnur and Braziel 9). It is this dual position that pushes her to a state of perpetual unbelonging, and liminal existence.

Thi and her younger brother were often left alone with their father, Bo—who terrorized and subjected them to various forms of psychological abuse and/or negligence. They were left under his sole care for an extended period when their mother had attempted suicide in the aftermath of Thi's older sister running away from home. Years later, soon after the birth of Thi's son, her mother unexpectedly brought up the incident. In a moment of an overdue emotional release, Thi exclaims, "Almost thirty years later, I didn't know I was still angry" (Bui 28). The act of drawing herself into a character and letting that character confront past traumas allows her to process the un-metabolized emotions that she carried for years on end. It is through comics that Bui "harness[es] the possibilities of the pictorial space" (Chute in *Graphic Women* 142), to revisit her childhood and simulate a reenactment of traumatic memories. Cathy Caruth, in *Unclaimed Experience*, theorizes: "Traumatic experience, beyond the psychological dimension of suffering it involves, suggests a certain paradox: that the most direct seeing of a violent event may occur as an absolute inability to know it; that immediacy, paradoxically, may take the form of belatedness" (92). Thus, revisiting the traumatic event via an image-textual reenactment, enabled by their cartoon avatar, allows the author-protagonist to access the memory in a way that is revealing, more so than when it originally occurred. Caruth explains that when trauma is experienced "too unexpectedly," its effect is not fully "available to consciousness until it imposes itself again" (19).

Figure 3.3. *The Best We Could Do*, page 312. Example of "braiding" or linking of unrelated images through visual sequence.

Bui's utilization of the visual grammar of the medium to mimic a to-and-fro motion across time and space not only helps simulate an environment to access past traumas safely, but it also aids in reproducing "the effects of memory" (Chute in *Graphic Women* 134). Furthermore, to quote Scott McCloud's astute understanding of the medium, "The cartoon is a vacuum into which our identity and awareness is pulled . . . an empty shell that we inhabit which enables us to travel to another realm" (McCloud 38). Making comics, he argues, "isn't just a way of drawing" but "a way of seeing" (31).

Similarly, Bui's reenactment—or simulation of her traumatic memories in the comic medium—aids in *seeing* and ultimately tracing the source of the trauma that is responsible for her ambivalent sense of self and unbelonging. The visuality of the medium not only cohesively holds together multiple intersecting but distinctly separate narratives but also cues the reader in to shifts in location, time, and space—thus minimizing the need for verbal transitions, which, in turn, enhance the effect of her images.

The raw depiction of a long, difficult labor makes birthing double as a metaphor for border crossing, which foreshadows in reverse chronology the precarious voyage the Bui family undertook from war-ridden Vietnam to the US in 1978. This metaphor also figures into the narrative's quest for self-invention. In the chapter called "The Shore," Bui writes that people took new identities at the UN refugee camp in Malaysia, where her family stopped for a few months before moving to the US. Some listed themselves as couples so that they could travel together; some changed their names and modified their age for better work opportunities; some even adopted orphaned children (Bui 269). Despite, or perhaps as a result of, their circumstances, the transitory period gave them a chance to build new identities for themselves to take to the next phase of their lives.

Another motif, that of a boat drifting perilously in tumultuous waters (312), visually braids Bui's family's migratory journey to Thi's challenging experience of caring for her newborn, who suffered from jaundice shortly after his birth (figure 3.3).

She describes how she did everything in her capacity to keep him alive, just as her parents did everything they could to keep Thi and her siblings alive as they left Vietnam under cataclysmic circumstances. The precariously drifting boat appears several times throughout the narrative, sometimes as the primary subject (Bui 30, 41) and at other times in the distance or as a blurred background (figure 3.4). The recursive occurrence of the motif in various visual states draws attention to how the trauma of war and migration manifests retroactively and continues to mediate the lives of refugees long after the immediate danger of war has passed. In figure 3.3, the juxtaposition of images connecting the textual present and the past (312) reveals to the readers how "the weight of history informs the entire narrative, at times foregrounded but always present" (Kirby). Moreover, the sepia-toned watercolor washes, by bleeding beyond their designated panels onto others throughout the narrative, consistently emphasize how the Bui family's past constantly impinges on their present. As McCloud writes, "When 'Bleeds' are used—i.e. when a panel runs off the edge of the page—this effect [of timelessness] is compounded. Time

Figure 3.4. *The Best We Could Do*, page 37. Recurring boat motif in the background. Researcher self is visible in the narrative.

is no longer contained by the familiar icon of the closed panel, but instead hemorrhages and escapes into timeless space" (103). By making use of the formal features of the medium, the author-protagonist in *The Best We Could Do* traverses between the past and the present fluidly, which aids in tracing her ubiquitous sense of (un)belonging to the original site of conflict.

GRAPHIC AUTOETHNOGRAPHY AND REINVENTION OF SELF THROUGH CULTURAL ANALYSIS

To unbelong is to live with an ambiguous or fragmented sense of Self—to live a life perpetually characterized by not knowing who you are, or who you are supposed to be, or where your roots, priorities, loyalties, or attachments lie. In the words of the inimitable postcolonial scholar Sara Ahmed: "The narrative of leaving home produces too many homes and hence no Home, too many places in which memories attach themselves through the carving out of inhabitable space, and hence no place that memory can allow the past to reach the present (in which 'I' could declare itself as having come home)" (78). It is this state of pervasive *not knowing* that motivates Bui's search for "an origin story that will set everything right" (Bui 41). However, since much of her unbelonging was prompted by conflicts arising outside the scope of the Self, she had to simultaneously look outward as well as inward to understand it. Consequently, she resorts to a form of inquiry that can be categorized as graphic autoethnography—a methodology that lets her locate (and thereby process) her individual position within the larger historical conflict, in part by enabling sociohistorical research to be presented both visually and narratively. Autoethnography, a method popularized largely by Carolyn Ellis and Arthur Bochner, can be understood as:

> an autobiographical genre of writing and research that displays multiple layers of consciousness, connecting the personal to the cultural . . . autoethnographers gaze, first, through an ethnographic wide-angle lens, focusing outward on social and cultural aspects of their personal experience; then, they look inward, exposing a vulnerable self that is moved by and may move through, refract, and resist cultural interpretations. (Ellis and Bochner 65)

In Bui's case, the autoethnographic method is useful in connecting her personal narrative with that of the sociopolitical narratives of communism, colonialism, and war in seventies Vietnam. It allows her to bind together many seemingly disparate but ultimately connected pieces of intergenerational memory that agglomerate to form a cohesive, single whole.

In addition to Thi's coming of age, the reader is privy to Thi's parents' childhoods as well as adulthoods, which they spent transitioning between different cultures and nations. The chapter appropriately titled "Rewind, Reverse" begins in 2015 California, travels back to 1999, then to 1993 Minnesota, 1987 San Diego, and then all the way back to 1978 Malaysia and 1975 Saigon, to the time when they were leaving Vietnam. To navigate a landscape of the lived experiences of war, trauma, conflict, migration, and refugeeism of not one but three consecutive generations, Bui had to conduct her autoethnographical inquiry via a medium that could accommodate multiple and simultaneous narratives, as well as one that could adequately depict the scale of the crisis while being rooted in the individual narrative. In other words, the multiplicity of events and characters with which she was dealing posed a narrative challenge that could be best streamlined through the image-textuality of the comic medium, as it is especially effective in taking the abruptness out of jump cuts by providing visual cues that bridge moments across time and space seamlessly. Secondly, while drawing on the collective memory of her family, she literally draws, i.e., gives visual shape to the memories that are not her own, which enables her to *see*, analyze, and empathize with the community she came from. Drawing her parents' childhood and transition to adulthood under the rising communist forces in Vietnam allows Bui to see them not just as parents with flaws but also as people broken by war who did the best they could (as implied by the title of her graphic memoir) under disastrous circumstances.

Figure 3.5. *The Best We Could Do*, page 128–29.

The Best We Could Do is largely characterized by what is known as "retroactive redescription and re-experiencing of human actions and behavior" (Ellis and Bochner, 252) in autoethnography—as Bui constantly goes back in time to contextualize her family's lived experiences in response to history or to locate the source of her trauma(s) by reenacting certain conflictual memories. In a particularly visually compelling scene, Bui illustrates afternoons spent with her father, Bo (Figure 5)—a taciturn man who minded Thi and her younger siblings while her mother worked a minimum wage job when they first moved to the US. To comprehend why her father terrorized them with his less-than-ideal parenting skills and strange quirks, she revisits her childhood by using a quick succession of panels, jumping from one moment to the next in a way that gives the reader almost a live-action view of how those afternoons unfolded. She goes back to Bo's childhood, tracing his journey from his native village to French-controlled Hai Phong to understand how she "grew up with a terrified boy who became [her] father" (Bui 129). In the process, she gives the reader a glimpse into how her father was psychologically abused, first by a mostly absentee father and then by an opportunist grandfather. As a result, when it was Bo's turn to assume parenthood, he did not exactly mirror the treatment meted out to him as a child; he simply did not know how to do better. In a haunting moment of narrative revelation, Bui writes that while growing up, she had "no idea that the terror [she] felt was only the long shadow of his [her father's] own" (Bui 129).

As observable in figure 3.5, there is an "inherent power in the immediacy of an image" (Joe Sacco qtd in *Why Comics* 35), which makes the reenactment of trauma feel tangible in its affective capacity, both to the creator drawing it and the reader engaging with it. Moreover, as time is measured through the "memory of experience" (Eisner 48), the simulation of the experience adds a temporal dimension to the reenactment. This further aids in "creating an experience of the experience" (Ellis 108), by means of which Bui invites the reader to participate in her literary catharsis. Bui also utilizes the comic medium's ability to shape "time by arranging it in space on the page in panels" like "boxes of time" (Chute, *Why Comics* 24). Since each panel is drawn to represent an individual moment, a succession of panels (71–72) creates a semblance of movement from one to the next. The white space between the panels makes the reader an active participant in creating meaning from the narrative, as they are compelled to imagine the action between the panels in order to transition from one to the next. Outside of reader response, although comics cannot be a substitute for therapy, in a rather curious paradox, the creator—by engaging with their traumas through their pictorial self—creates distance between the character and the Self, which expedites the processing of trauma. Having re-created or emulated the passing of time and having reenacted their trauma through their pictorial Self, the author is finally able to wholly see (as Caruth theorizes), process, and let go of the repressed feelings that destabilize their sense of self. Essentially, Bui here is using comics to address the gaps left by verbal language and filling them with the pictorials. The comic form enables Bui to use herself both as a character—to animate the story—and as a subject of research to get to the bottom of her narrative quest. Thus, not only does the comic form enable laying out three generations' worth of trauma in a unified structure, but it also allows her to make visible her investigational process, i.e., how she accessed the records that allows her to trace the source of the primary conflict. The conspicuous presence of her researcher-self cues the reader into how her writing and drawing process is fundamental to her inquiry. She writes—or, more accurately, draws—not just to put an end to emotional suffering but to trace the root cause of her unbelonging. She draws to "bridge the gap between the past and the present" to "heal the void" between her and her parents (Bui 36). In a move that is distinctly reminiscent of Bechdel's creative process in *Are You My Mother?* (2012), Bui arranges and re-orders her memories in conjunction with her family's history against Vietnam's sociopolitical backdrop till it starts making sense to her. Eventually the various disparate pieces of memory fall together in cohesion, making her narrative part literary nonfiction, part imaginative sociological inquiry rendered stylistically through the comic form.

In 1965, when Bui's parents were working in primary education in Ha Tien, "American planes carpet-bombed a country dependent on agriculture . . . money ruined everything else" (200–201). It soon led to "skyrocketing inflation" (201), while cities across Vietnam gradually turned into police states as the war intensified. By the Tet Offensive of 1968, all citizens could be suspected of being "enemies of the state" (202). Bui's parents were detained until they could satisfactorily verify their allegiance to their own government. In the name of protecting the country against foreign power, Vietnamese citizens were treated as criminals and outsiders in their own nation. Subsequently, the day South Vietnam lost the war (April 30, 1975) is regarded as the day they lost their country (211), at least by the common people such as Bui's family. With communist forces approaching Saigon, Bui's parents were given a new—censored and ultra-nationalist—curriculum to teach; neighbors were encouraged to spy on each other, many literary fictions were banned, and their house was raided by the military. Eventually, Bo was fired from his job as an educator and was forced into hard manual labor in "the New Economic Zones" where the government exiled citizens they did not trust. In school, Bui and her sisters were taught to report suspicious antinationalist behavior, even if the "suspects" were their own parents. They were essentially turned into strangers in their country of birth and were dismissed as "Nyguy" by the State. Bui explains, "[Nyguy] meant "false lying deceitful"—but it could be applied to anyone in the South. It meant constant monitoring, distrust, and the ever-present feeling that our family could, at any moment, be separated, our safety jeopardized" (Bui 221). Soon after this, they decided to flee Vietnam for the US, despite Thi's mother being eight months pregnant at the time.

STRANGERS IN ONE'S OWN HOME

Separated by three countries from Vietnam, in between India and Pakistan, lies Kashmir—a state that has been occupied by external forces for centuries, from Sikhs, to Afghans, to British, to Dogras, and finally, the Indian military in the present. Malik Sajad, a cartoonist from the valley, writes that Kashmir was sold to the Dogras by the East India Company (when India was a British colony) for INR 7.5 million.

Following India's Partition (1947) and decolonization, 200,000 Muslims were killed in Kashmir, following which the Indian Army invaded the territory. They have been there ever since. Sajad's 2015 graphic narrative, *Munnu: A Boy from Kashmir*, embodies this peculiar kind of disenfranchisement, the same kind experienced by the Bui family in Vietnam, where people are treated as outsiders by their own government, but in the context of Kashmir. In *Munnu*, Sajad emphasizes that although the Indian government insists on calling Kashmir a "disputed land," it is, in truth, an occupation (191). By claiming that it is an internal issue (335), India has prevented international humanitarian intervention that would benefit the common people of Kashmir. Sajad, in a style strongly reminiscent of Spiegelman's formative work *Maus*, draws Kashmiris as Hanguls, a species of endangered deer native to the land. Like the people of Kashmir, external forces threaten their habitat. The generative use of anthropomorphism here helps emphasize how Kashmiris—like the endangered Hangul—are battered, butchered, and pushed into a state of exile in their own home. By visually portraying Kashmiris as Hanguls, Sajad implicitly conveys how they are seen as an indistinguishable mass by both India and Pakistan, to be used and abused in the opposing countries' respective propaganda. The visual characterization makes the characters appear identical with no distinct individuality, which underscores the identity crisis Kashmiris live with as collectives and as individuals. In contrast, the occupying forces—the Indian Army—as well as non-Kashmiris (tourists or non-Kashmiri journalists) are drawn as humans, which further emphasizes the hierarchy between the oppressor and the oppressed. Sajad's visual rhetoric investigates how India's need to occupy Kashmir has little to do with the welfare of its people and more to do with the volatile political dynamic India shares with its neighbor Pakistan, ever since the Partition. Consequently, while claiming that Kashmir is integral to India, both the Indian government and its people at large treat Kashmiris as suspects of terrorism, as Pakistani allies, as traitors, and as threats to national security, which pushes Kashmiris to the margins of the nation—a liminal position where they belong to India cartographically, but not as far as basic rights of citizenship are concerned. Sajad's demonstration of the unbelonging specific to Kashmir, by way of multiple accounts of lived experiences, serves as an imperative sociology of life under occupation, and it complicates the notion of citizenship. It points out the irony of a country that prides itself on being the largest democracy in the world yet enforces the national elections in Kashmir in a way that not only makes voting compulsory but criminalizes noncompliance. On Independence Day, even as the army hoists Indian flags across Kashmir, its citizens are placed under strict curfew (Sajad 180). Sajad writes—

> At the polling booths, each voter would be marked with purple ink on their index finger. The mark was permanent like Henna, and it

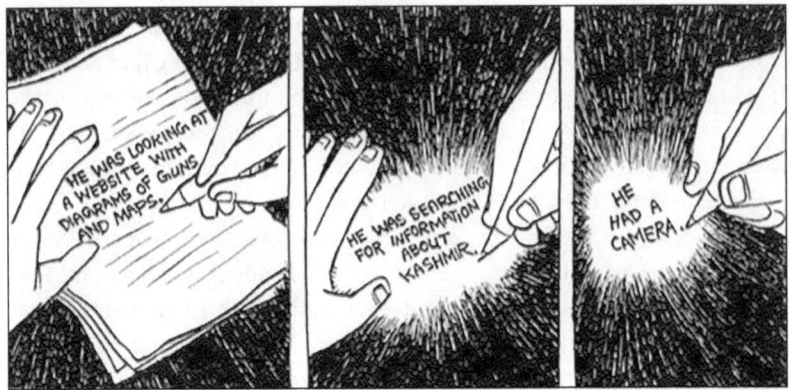

Figure 3.6. *Munnu: A Boy from Kashmir*, page 301.

was necessary to avoid the wrath of the army during random raids, crackdowns, and frisking. But it also marked you as a traitor to the resistance movement in the eyes of the militants. (108)

Belonging—at least a significant aspect of it—depends on a stable sense of community. In Kashmir, due to conflict between the many political factions (the Indian Army, the Pakistan Army, or the Separatist or Resistance Movement), all semblance of community is lost. The resistance movement, despite their ideological progressivism, often resorted to violence to achieve their goals, which hurt the very civilians whose rights they were fighting for, leading to the common people being cornered by all sides. Sajad shows his readers how he himself was on the verge of being detained by the army for his political cartoons while simultaneously being threatened by the resistance party for portraying them in a less than complimentary manner (215). When he visits Delhi to exhibit his artwork, he is accused of terrorism since his visit inopportunely coincides with a bomb blast in the capital. Even as Sajad verifies his identity as a cartoonist who was invited to Delhi to exhibit his work, he is arrested simply for having surfed the web for news about Kashmir in a cybercafé (296).

In figure 3.6, Sajad, by drawing the reasons that the police stated for arresting him—each reason suspended in isolation against a dark background—captures the absurdity of his arrest. The text functions as "an extension of the imagery" as it is intentionally produced graphically "in service of the story ... [and to] support the climate" (Eisner 10). The technique aids in emphasizing how little Kashmiri lives matter, even in their country of birth. Sajad explains that the police only cared to listen to his explanation once he started speaking in Hindi, the dominant language of North India and foreign to Kashmir. The incident reveals how linguistic Othering further disenfranchises Kashmiris, as they are forced to forgo their native tongue in favor of Hindi and English.

Belonging in Kashmir is also fractured by the constant fearmongering by the Indian army, which seeps into the Kashmiri people's interpersonal relationships and further disintegrates their sense of community through systemically manufactured isolation. When Paisley, Munnu's (Sajad's character in the comic) girlfriend from New York, borrows and eventually loses his cell phone, the seemingly innocuous episode turns ugly because it threatens his safety. When Paisley argues that he is overreacting, Munnu explains:

> This is KASHMIR. You need to submit official documents. I had to give a photocopy of my passport . . . What if the police or the army finds the mobile? They might think it belongs to a militant . . . Kashmir's a prison you know. And a passport is your bail contract, a reward for behaving. Get it? It's not all f*****g breathtaking here. (Sajad 291–92)

Sajad's visual storytelling formulates how Kashmir's lack of distinct identity operates through, as well as impinges upon, its people. Their individual identities are impacted adversely by the disparate political factions that try to own Kashmir's narrative, each with their own ideologies and cultures. Being marginalized by the state and internal politics alike, the common people of Kashmir were/are not privy to a sense of security and belonging that usually comes with citizenship, one that somewhat mitigates the division caused by caste, ethnicity, and religious hierarchies.

"A CARTOON IS WORTH A THOUSAND WORDS": PROCESSING GRIEF VIA THE COMIC FORM

In a childhood spent worrying about whether his father would return safely from the military crackdowns, being tear-gassed by the army during a school-led protest, watching neighbors being killed without trial for allegedly being militants, being sexually abused by military personnel, Sajad depicts himself as somebody who found solace in his art. Eventually, he starts using political cartooning to make sense of Kashmir's history. His first editorial cartoon— an incisive take on how Kashmir generates electricity for North India but is deprived of the product of its own labor—appeared in the regional daily when he was only sixteen. Soon after, political cartoons became not only a way for him to lucidly communicate Kashmir's plight to a wide range of readers but also to navigate Kashmir's complex sociopolitics for his own understanding. Over the years, his editors advised him to fashion "a graphic novel" (217) in a style comparable to Joe Sacco's. Sajad is asked to interview victims of military violence in Kashmir to gather primary material for his book. However, in the process of interviewing the victims (223–25), Sajad realizes that under Kashmir's circumstances, that approach bordered on voyeuristic at best and exploitative at worst. He explains that "[interviews] won't change anything for these people. They need our compassion, not questions. We're just rubbing salt in their wounds and toying with their emotions by giving them a fake hope that someone will come and rescue them after reading their stories (226). As Sacco did with Palestine, Bosnia, and other conflict spaces,[1] Sajad wanted to draw attention to the occupation and insurgency in Kashmir through a visually compelling graphical account. However, instead of resorting to journalistic style reportage, he combined the sociopolitical narrative with intimate experiences of life under occupation, told from an autobiographical perspective. While there is a sizable amount of journalistic reporting of the conflict, there is an absence of personal narratives that could potentially make Kashmir's crisis palpable to Indian citizens and foreigners alike, who are often apathetic to impersonal media coverage that does not quite focus on the plights of the ordinary Kashmiri citizen. Sajad fills this gap through his graphic autoethnography, which highlights lived experiences and sheds light on the sociopolitical situation in Kashmir without exploiting the grief of those who have already lost so much. As comics allow a "multiplicity of autobiographical I-s" (Chute, *Graphic Women* 144), Sajad, like Bui, can accommodate both his researcher-self as well as his character Munnu, where the former sociohistorically contextualizes the personal narrative provided by the latter.

Furthermore, similar to Bui's visual praxis in *The Best We Could Do*, Sajad uses the graphic space to perform trauma retroactively and process repressed emotions. Through the redrawing of his memories, he revisits the harrowing event he witnessed as a child when his neighbor Mustafa was shot to death by the army for being suspected of militancy. Mustafa's body was dragged through the streets of Batamaloo, and his face was skinned in the process (Sajad 43). The gruesome image haunted young Munnu for months afterward.

Through a quick succession of panels, narrowly positioned against each other, Sajad demonstrates how he had nightmares about Mustafa suffocating in his grave (342). Some panels are blank except for a pitch-black ink wash that is suggestive of the darkness of a grave, where Munnu imagined Mustafa to be gasping for air. The temporal unfolding of the event aids in an active simulation of the traumatic memory and, in turn, gives Sajad a second

Figure 3.7. *Persepolis*, Marjane Satrapi, page 1.

chance to process his discomfort and manufacture an ending toward closure. In essence, Sajad, secure in the knowledge that the past cannot yield any different outcome than the one with which he is familiar, deliberately places Munnu squarely in the middle of his most traumatic memory through an affective pictorial reenactment. He explains, "There was once Munnu, who loved drawing. Munnu never sought any meaning from his scribbling, but after growing into Sajad he used it to criticize, to express, to expose, to seek revenge against time passing by without fulfilling the promises" (339–40). The comic medium then allows one to not just recall memories but map them spatio-temporally and, in doing so, produces a controlled environment with a predetermined outcome, which one can revisit to find "a safe context to feel pain" (Ellis 115), and process traumatic memories.

CULTURAL HOMELESSNESS AND BEING TWICE-OTHERED

In *Persepolis* (2000), Marjane Satrapi uses the comic form in a way that employs her lived experiences to comment on life under fundamentalist occupation in Iran and, in the process, creates a collective narrative of dislocation, liminality, and transcultural identity, that transcends the individual. On being asked where she comes from, Satrapi explains that "A simple question that for everyone is a one-word answer . . . for an Iranian it's a one-hour explanation: 'I am Iranian, but . . .'" (qtd. in Adams 74).

The *autobio-graphic-al* fabric of Satrapi's narrative enhances the readers' understanding of her unbelonging by enabling them "to read beyond the narrated, toward the embodied—physically and emotively" (Davies 253). Satrapi foreshadows the complex interrelation between the Self, identity, and Othering at the very beginning of the narrative. In figure 3.7, she draws

Figure 3.8. *Persepolis 2*, page 155. The death of Farzad, Marjane's friend, who died in an encounter.

herself outside the panel that encompasses her classmates, indicating a clear disjoint between her and her surroundings. In the words of Chute, Satrapi uses the "spacing within the pictorial frame as the disruption of her own characterological presence" (*Graphic Women* 141) to present herself "fragmented, cut, disembodied, and divided between frames" (*Graphic Women* 141), which is symptomatic of her state of unbelonging.

Through the characterization of Marjane's family, it can be inferred that twentieth-century Iran, especially for the upper classes, was highly Westernized due to years of Western cultural imperialism and colonial histories. However, the society's affinity to the West led to the hybridization of cultures, eventually culminating in a strong backlash from Islamic Fundamentalist leaders, who wanted to purify Iran's cultural fabric of foreign influences. When the Guardians of the Revolution reprimand Marjane for possessing signifiers of Western "decadence" (133), to avoid punitive legal repercussions, she lies that her Michael Jackson badge is instead of "Malcolm X, the leader of black Muslims in America" (133). All Iranians, regardless of their ideological leanings in the era preceding the revolution[2], were compelled to forgo anything Western; anybody who did not comply was considered a traitor to the country. In some extreme cases, civilians were killed for something as simple as being caught in a house party (figure 3.8), which was also considered a sign of Western decadence. In the wordless spread on the left, both the pursuers and the pursued are drawn as silhouettes.

The indistinguishability between the shapes indicates how identities are formed under duress and in the absence of choice and agency, while the lack of dialogues in the frame "reinforces [the] action" (Eisner 16). The last three panels, where Farzad tries to leap across the gap between two buildings but misses, make it look like he is trying to reach for the moon (signifying escape and freedom) but fails and falls instead. In the last panel, all that remains are two buildings and the moon high up in the sky—something distant and unachievable, as is personal liberty for Iranians at this juncture of history. As culture "involves a recognition of commonality, a subjective consciousness of who we are, an awareness of us" (Anand 12), by impinging on the ways Iranians connected with each other and built a sense of community, the Islamic Fundamentalists disenfranchised its citizens through a pervasive form of social isolation that permeated their daily lives. Satrapi demonstrates how civilian resistance is eventually reduced to little, almost inconsequential acts of resistance, such as showing an extra inch of skin or listening to Western music within the safety of indoor spaces, instead of larger acts, such as organizing against the regime or demanding the release of political prisoners (148). By drawing isolated images of outlawed activities such as wearing makeup, she demonstrates how the Iranian community lost its "sense of analysis and reflection" due to fear of the consequences of free thinking.

Through her image-textual inquiry, Satrapi infers that The Regime had understood that one person leaving her house while asking herself: 'Are my trousers long enough? Is my veil in place? Can my makeup be seen? Are they going to whip me?' no longer asks herself: 'Where is my freedom of thought? Where is my freedom of speech? My life, is it livable? What's going on in the political prisons?' (*Persepolis 2*, 148).

Marjane's personal unbelonging is two-fold. Born and raised in Iran, she is sent to Austria as a young adult when rising Islamic Fundamentalism makes the country exceptionally unsafe for young women. Subsequently, she is first Othered in her own country by the regime that enforced systematic marginalization of those with Western affinities, followed by being racially discriminated against in Austria as a foreigner. The nuns in her hostel in Austria humiliate her for improper etiquette, a lack that they attribute to her ethnicity. Amongst other traumatizing incidents, she is thrown out by

Figure 3.9. *Persepolis*. On Being Twice-Othered

her boyfriend's mother for being Iranian and disbelieved/ridiculed by her Physics teacher about her lived experiences of war in Iran. In *Persepolis: The Story of a Return* (2005), Satrapi writes, "My calamity could be summarized in one sentence: I was nothing. I was a Westerner in Iran, and Iranian in the West. I had no identity. I didn't even know anymore why I was living" (118). Due to her existing memories of oppression from Iran, the form of systemic othering she faces in Austria becomes doubly marginalizing—situating her in a liminal position where she ceases to fully belong in either country. Diasporic loss is not "the loss of homeland" but a loss of "relationship to history," to the past, and not just "land or territory" (Cho 7). Cho writes that "Diasporic subjectivity lies in thinking through how the memory of oppression lives on in the present through the processes of racialization" and that "these processes do not emerge in isolation but through difference" (12). To avoid constant othering, Marjane tries to pass as French, justifying that "being an Iranian was a burden to bear" and "it was easier to lie than assume that burden" (*Persepolis 2*, 41). She is compelled to fabricate a twofold projection of Self in an attempt to belong, as indicated in figure 3.9, where Satrapi's stylistic abstraction "strips down [the] image [to amplify] its essential meaning" (McCloud 30), i.e., her *inbetweeness* of being. The graphic autoethnography Satrapi conducts helps her let go of her guilt of inhabiting this dual identity and accept that cultural identity is "a matter of 'becoming' as well as of 'being,'" which are subject to change due to "the continuous 'play' of history, culture and power" (Hall qtd. in Braziel and Mannur 234).

Moreover, Satrapi's autobiography is "split into two voices"; the "captions are narrated by the adult Satrapi reflecting upon her experiences," while her younger self Marji "participates directly in the story dialogues" (Kuhlman 117). The double narration not only indicates Marjane's "evolving sense of identity," as Kuhlman suggests but also enables Satrapi to focus on her personal life in tandem with the sociohistorical context that mediates it. The fluidity of the image-textual space allows her to conjure her mother's and grandmother's memories simultaneously, through first-person narration, that is in conversation with the other through narrative braiding, which "proliferates [multiple] selves on the page" and "allows for a dialectical conversation of different voices to compose the position from which Satrapi writes" (Chute 144). Satrapi's process of narrative drawing also "offers a constant self-reflexive demystification of the project of representation" (Chute, *Graphic Women* 8) and "pushes outward to consistently visualize publics—collectivities of people—aside from herself and thus shifts the narrative attention to a broad public sphere" (139).

The evocative appeal of the visual aids in removing the 'alien-ness' of Others, as its "icon signs" (Duncan, Smith, and Levitz 10) or conventions' universality, which solicit identification from a diverse range of recipients. As a text that is widely taught worldwide (despite periodical calls for banning it), *Persepolis* becomes an object that circulates as an implicit act of resistance, building empathy and understanding across ethno-racial borders and cultural gaps. It resists the dominant discourse that is "created, and distorted, by overt state mechanisms like censorship or covert ideological pressures" (Adams 54). Given comics' history with censorship and that the 'Comic Code' had once systemically tried to prevent 'aberrant' content from being published, Satrapi's move to undo cultural, gendered, and ethnoracial biases via artistic expression becomes especially subversive. In tracing the history that culminated in her unbelonging, but doing so in a public capacity, she is essentially speaking out against the atrocities of the fundamentalist regime in Iran. This, in turn, enables Satrapi to assuage her guilt of leaving her country of birth both physically and, to an extent, psychologically.

AMBIGUITY, DOUBLE CONSCIOUSNESS, AND TRANSCENDENCE

Graphic Narratives that draw on the sociohistorical in tandem with the personal, such as the ones discussed in this chapter, tend to "revise' and 'rewrite' previously held notions of history" that gloss over "exclusion, ethnoracial violence and systemic oppression" (Cutter and Schlund-Vials 1). By converting memory into readable images, these intimate pictorial accounts allow the "author to literally reappear—in the form of a legible, drawn body on the page—at the site of her inscriptional effacement" (Chute 5). Satrapi uses this manifestation of a cartoon self as a visually readable entity in *Persepolis* to play the role of both author and protagonist, which allows her to intervene in the narration and serve as a narrative bridge between the historical account and the present. In turn, the medium, by helping the author-protagonist locate and process their inherited trauma, aids in finding their "elsewhere-within-here"—a hybrid space that forms from coming to terms with one's state of unbelonging. Instead of "simply adding a here to a there" (Minh-ha 37), this hybrid space combines the best of two worlds, giving rise to a home that is "both too recognizable and impossible to contain" (37), a space that is well-suited to house the double consciousness of displaced/diasporic/immigrant lives. Similarly, in Sajad's case, he finds comfort in drawing and making legible the geopolitics of a place whose struggles are obscure to the world. He had said, "It is only by sharing stories that a place like Kashmir begins to exist" (Recchia). Indeed, as is visible from the popular reception of Sajad's text, accounts such as these create a space for marginalized groups to recognize themselves in the author-protagonists' lives and for others to recognize state-sponsored atrocities. Bui, on the other hand, concludes that family is not just something she was born into and that identity is not something that is predetermined at birth. In contrast to the beginning of the narrative, where she is visibly concerned about passing on her shaky sense of identity to her child, by the time she nears the end, she concludes that she "no longer needed to reclaim a homeland" (326). Although "the ground beneath [her] parents' feet had always been shifting . . . by the time [she] was born, Vietnam was not [her] country at all. [She] was only a small part of it" (326). To borrow from the astute nuance offered by Stuart Hall, identities, instead of solely "being grounded in a mere recovery of the past," are "the names we give to the different ways we are positioned by and position ourselves within" (qtd. in Braziel and Munnur 244). By performing their position of being suspended in-between spaces and cultures with the help of a *comic-ally* rendered image-textual self, the three author-protagonists eventually process and revise their notions of identity and sense of self.

AFTERWORD

I wrote this chapter towards the beginning of my PhD, all the way back in early 2019. Since then, barring book reviews, I have mostly pivoted from writing about comics to drawing about comics. I even decided to draw my entire doctoral dissertation, "Drawing Unbelonging," as a comic. Early in the pandemic, I used the comics medium to approach the sociopolitical through the lens of the personal, to work through my grief at losing a loved one. Currently, as I revise this conclusion in January 2022, I am less than four months away from graduating. In the time since I started writing the above chapter, over five million people have died of the virus, socioeconomic inequalities have exacerbated manifold, and the world as we knew it has changed.

On the academic side of things, a lot has been written about COVID and public health, COVID and the role of humanistic inquiry in addressing health inequities, and yes, on COVID and comics. The last couple of years have witnessed a rapid expansion in the field of Graphic Medicine, a field that lies at the intersection of comics and medical humanities. During the first few months of pandemic-spurred isolation, many took to drawing comics to express the relationship with their bodies, to bear testimony to a global crisis, to process grief, to document, and to connect with community. Being fascinated with the medium, I read as many of these comics as I could, contributed to one of the first pandemic anthologies (Graphic Mundi/PSU Press's COVID Chronicles), and cocurated an edited collection of graphic scholarship and commentaries focusing on creative-critical responses to the pandemic for The Comics Grid: A Journal of Comics Scholarship. In all my encounters with such comics, particularly those that explore grief from an autobiographical perspective, what I found was common to all these works was a distinct sense of processing. In that vein, I would like to make the distinction between 'cathartic' and 'therapeutic,' considering that the former indicates some sort of purging or cleansing, while the latter suggests processing or an ongoing process of recovery. In my experience, grief and trauma are both complex and often cyclical.

To suggest that all comics making is cathartic would be glib in that it assumes that one can simply write or draw oneself out of a traumatic memory. For most people, grief is something that comes and goes. Drawing grief, giving shape to my traumatic memories on paper, has been revelatory in many ways; it has provided distance and perspective; it has even, at times, provided momentary relief. Is that enough to call it catharsis? In my experience, it is not, especially since drawing autobiographical comics involves engaging deeply with a subject. For weeks and months on end. For me, as a method, it bordered on rewarding and excruciating in equal measures, and while it almost certainly helped me process difficult memories, to work through complexities, processing isn't the same as purging.

Of course, this is only my opinion based on my personal experience. By the nature of such things, this view is entirely subjective. But so is literary criticism, even when we do omit the informal sounding I's. The truth is that unless the authors whose works I discuss in this chapter have explicitly mentioned it in any of their interviews, it is impossible to know through close reading alone whether the process was cathartic for them. Consequently, I am more interested in reader responses in the shared spaces that reading comics engenders. I am, of course, referring to scholarly and literary spaces and to online spaces. But even in the ostensibly solitary act of reading (which isn't solitary at all, if you think about it), comics, in all its additive glory, enables us readers to synthesize our imagination with that of the drawer's, to fill in the gaps, to draw from our own experiences to leap from one panel to the next, to create a moving story out of stillness. Can comics be cathartic to readers? Maybe, depending on how they engage with the text, and/or how they understand the concept. But the very acts of reading about gut-wrenching grief, engaging with the vulnerabilities of others, witnessing trauma, and, more topically, participating in the act of remembering are noteworthy in the context of comics and Graphic Medicine. Perhaps, in this shared space of meaning-making, augmented by the immersive environment of comics, lies the therapeutic possibilities of the medium.

NOTES

1. In *Palestine* (1993), *Safe Area Gorzade* (2000), and *Footnotes in Gaza* (2009).

2. The Islamic Revolution overthrew the Shah of Persia in 1979. Satrapi writes that, ironically, although the revolution was a leftist one, the leaders that emerged post-revolution, the Islamic Republic, were conservative extremists.

WORKS CITED

Ahmed, Sara. *Strange Encounters: Embodied Others in Post-Coloniality*. New York: Routledge, 2000.
Anand, Dibyesh. "Diasporic Subjectivity as a Subject Position." In *Diaspora and Identity: Perspectives on South Asian Diaspora*, ed. Ajaya Kumar Sahoo and Gabriel Sheffer, 12–20. New York: Routledge, 2014.
Ashcroft, Bill, Gareth Griffiths, and Helen Tiffin. *The Empire Writes Back: Theory and Practice in Post-Colonial Literature*. New York: Routledge, 2002.
Bochner, Arthur, and Carolyn Ellis. *Evocative Autoethnography*. New York: Routledge, 2016.
Braziel, Jana Evans, and Anita Mannur. *Theorizing Diaspora: A Reader*. Hoboken: Wiley-Blackwell, 2003.
Bui, Thi. *The Best We Could Do: An Illustrated Memoir*. New York: Abrams Comicarts, 2018.
Cho, Lily. "The Turn to Diaspora." *Topia: Canadian Journal of Cultural Studies* 17 (Spring 2007): 11–30.
Chute, Hillary. *Graphic Women*. New York: Columbia University Press, 2010.

Chute, Hillary. *Disaster Drawn: Visual Witness, Comics and Documentary Form*. Cambridge: Harvard University Press, 2016.
Chute, Hillary. *Why Comics: From Underground to Everywhere*. New York: Harper, 2017.
Chute, Hillary L., and Patrick Jagoda. *Comics & Media*. Chicago: University of Chicago Press, 2014.
Cutter, Martha J., and Cathy J. Schlund-Vials. *Redrawing the Historical Past: History, Memory, and Multiethnic Graphic Novels*. Athens: University of Georgia Press, 2017.
Davies, Rocio G. "Layering History: Graphical Embodiment and Emotions in GB Tran's *Vietnamerica*." *Rethinking History: The Journal of Theory and Practice* 19, no. 2 (2015): 252–67.
Duncan, Randy, Matthew J. Smith, and Paul Levitz. *The Power of Comics: History, Form and Culture*. London: Bloomsbury Academic, 2015.
Eisner, Will. *Comics and Sequential Art: Principles and Practices from the Legendary Cartoonist*. New York: W.W. Norton, 2008.
Groensteen, Thierry. *The System of Comics*. Oxford: University Press of Mississippi, 2007.
Hirsch, Marianne. *The Generation of Postmemory*. New York: Columbia University Press, 2012.
Kirby, Robert. "Review: *The Best We Could Do*." *The Comics Journal*, http://www.tcj.com/reviews/the-best-we-could-do/
Kuhlman, Martha. "The Autobiographical and Biographical Graphic Novel." In *The Cambridge Companion to the Graphic Novel*, ed. Stephen Tabachnick, 113–29. Cambridge: Cambridge University Press, 2017.
McCloud, Scott. *Understanding Comics: The Invisible Art*. New York: William Morrow, 1994.
Recchia, Francesca. "Malik Sajad's 'Munnu': A Graphic Novel From Kashmir." *Warscapes* 4 (November 2015): http://www.warscapes.com/reviews/malik-sajads-munnu-graphic-novel-kashmir.
Sajad, Malik. *Munnu: A Boy from Kashmir*. London: Fourth Estate, 2015.
Satrapi, Marjane. *Persepolis: The Story of a Childhood*. New York: Pantheon Books, 2000.
Satrapi, Marjane. *Persepolis: The Story of a Return*. New York: Pantheon Books, 2004.
Trinh, T. Minh-Ha. *Elsewhere, Within Here: Immigration, Refugeeism and the Boundary Event*. New York: Routledge, 2011.
Whitlock, Gillian. "Autographics" in *Comics Studies: A Guidebook*. New Brunswick: Rutgers University Press, 2020.
Yu, Mallory. "Cartoonist Thi Bui Weaves Together Personal and Political History." NPR, 1 Aug. 2018, www.npr.org/2018/08/01/634606313/cartoonist-thi-bui-weaves-together-personal-and-political-history.

III. DRAWING TOGETHER:
NATION AND NARRATIVE

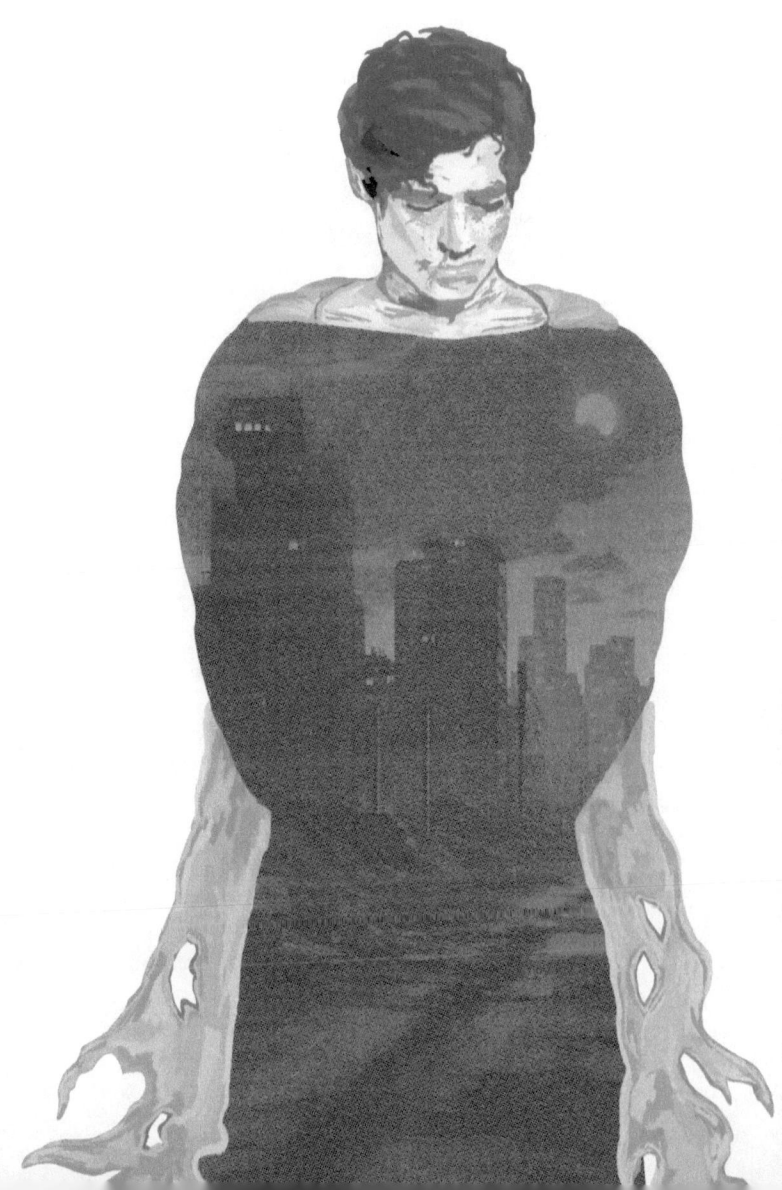

CHAPTER 4

THE BURDEN OF TRANSLATING HISTORY IN LI KUNWU'S
A CHINESE LIFE

ANGIE CHAU

In 1935, the American missionary Pearl Buck introduced English-language readers to Lin Yutang's *My Country and My People* (1935), declaring the soon-to-be bestseller "the most important book yet written about China," while touting its greatest feature: "[B]est of all, it is written by a Chinese, a modern, whose roots are firmly in the past, but whose rich flowering is in the present" (Lin, xii). Lin Yutang's ensuing "Preface" reciprocally praised Buck, "who, from the beginning to the end, gave me kind encouragement and who personally read through the entire manuscript before it was sent to the press and edited it" (Lin, xiv). At the time of *My Country*'s publication in the United States, Buck was an established author, riding on the success of her critically acclaimed Pulitzer-winning *The Good Earth* (1931), and Lin Yutang was nearly as well-known among intellectuals in mainland China as the founder of the satirical magazine *Analects Fortnightly* (Lunyu banyuekan).

More recently, in 2009, the comic *A Chinese Life* (Une vie chinoise), the first of a three-volume serial, was published in France by the manga publisher Kana. The comic memoir, like *My Country and My People*, was also the result of a cross-cultural literary partnership—the 2005–2010 collaboration between the Chinese cartoonist Li Kunwu (李昆武, b. 1955), a former illustrator for the newspaper *Yunnan Daily* (Yunnan ribao), and the French writer-diplomat Philippe Ôtié (née Philippe Autier, b. 1964). *A Chinese Life* has since been translated into fifteen languages, including Edward Gauvin's English version, published by SelfMade Hero in 2012. The story takes place over the span of sixty years, from the first-person narrator's birth in 1955 to the 2008 Beijing Olympics.

The conception of *A Chinese Life* differs from the earlier literary pairing of Pearl Buck and Lin Yutang in *My Country and My People* in three obvious but nonetheless important ways. For one, in terms of medium, the latter is a collection of humorous prose essays about Chinese politics, culture, and society from the first-person perspective, targeted for English language readers, whereas *A Chinese Life*, while also narrated in the first-person, was written initially for French readers, and appears in the combined form of black-and-white illustrated panels (peppered with the occasional photograph) accompanied by textual dialogue and narration. Second, Lin Yutang is the sole author of *My Country*, whereas *A Chinese Life* recounts the life of its artist Li Kunwu: story and images are ostensibly produced by Li, but the text that appears on the page is attributed to both Ôtié and Li Kunwu. Third, in the nearly seventy-five-year difference in publication date, the position of China has shifted in the world cultural sphere, including what Pascale Casanova has called the "world republic of letters," a field closely linked to the nation's status as an increasingly powerful world economic leader. As such, Li Kunwu's underlying objective is to make China's recent development accessible to world readers, in contrast to Lin Yutang's ambitious project in the early 1930s, whose aim was essentially to explain how China ended up afflicted by political chaos domestically amidst the turmoil of the Civil War (1927–1950) and by foreign encroachment on the eve of the Second Sino-Japanese War (1937–1945) in WWII.

Yet, in both instances, the East-West literary relationship is framed as one in which the authentic Chinese source relies on an outsider with China familiarity as the liberating force that facilitates the creative process. Even more significantly, the ability to translate Chinese history from a personal narrative to link the past with the writer's grounded position in the present-day, is depicted as the defining trait of cultural authenticity. In the list of acknowledgments, which precedes the informal preface to *A Chinese Life*, Li thanks his family and friends, especially his cowriter, for "having unveiled the mysteries of the Western mind and given me the strength to bring to light all the memories and feelings my subconscious had buried so deep inside" (Li 2012, np). In an interview with *Le Petit journal* in 2012, Ôtié described the relationship between his role and Li's in the project, "My job was to make the story comprehensible to a foreigner, without whitewashing it. We were constantly trying to walk the line between Chinese propaganda and western critique" (Delaisse). This cultural sensitivity is not unwarranted, as literary scholars like Julia Lovell have pointed out the tendency of western readers to be obsessed with politically controversial (and usually banned in China) topics in recent Chinese history. Lovell questions whether the "Western interest in Chinese political suffering," as indicated by fetishization of the historical trauma inflicted by the Cultural Revolution and June 4, 1989, are "no more than junk-food literary topics designed for Western appetites" (Lovell, 32). The global reception of *A Chinese Life* certainly speaks to Lovell's contention that "Western audiences are happy to encourage politicized Chinese literature, as long as the politics are correct" (Lovell, 19).

The family memoir graphic novel subgenre, within which *A Chinese Life* occupies an uneasy position, was established by its critically acclaimed predecessors, such as Keiji Nakazawa's *Barefoot Gen* (1973–1974), Art Spiegelman's *Maus* (1980–1991), and Marjane Satrapi's *Persepolis* (2000–2003). The success of these works relies on the "new seeing" that the medium offers, according to scholars like Hillary Chute, who have demonstrated the potential of comics to reclaim otherwise lost histories: "Extending forward from a rich tradition of forms, comics has reemerged after the age of the camera through urgent acts of witness" (38). This chapter examines what happens during exchange and circulation when a graphic novel fails to conform to the reader's expectation of encountering "urgent acts of witness" and expressions of cathartic release. Attentive to Richard Kearney's cautionary warning in "Narrating Pain: The Power of Catharsis" that "History-making and story-telling can just as easily result in propaganda and distortion as in healing and release" (Kearney, 63), my essay asks, can a "new seeing" still arise when a graphic novel refuses to bear witness and address the burden of historical memory in the accepted way?

The chapter addresses this question by surveying the epic autobiography's varied global reception. As stated by Ôtié's aforementioned interview with *Le petit journal*, the work's aim is twofold: to avoid being perceived as the voice of Chinese Communist Party (CCP) propaganda, and to avoid taking the position of western critique. Anglophone, Chinese, and French readers of *A Chinese Life* disagree, however, whether this aim has been accomplished.[1] Reception of the English translation of *A Chinese Life* has focused on the element of propaganda, and in particular, the depiction of traumatic moments in recent Chinese history, especially the June 4, 1989 massacre in Tiananmen. As one blogger shares, "[R]eading the book was an uncomfortable experience because I couldn't shake the notion that the book is a work of propaganda" (Clough). While Li and Ôtié's book claims to "journey back to distant memories" and "plunge into forgotten emotions" (Li 2012, np), the narrator of *A Chinese Life* refuses to engage in direct condemnation of the CCP, thereby failing to live up to contemporary anglophone readers' expectations of the graphic novel as a distinctly subversive, counter-cultural literary genre. Yet for reasons of mutual benefit, French and Chinese readers have celebrated the book's achievement in the world literary sphere. Considering Casanova's contested claim that "Paris has become the place where books— submitted to critical judgment and transmuted—can be denationalized and their authors made universal" (Casanova, 127), this chapter argues that the book's global success relies on the Sino-Franco literary sphere's perception of *A Chinese Life* as a truthful and representative historical account, at the cost of overlooking the highly complex role the literary collaboration of Li and Ôtié plays, as well as the book's purported focus on economic development.²

As critics have pointed out, nostalgia is closely tied to "the rapidly changing social reality consequent upon China's entry into the global market economy" (Yue, 49). When it comes to modern Chinese history, particularly in the production of nostalgia and consumer culture related to the Cultural Revolution (1966–1976), Ming-Bao Yue has coined the term "obscene pleasure" to describe transnational Chinese narratives about the period that fall outside typical memoirs emphasizing the "ideology of victimization or personal suffering" (Yue, 47). Examining English-language Cultural Revolution memoirs by Anchee Min and Liu Sola, Yue argues that these texts deviate from more conventional narratives in large part due to Min and Liu's transnational identities as overseas authors. Testimonial literature about the Cultural Revolution is connected to its literary predecessor, "scar literature" (*shanghen wenxue*), or the literature of trauma that was published in the immediate post-Cultural Revolution period beginning in the late 1970s. Criticized as a superficial forum for moral reflection and victimization, this mode of literary production was seen as ineffectual in the healing process, particularly in its refusal to assign blame for the Cultural Revolution to the CCP: "Rather than probing the deep-rooted historical and political reasons for people's sufferings, Literature of Trauma often appears to be a mere cathartic expression of individual grievances, which is mistakenly thought to be capable of healing the historical trauma" (Li and Tam, 443). In addition to taking an ambivalent position on the issue of government accountability, *A Chinese Life* further complicates the familiar narrative mode of Cultural Revolution memoir by extending its trajectory into the less familiar territory of the twenty-first century and China's economic ascent. Chute has convincingly shown how comics operate as an experimental documentary form that "proposes an ethics of looking and reading intent on defamiliarizing standard or received images of history while yet aiming to communicate and circulate" (31). For non-Chinese graphic novel readers, even if the Cultural Revolution is accessible as a historical and literary topic, its association with China's subsequent growth and development in *A Chinese Life* stymies the reading process. Similarly, iconic images of the Tiananmen Square Massacre in 1989, well-circulated outside of mainland China, may render the book's ambivalent treatment of the atrocity an unexpected affront.

WALKING A NARROW RIDGE: RECEPTION OF *A CHINESE LIFE* IN ENGLISH

The issue of what exactly happened on June 4, 1989 continues to be a highly controversial topic, if not entirely glossed over or banned and forgotten in mainland China, and this section analyzes how Li and Ôtié address this contentious issue in the book, as well as the reasons for readers' dissatisfaction with their treatment of history and traumatic memory. Book 3 of the trilogy begins with Chapter 7, which is titled "The First Golden Bowl," and takes place in Wuhan in January 2010, as Li and Ôtié meet up to look over the published version of the second volume and discuss laying out Book 3. Apart from the book's color preface and the title page for Chapter 10, this is the only time readers see the illustrated image of Ôtié in the body of the book as Li admonishes him in one panel, "Sometimes you stray too far from a Chinese mindset. But they're mostly fine" (Li 2012, 484). The two characters brainstorm how "to settle the '6/4 question,'" as Ôtié growls, "We've been banging our heads against it for six months!" Ôtié continues, "Curfew, arrests, disappearances, deaths—we'll have to try harder than usual to stick to the objective viewpoint of a simple witness." Li jumps on this last word: "'Witness,' 'Witness'—but what did I see? I told you before: in June '89, I was studying sculpture near the border. What little I know about Tiananmen I heard on the radio. I want to bear witness to what they said, but I'm afraid that . . ." Comparing the Chinese version to the English and French versions reveals that while the latter delineate the "curfew, arrests, disappearances, deaths" associated with June 4th, the former has Ôtié leaving out the details, opting instead to state the duo's objective as "In order to give an objective introduction" [为了客观介绍] (Li 2015, 50). Li ponders one alternative, skipping the event altogether and jumping ahead in time before announcing decisively, "You know what? This is one time when I'd just like to come out and say what I think." For Ôtié, who is portrayed as more cautious, depicting Li's opinion over eyewitness account ("what you think instead of what you saw") necessarily "means an end to the neutrality" they've tried to maintain. While Ôtié's concern is one of narrativization and representation (i.e., how

Figure 4.1. *A Chinese Life*, page 488.

to tell the story), Li faces the burden of individual responsibility. When Ôtié suggests telling the story of what happened from someone who was there, Li counters, "You know I don't know anyone like that! Not only because so few people in Kunming were affected, but because with my professional, familial, and political circles, I was far removed from all of that" (Li 2012, 486). The crux of the problem lies here: how to address this significant historical event that all foreign readers would expect some reaction to.

As the autobiographical storyteller, even if he does not have firsthand lived experience of being physically in Beijing during the massacre, Li is confronted by the personal duty to address this historical trauma, which, for Ôtié, a foreign "outsider," is only a second-hand pressure. *A Chinese Life* offers two approaches. The first is the character Li's voiceover narration, a first-person address to the reader. Unlike the rest of the text that appears in *A Chinese Life*, this is not dialogue voiced in speech bubbles but neatly contained in text boxes that overlap the illustration panels.

In this two-page-long narration, Li acknowledges two opposing views between overseas and domestic audiences: "internationally, there is a very dark view of 6/4," and "here, in China, those events caused great suffering. Lives were shattered, some even lost. I know all that" (2012, 488). What the western reader may find unconscionable hinges on this turn: "But the truth is, like almost all my countrymen, my mind is occupied with so many other things I find even more important." While both the French and English versions emphasize the national specificity of Li's perspective ("like almost all my countrymen" translated from "comme presque tous mes concitoyens"), the Chinese version adopts a more universal tone ("like almost all people" 和几乎所有的人一样). Li continues, "Partly because all that happened twenty years ago, and I have a habit of putting behind me parts of the past that are liable to make me uncomfortable. Also, because I didn't personally suffer as a result . . . And partly because I'm convinced that, above all, China needs order and stability to develop. The rest is secondary, in my view" (Li 2012, 488–89). Li's narrative of personal (hence insignificant) suffering is overshadowed by the burden of the nation's "growth and rebirth" (Li 2012, 489), and his lengthy monologue, repeatedly invokes CCP keywords "stability," "order," "growth," "rebirth." The Tiananmen Square massacre is invoked here on the same page as merely one in a series of "uncomfortable" or uneasy ("mal à l'aise") historically unfortunate events, including hardships from before Li's time ("invasion, plunder, 'unequal treaties,' internal divisions, battles among warlords") and those experienced firsthand (Cultural Revolution, "the opposing movements, struggles, drought, famine, electricity shortages, penury"). As such, Li frames the violence of June 4th in the longer legacy of political turmoil and human suffering in modern Chinese history in order to reduce the distance between western expectations and what has been broadly read by anglophone readers as CCP propaganda.

The second approach to the problem of how to depict June 4th is in terms of commemoration. Immediately after Li's monologue, the next page begins with a panel that states the date June 1990. The plot moves to ways of money-making, which is in line with the chapter's focus on the economic development of the 1990s. As Li searches for leads for a bubble-wrap supplier in the local papers, the bottom panels on page 491 depict a close-up of the *Yunnan Daily* masthead for the June 4, 1990 issue.

Figure 4.2. *A Chinese Life*, page 491.

Three panels reveal the patriotic party slogan, "Our love for the country does not change, our gratitude toward our country is unwavering" (Aiguo zhi xin bubian, baoguo zhi zhi buyi 爱国之心不变, 报国之志不移) and also a section from the paper featuring a *Peoples Daily*'s editorial with the characters "Stability" (wending 稳定) in bold. While these have been rendered into pinyin and translated into English, decoded for the reader, much remains enigmatic, still in code. What is the purpose of these panels? Just as mysteriously, the top of the next page shows Li reading the paper, with the speech bubble questioning, "Huh? 4 June? A year already!"

Figure 4.3. *A Chinese Life*, page 492.

Without further reflection, the plot continues with the search for bubble wrap as a money-making scheme. The commemoration of June 4th appears as a blip on the screen, overshadowed by more important pressing issues filling the crowded street scenes with the materiality of everyday life in the early 1990s, such as the boxed goods related to growing international trade (Sony TVs), and official banners announcing official policies such as family planning and education. The passing of time from 1989 and Li's reflection on the dilemma of how to depict June 4th indicates that exactly one year later, public concern has shifted to ways of making a profit as the official way to support the nation's stability. The number of panels devoted to this date, through the close-up view of the masthead and the zooming in on particular phrases of patriotism, emphasize the importance of remembrance. The gutter space surrounding the panels on page 491 reinforces the depiction on page 492 of Li holding the newspaper as he remarks on the date; the narrative device of perusing ads in the search for business leads jolts the reader into pausing sporadically, without any possibility of overlooking the one-year anniversary of June 4th. Chute's analysis of the usually overlooked gutter space can be instructive in thinking about what is not said in dialogue or narration but in visual language unique to the medium:

> This blank space, which translates as *blanc* in its French usage, is constitutive of comics logic and grammar. It is where a reader, conventionally, projects causality, and where the division of time in comics is marked, providing a constant source of tension, a constant proffering of the unmarked in spaces that are carefully bounded and marked out. At the heart of the attention to the gutter is the fact of its *constitutive* absence. It is not merely like a seam or a margin (although it bleeds out into margins often, suggesting a kind of narrative ceaselessness, an unendingness); rather, its present blankness, often implying duration, is laid out for readers as part of the narrative encounter. (Chute 35)

As Li looks through the cacophony of printed material, the division of panels and gutter space on the bottom of page 491 accentuate the sudden shift in narrative perspective as the reader becomes Li, holding the *Yunnan Daily* paper, unable to look away. The juxtaposition of official party slogan with individual reaction can imply disbelief in the passing of time ("already" a year) as well as in the unnatural washing over and awareness (or the ability to express anything beyond the mundane observation) of historical trauma. The reader can perceive what is not being said or what cannot be directly stated simply by reading the paper headlines: as Li explained pages earlier, the official position of prioritizing "order and stability to develop" may temporarily occlude historical trauma or serve as a distraction, but this cannot prevent individuals from personal reflection or remembering.

Most anglophone readers have been dissatisfied with the way that June 4th is depicted in *A Chinese Life*, arguing that contrary to Ôtié's stated objective of avoiding whitewashing history and siding with the CCP, the discussion of the massacre in the graphic novel fails to take on the responsibility of memory work commonly practiced in other "world" historical graphic novels based on autobiographical experiences. In one analysis of the book, for example, Jeffrey Mather argues that Li's professional background in propaganda art is a destructive force:

> Similar to graphic autobiographies like *Maus*, *Fun Home*, and *Persepolis*, *A Chinese Life* is structured as a künstlerroman narrative as it traces the struggle and development of the autobiographical subject into an artist. However, unlike the rebellious artist who is shown to have broken free of social constraints, the protagonist of *A Chinese Life* is unable to separate himself from, and in many ways actually becomes, that which oppresses him. (102)

In a review for *Yishu* journal, Ryan Holmberg concludes that the book "seems ready to accept the continuing authoritarianism of the Chinese government in the name of economic growth and global prestige" (97). Similarly, in a review of the book for *Paste Magazine*, Hillary Brown complains, "Most troubling of all is his persistent justification for problematic or horrific policies, as with the crackdown in Tiananmen Square in 1989 and the shrugging off of state-caused famine and the excesses of the Cultural Revolution." Another reviewer echoes this disappointment even more cynically: "[W]e'll unfortunately always be left wondering how many other panels of the graphic novel have conveniently been 'forgotten' by the author" (Hertzberg).

These readers' expectations and their subsequent disappointment with *A Chinese Life* can be better understood given the book's stated purpose, along with the way that memory work has been depicted in other internationally recognized graphic novels of this genre. In the prologue of *A Chinese Life*, the hesitant Li Kunwu is drawn to the promise that the project will allow him to engage in "real memory work" with the help of his diary and *Yunnan Daily* newspaper archives: "With all that, you'll be able to reconstruct everything" (Li 2012, np). However, the three volumes prove the lofty dream impossible to achieve due both to the narrator's voluntary reluctance to remember and his involuntary blocking out of traumatic events. For instance, as he recalls the early days of the Cultural Revolution in hindsight, an image of Old Li is accompanied by the reflective confession, "Like many others, I try not to look back too often, to let memory tug me down the slope of remorse" (2012, 131). Contrary to the belief that "One can forgive but one should never forget" presented in narratives like Satrapi's *Persepolis* (Satrapi, Introduction), readers here are likely to be offended by Li's reluctance or outright ability to remember. Narrating a violent Red Guard struggle session against schoolteachers, a middle-school-aged Li is shown in a series of increasingly hazy panels, "What happened next . . . what happened next has been erased

Figure 4.4. *A Chinese Life*, page 141.

from my memory" (Li 2012, 141) [illus. 4]. Compared to the Chinese version, which narrates neutrally, "Inside my mind . . . a blank . . ." (Li 2015, 141), the English translation is heavy-handed in depicting the act of forgetting as an externally enforced process of erasure.

Not only are personal attempts to reconstruct history thwarted, but the transmission of history is also obstructed. Multiple characters at various points in the narrative are depicted urging family members and friends to forget the past, either because "You can't say such things" (Li 2012, 276); "[N]ow all that's settled" (Li 2012, 294); or "for fear of waking ghosts—there were so many" (Li 2012, 341). In contrast, the dialogue from *Persepolis* between Marji and her uncle Anoosh takes the opposite stance: "I tell you all this because it's important that you know. Our family memory must not be lost. Even if it's not easy for you, even if you don't understand it all." "Don't worry, I'll never forget" (Satrapi, 60). Discussing the responsibility of historians and the challenges of Holocaust historiography, in particular the inextricability of writing Holocaust history with its "unavoidable use in its interpretation and narration of implicit or explicit moral categories," Saul Friedlander asks, "Is the real impact of this history solely in the memory it has left?" (Friedlander 2000, 12). In the specific context of Chinese history, Ian Johnson has described history as both "the benchmark for legitimacy in the present" as well as "a beast that lurks in the shadows" (Johnson 2016, 303). For Li and Ôtié, one way to resolve this moral dilemma without challenging the Party's legitimacy is to displace historical trauma with the promise of what is to come. For instance, in Part II of *A Chinese Life*, the last page of Chapter 3 ends with a full-page panel about the end of the Cultural

Revolution, describing the effects of the decade as "expunged memories better forgotten," concluding triumphantly, "With the disturbing past behind us, all that remained was to invent an ever more glorious future" (Li 2012, 267). Li implies that the nation's development depends on the erasure of history.

In an op-ed for the *New York Times*, the author Yan Lianke describes the "state-sponsored amnesia" that has resulted in the Chinese censorship of much of twentieth-century history, such as the number of starvation-related deaths during the Great Leap (1958–1961). Yan writes, "While the whole world still vividly remembers the tragic end of the June 4 student movement in 1989, the painful memory is lost in the country where the bloodshed took place, in the midst of cheers for China's economic growth and increased influence" (Yan 2013). *A Chinese Life* defies this forgetting by directly depicting the moral dilemma of duty to bear witness, yet also delineates the limits of personal memory through the narrator Li's avoidance of confronting trauma head-on and the narrator's faith in the nation's future prospects. Compared to the case of the CCP's official position on June 4th, one's sense of social responsibility diminishes—and is made impossible—when suppression of history is state-condoned and continues to be censored by state institutions. Unlike Satrapi's narrative, which emphasizes the necessity of preserving family history, Art Spiegelman's *Maus* actually more closely reflects the realization in *A Chinese Life* that to reconstruct everything is an untenable project. The rejection of the notion of memory work through comics as necessarily cathartic, along with the recognition that one's reckoning with historical trauma is an ongoing process, lie at the heart of Spiegelman's *Maus*: "Some part of me doesn't want to draw or think about Auschwitz. I can't visualize it clearly, and I can't begin to imagine what it felt like" (Spiegelman, 206). Spiegelman problematizes the burden of what Marianne Hirsch has called postmemory, which refers to the transmission of traumatic experiences from one generation to the next: "The growth of the memory culture may, indeed, be a symptom of a need for inclusion in a collective membrane forged by a shared inheritance of multiple traumatic histories and the individual and social responsibility we feel toward a persistent and traumatic past" (Hirsch, 111). Artie's social responsibility manifests in the guilt he feels for not having firsthand lived experience of the Holocaust: "It's just that sometimes I'd fantasize Zyklon B coming out of our shower instead of water. I know this is insane, but I somehow wish I had been in Auschwitz with my parents so I could really know what they lived through! ... I guess it's some kind of guilt about having had an easier life than they did" (Spiegelman, 176). Unlike Artie, Li can claim firsthand lived experience, but his insistence on looking forward not backward, reflects Yan's concern

Figure 4.5. *A Chinese Life*, page 131.

that eventually "we lose our memories of what happened to our nation in the past, then we lose the sense of what's happening in our nation at present, and, finally, we run the risk of losing memories about ourselves, about our childhood, our love, our happiness and pain" (Yan 2013).

A closer reading of *A Chinese Life* reveals, however, less a total rejection of the value of memory work than a realization that the traumatic past always finds a way to resurface. There are two specific examples in which Li's graphic novel implies a more critical and nuanced reflection on the relationship between historical trauma and the passing of time than has generally been acknowledged by the accusations of propaganda. First, the repetition of an image that first appears on page 131 reappears on page 489.

In both cases, Old Li sits resignedly in profile view, shoulders hunched over, atop an old tree stump that rests upon a mountain of tangled roots, facing the setting sun overlooking a distant cityscape of high-rise buildings that jut out against a remote mountainscape. On the first occasion, following a three-panel sequence depicting the broken remnants of artifacts destroyed during the Cultural Revolution, Old Li reflects, "In truth, he who once, with the insouciance of youth, destroyed so many wonders would give so much today to find just a few of those marvelous objects intact, bearers of our history" (2012, 131). Li's retrospective and nostalgic interjection in the Cultural Revolution narrative calls on the reader to acknowledge the loss and destruction of material goods, as well as the emotional burden of being personally responsible for those acts of destruction yet being a relatively powerless observer in the present moment. This same image is repeated on page 489 in Old Li's reflection on June 4th. If the gutter is "a space of movement: it is where, in a sense, the readers makes the passage of time in comics happen" (Chute, 35), then this repeated image also requires the reader to interpret what happens between June 4, 1989, and Li's struggle to bear witness in the writing of the book, leading to his drawing the connection these two historical moments of trauma, as a way to emphasize the "indescribable torments we suffered for far too long" (Li 2012, 489).

Another example that complicates accusations of *A Chinese Life* as political propaganda for the CCP takes place in Chapter 8, "The Character 'Chai,'" of the last volume when June 4th resurfaces in the daily street conversations about economic reforms. As Li's mother and her friend Mrs. Ding debate the pros and cons of new developments such as bank cards, they recount the story of Mrs. Ding's nephew, who was forbidden by his parents to go to Tiananmen. The two elderly women draw a connection between this nephew and his generation of young people, "full of fervor, ideals, always ready to take on the world" (Li 2012, 561), and then relate this youthful idealism to their personal memories of Red Guards during the Cultural Revolution.

As they reminisce, Mrs. Ding exclaims, "I'll never forget them! And when I saw the students flood Tiananmen Square last year on TV, I couldn't help thinking, can it mean the Cultural Revolution will be starting all over again?" (Li 2012, 561). Immediately, Li's mother responds, "Before I forget, did you know our singing class was moved to Saturday?" This brief exchange, like the earlier moments about the seemingly conflicting necessity of forgetting, coupled with the impossibility of forgetting, fit the book's underlying obsession with the persistence of memory, linkages to historical political movements,

Figure 4.6. *A Chinese Life*, page 561.

and their implications for the uncertainty of the future. These examples in the graphic novel illustrate the element of compromise that Li and Ôtié address explicitly in the prologue, "With every subject, we always had to walk a narrow ridge between critique and propaganda, with steep drops on either side. A path that remained faithful to Lao Li's life, even as it allowed the reader to make his or her own assessments and judgments" (Li 2012, np). The next section will discuss the assessments and judgments of Chinese and French readers and how the book's circulation has shaped the way that contemporary Chinese literature is viewed in the world literary sphere.

CHINESE LITERATURE AND THE GLOBAL GRAPHIC NOVEL: RECEPTION OF *A CHINESE LIFE* IN FRANCE AND CHINA

On October 12, 2011, China's state-mouthpiece Xinhua News announced proudly, "The cartoon trilogy *A Chinese Life* documents one person's life, introducing foreign readers to a complete, authentic, and open [完整, 真实 和开放] China" (Wang 2011). Domestic news media drew from this description of the book, and the tripartite phrase—consisting of adjectives rarely used to describe state-sanctioned works of contemporary Chinese literature—became prominently circulated. For French readers, *A Chinese Life* is described by Kana as "narrated from the inside by a Chinese author who has lived through the dizzying ascent of communism under Mao." According to the French-language version of its website, Li's narrative takes the reader on a journey that blends "nostalgia and awareness, with faith to facts and historical references through a nearly clinical approach to the subject." This section of the chapter reveals how the French and Chinese reception of *A Chinese Life* share some overlapping interpretations of the work's intended audience and message. The book's Chinese version was published by Sanlian Shudian in 2013 and titled *From Little Li to Old Li* (Cong xiao Li dao lao Li). Chinese readers have seized on the importance of the work's global influence, namely how well the work has been received and translated worldwide, and Li Kunwu's path to French literary celebrity read as evidence of the success of a Sino-French partnership. *Nouvelles d'Europe* (Ouzhou shibao 欧洲时报), a Chinese-language newspaper based in Paris, identified the primary allure of *A Chinese Life*: "The book reveals many aspects of Chinese people's everyday lives, exposes the ordinary life of an average Chinese, which is something that any official propaganda cannot achieve, and satisfies the yearning of European readers to understand the reality of China from an individual's standpoint" (Ze 2016). This kind of testament affirms the existence of a French readership invested in more than navel-gazing; at the same time, it affirms the book's subversive counter-narrative.

But arguably the work's greatest accomplishment is how it has helped elevate the status of Chinese comics in the eyes of the global comics prize circuit. *Chinese Life* received an impressive number of international prizes, including the Reader's Choice Award at the 2012 Saint-Malo Comics Festival, the 2013 Best Foreign Language Comic at the Algeria Comics Festival, the Golden Dragon Award in the 2012 China Animation and Comic Competition, and the 2014 Japanese Culture Department Award (Wang 2017). In a 2015 interview published in *L'est républicain* titled "The wakening of Chinese comics," Angoulême BD festival programmer Nicolas Finet explains the tradition of Chinese comics by positioning it as the next hot thing to follow in the footsteps of Japanese manga: "If the word 'manga' is outdated, it's 'manhua's' turn to try" (Ganousse). Finet also recognizes Angoulême's role in facilitating China's entrance into the world of international comics by creating the Pavillon China and inviting a special delegation of Chinese authors. Li Kunwu echoed this sentiment in an interview with *Global People* (Renwu zhoukan), describing his feelings at attending a comic book exhibit in Paris where Japanese books occupied an entire wall, compared to the Chinese tradition as represented by him solely in one corner: "Our [China's] 'stories' are still too weak . . . the discrepancy between the state of Chinese comic publishing and foreign readers' demands is still too vast" (Huang). According to Li, while other Chinese comics are merely a poor imitation of Japanese manga, *A Chinese Life* is a uniquely Chinese product (Zhongguo zhihao) (Huang). Just as importantly, it's about the recognition of China (as represented by Li Kunwu) as a global player in the comic scene: "From a Chinese comic artist's contribution in Europe and the Sino-French partnership to observations of contemporary life and the exploration of historical details, Chinese comic artists are in the midst of trying to get Europeans to 'see' that distant, thousand-mile away Asian country" (Ze).

The main reason why *Chinese Life* is perceived as having been able to successfully transcend national borders is because of Li's partnership with Ôtié and, from a broader perspective, the prestige of the French literary tradition. Clément Bénech, writing on Li's exhibit at the FRAC Auvergne in early 2018, titled "La Formidable épopée du Yunnan de Li Kunwu," describes Li Kunwu as someone whose graphic novels have found great success in France, "the country that [Li] treasures, and that which has treated him well," describing *Une vie chinoise* as a near equivalent to Jean-Paul Dubois's *Une vie française* "only . . . in Chinese" (Bénech). Dubois's book, published in 2004 and winner of the Prix Femina, follows the life of protagonist Paul Blick, as organized in chapters named after the presidents of the Fifth Republic, beginning with Charles de Gaulle leading up to Jacques Chiraq. While the book intersects with *A Chinese Life*'s tragicomic tone in depicting everyday life and the effects of globalization in the second half of the twentieth century from an average individual's perspective, there is little else that the two works share.

Mainland Chinese press also tried to draw comparisons between *A Chinese Life* and another work with an "outsider's view" on China; surprisingly, *Beijing News* likened *A Chinese Life* to American journalist Peter Hessler's *Country Driving: A Journey Through China from Farm to Factory* (2010) by "using an outsider's vision to discover the everyday details that often get overlooked" (*Beijing News*). Categorizing *A Chinese Life* as a work of *chukou zhuan neixiao* (除口转内销), a label designating "successful" exported works that are imported back for domestic sale, the review lauds the book for allowing Chinese readers to "experience fresh feelings and emotions upon encountering elements either familiar or strange." *Yunnan Daily* quotes Li Kunwu on enumerating similar reasons for his book's success: "What have Chinese people experienced in the last sixty years in the transformation of New China? What were their lives like? In foreigners's eyes, this is very much a puzzle. As China rises once again, more foreigners really wish to understand life for the average commoner in this great Asian nation, but the news they receive isn't necessarily sufficient" (Li 2011). According to Li, this is the "first time that overseas readers have access to a complete, authentic, open history about contemporary China. This is also most likely why the book was so quickly translated into seven languages and won the Golden Dragon award" (Li 2011). The same article credits the book for using the comic medium to "transcend the world [超越世界], evoke human emotion, receive world's foremost nations' people's love [受到世界名国人民的喜爱]" (Li 2011).

Global People (Huanqiu renwu), a magazine published by *People's Daily*, quotes Li Kunwu's reason for why a Chinese writer's work would attract so many readers from around the world: "The story I'm telling is the most authentic (zhenshi) story" (Huang). In the same interview with Li, the reporter asks him about politics: "Any 'comprehensive, true, lively, and open' [view] of China must include those political events that have influenced China's development; what is your response when you encounter those topics?" (Huang). Li responds, "I wholly stick to my own personal experiences; if there's any time in my life that is related to politics, then I address the politics; if there's a part of my life that is not political, then what I introduce will not be political." This interview response fits with what is depicted in the first-person monologue by Old Li in Part III, as he and Ôtié debate whether he should comment on June 4th despite not having been in Beijing at the time.

On Douban, the Chinese version of the book review site Goodreads, the first volume of the trilogy has 203 reviews and three out of four stars. One Beijing-based reviewer writes on the book review site: "Average, very obviously made for foreign readers" (paolu de tuzi, Douban, Feb. 15, 2014). Another reviewer, 牵手到老 from Suzhou, writes, "To use the graphic novel medium as a way to document Chinese history from the eyes of a Chinese commoner, in order allow foreign readers to understand China, the author has done a good deed" (Qianshou dao lao, Douban, Dec. 10, 2013). These reactions from popular readers and literary critics alike fit what Marie Ostby has identified as a shared trait of the "global graphic novel" genre, as one that "simultaneously locates and alienates, embraces and interrogates the author, character, and reader, all of whom consider themselves global citizens" (Ostby, 560). In order to classify an imagined group of "foreign readers," each individual Chinese reader must position him or herself in an ambivalent relationship to the intended readership of this book. This is further complicated by the fact that Ôtié has explained that editors initially proposed the project to the duo in 2005 due to two main factors related to that particular moment in time: the "tremendous success of *Persepolis* and of graphic novels in general" combined with Europe's interest in China (Delaisse). Here, in this conception of literary-cultural relations, *A Chinese Life*'s existence is construed only in the aftermath of global bestsellers like *Persepolis* and warranted by European affirmation of "China" as an object of knowledge. Furthermore, this uneven power dynamic is bolstered by author interviews, popular online reviews, publishers, and mainstream news media alike.

How can we reconcile these drastically divergent reactions to *A Chinese Life* between anglophone readers versus their Chinese and French counterparts? Julia Lovell has written on China's Nobel complex and the work of award winner, dissident author Gao Xingjian: "Since intellectuals began to view China as a participant on a global stage, writers have found themselves caught in a double-bind: that of representing 'China' while achieving international plaudits through their individual literary achievements. This double-blind has meant extending the appeal of literary works both to the ill-defined category of the 'Chinese people' *and* to ideologically suspect foreigners" (Lovell, 6). Like Gao Xingjian, Li Kunwu is a Chinese-born person of Chinese ethnicity whose cultural identity as Chinese is called into question because of what is perceived as his international position. In the case of Gao, it is his citizenship status; in the case of Li, his partnership with Ôtié renders *A Chinese Life* as a product for foreign consumption.

CONCLUSION

As writers and artists continue to grapple with the challenge of making China readable and comprehensible to outsiders, one key question that remains unresolved can be found in Lin Yutang's prologue to *My Country*, "But do the Chinese understand themselves? Will they be China's best interpreters?" (Lin, 12). Lin provides his own ambivalent explanation for why the Chinese interpreter is superior to a foreign outsider: "For he is a Chinese, and as a Chinese, he not only sees with his mind but he also feels with his heart, and he knows that the blood, surging in his veins in tides of pride and shame is Chinese blood, a mystery of mysteries which carries within its bio-chemical constitution the past and the future of China bearer of all its pride and shame and of its glories and its iniquities" (Lin, 13). This self-orientalist view may also illustrate the dilemma that writers like Li Kunwu face as they attempt to balance readers' preconceptions of CCP propaganda on the one hand, with foreign critique on the other, in the search for world (European) recognition. While contemporary Chinese artists like Ai Weiwei have found commercial and critical success on the international art circuit,[3] Li Kunwu who has attested to the importance of knowing history, especially for younger people who ignore or do not care about history (ARTE, 00:37), is in a markedly distinct and more precarious position that relies on both a domestic market in China and one with different demands overseas. As this chapter has shown, *A Chinese Life* challenges readers' expectations of the family memoir graphic novel genre narrative of individual and collective memory by refusing to bear witness in the accepted way and instead seeming to celebrate China's rapid growth in place of cathartic healing. But, a closer examination of the book shows the author's anxiety over China's ascendant role in the global economy and the persistence of memory. As such, translating history for a global readership becomes a burden, resulting in a divided reception that claims to prioritize historical accuracy but ultimately values literary prestige.

In 2019, as the thirtieth anniversary of June 4th approached, American media continued to emphasize the importance of commemorating the massacre. Writing for *ChinaFile*, Perry Link insisted, "We remember June Fourth because, if we didn't *remember* it, it could not be in our heads any other way. Could we possibly have *imagined* it?" (Link). Link is correct to point out the coercive tension between "people who dearly *want* us to remember" and the people "who desperately want us *not* to remember" (emphasis in original). The official Chinese narrative of June 4th as a "counterrevolutionary riot" gives an additional layer of meaning to the "counterfactual worldmaking" that Aanchal Vij explores in the following chapter. *The New York Times* quoted Jiang Lin, former People's Liberation Army lieutenant, in an interview, "Everyone who took part must speak up about what they know what happened. That's our duty to the dead, the survivors, and the children of the future" (Buckley 2019). This kind of discourse, which places the burden of memory on survivors, echoes the conclusion of the first volume of Nakazawa's *Barefoot Gen*, as Gen's mom holds up his newborn baby sister and vows, "Remember this, my little one. This is war. This what took your father, sister, and brother from us ... When you grow up, you must never, ever let this happen again!" (Nakazawa, 284). If the Chinese government has yet to come up with a historically accurate account of historical events like the Cultural Revolution or June 4th, does the burden of translating history rest on Chinese artists and writers, and do readers have the right to demand this of so-called world artists and writers? The implicit hope for future generations, as memories are transmitted, requires a refusal to forget and also the refusal to remain silent as a way to prevent future violence. This may be feasible for people like Jiang Lin, who is described by the *Times* as just about to leave Beijing after giving the interview. But for those like Li Kunwu who remain in China and hope to continue working and publishing in China and overseas, speaking up in the way that anglophone readers demand is still impossible.

NOTES

1. These three versions of the work have been chosen because of its Sino-French origins, with the English translation (and its reception) as most representative of the title's foray into the contested category of world literature.

2. For an example of the book's French reception, see Zhou Lin's article for *Chine-Info*, a website that promotes China-France relations, which credits Ôtié's influence for the book's departure from Li Kunwu's earlier aesthetic style: "Before this graphic novel's publication, Li Kunwu's style was more fluid, light, almost timid, but could not delve into the deepest feelings of his characters. With Philippe Ôtié's advice, he abandoned all flourish to seek a more personal drawing style that allows him to express himself more honestly and to incorporate the *lianhuanhua* (Chinese comics) with western BD" (Zhou).

3. For more on Ai Weiwei, see Hans Werner Hozwarth, ed. *Ai Weiwei*. Taschen, 2019.

WORKS CITED

Bénech, Clément. "Expo: Li Kunwu, le Yunnan de rails et d'os." *Libération*, February 23, 2018. https://next.liberation.fr/arts/2018/02/23/expo-li-kunwu-le-yunnan-de-rails-et-d-os_1631947.

Brown, Hillary. "*A Chinese Life* by Li Kunwu and Philippe Ôtié." *Paste Magazine*, Comic Book & Graphic Novel Round-Up, September 12, 2012, https://www.pastemagazine.com/articles/2012/09/comic-book-graphic-novel-round-up-91212.html.

Buckley, Chris. "30 Years After Tiananmen, a Chinese Military Insider Warns: Never Forget." *The New York Times*, May 28, 2019, https://www.nytimes.com/2019/05/28/world/asia/china-tiananmen-square-massacre.html.

Casanova, Pascale. *The World Republic of Letters*, trans. M.B. Debevoise. Cambridge: Harvard University Press, 2004.

Célérier, Philippe Pataud. "Li Kunwu, l'humour face à l'absurde." *Le Monde Diplomatique*, October 6, 2015, https://blog.mondediplo.net/2015-10-06-Li-Kunwu-l-humour-face-a-l-absurde.

Chute, Hillary. *Disaster Drawn: Visual Witness, Comics, and Documentary Form*. Cambridge, MA: Belknap Press of Harvard University Press, 2016.

Clough, Rob. "Pride or Propaganda? A Chinese Life." *High-Low Comics Blog*, July 31, 2014, http://highlowcomics.blogspot.com/2014/07/pride-or-propaganda-chinese-life.html.

Delaisse, Morgane. "Interview avec l'Auteur Francais de 'Une Vie Chinoise.'" *Le Petit Journal*, January 19, 2012. https://lepetitjournal.com/p-otie-interview-avec-lauteur-francais-de-une-vie-chinoise-195348.

Friedlander, Saul. "History, Memory, and the Historian: Dilemmas and Responsibilities." *New German Critique*, no. 80 (Spring–Summer 2000): 3–15.

"From Little Li to Old Li: The Life of One Chinese." (Cong xiao Li dao lao Li: yige Zhongguo ren de yi sheng《从小李到老李:一个中国人的一生》). *Beijing News* (Xinjingbao wang 新京报网), April 27, 2013. http://www.bjnews.com.cn/book/2013/04/27/260936.html.

Ganousse, Lysiane. "Quand la BD Chinoise se Réveille." *L'Est Républicain*, January 27, 2015. https://www.estrepublicain.fr/blog/2015/01/27/quand-la-bd-chinoise-se-reveille.

Hertzberg, Andrew. "Big Red Book: A Review of Li Kunwu, A Chinese Life." Originally posted on *Frontier Psychiatrist* (no longer online). Excerpted by Edward Gauvin at "A Chinese Life: A Reception Part II," January 23, 2013. http://www.edwardgauvin.com/blog/?m=201301.

Hirsch, Marianne. "The Generation of Postmemory." *Poetics Today* 29, no. 1 (Spring 2008): 103–28.

Holmberg, Ryan. "Li Kunwu: A Chinese Life." *Yishu*, 12, no. 1 (2013): 95–105.

Huang Ying 黄滢. "Li Kunwu's 'Epic of a Commoner'" (Li Kunwu huachu yibu pingmin shishi 李昆武画出一部'平民史诗'). *Huanqiu Renwu* 13 (2013). http://paper.people.com.cn/hqrw/html/2013-07/16/content_1270466.htm.

Johnson, Ian. "The Presence of the Past—A Coda." In *The Oxford Illustrated History of Modern China*, ed. Jeffrey N. Wasserstrom, 301–23. Oxford: Oxford University Press, 2016.

Kearney, Richard. "Narrating Pain: The Power of Catharsis." *Paragraph* 30, no.1 (Mar. 2007): 51–66.

Li Kunwu and P. Ôtié. *A Chinese Life*, trans. Edward Gauvin. London: SelfMade Hero, 2012.

Li Kunwu and P. Ôtié. *Une Vie Chinoise*. Brussels: KANA, 2015.

Li Kunwu 李昆武 and Ou Lixing 欧励行. *From Young Li to Old Li: The Life of a Chinese I-III* (Cong xiao Li dao lao Li: yi ge Zhongguo ren de yi sheng I-III从小李到老李:一个中国人的一生I-III). Beijing: Sanlian shudian, 2013.

"Li Kunwu: la formidable épopée du Yunnan." ARTE, January 24, 2018. Interview on video. https://www.arte.tv/fr/videos/080712-000-A/li-kunwu-la-formidable-epopee-du-yunnan/.

"Li Kunwu's Autobiographical Cartoon Warmly Welcomed in France" (Li Kunwu zizhuan manhua darefaguo 李昆武自传漫画大热法国). *Beifang ribao*, December 12, 2011. http://comic.people.com.cn/GB/122401/16671474.html#.

Li, Meng and King-fai Tam. "Literature of Trauma and Reflection." In *Routledge Handbook of Modern Chinese Literature*, ed. Ming Dong Fu and Tao Feng, 439–49. London: Routledge, 2018.

Li Yuechun 李悦春. "The cartoon path from Kunming to Paris" (Cong Kunming dao Bali de manhua zhi lu 从昆明到巴黎的漫画之路). *Yunnan ribao*, November 18, 2011. http://yndaily.yunnan.cn/page/1/2011-11-18/09/90601321558537189.PDF.

Lin Yutang. *My Country and My People*. Oxford: Oxford City Press, 2010.

Link, Perry. "Why We Remember June Fourth." *ChinaFile*, May 28, 2019, http://www.chinafile.com/reporting-opinion/viewpoint/why-we-remember-june-fourth.

Lovell, Julia. "Gao Xingjian, the Nobel Prize, and Chinese Intellectuals: Notes on the Aftermath of the Nobel Prize 2000." *Modern Chinese Literature and Culture* 14, no. 2 (2002): 1–50.

Mather, Jeffrey. "Propaganda and Memory in Li Kunwu and Philippe Ôtié's *A Chinese Life*." *Concentric* 42, no. 1 (March 2016): 99–118.

Nakazawa, Keiji. *Barefoot Gen: A Cartoon Story of Hiroshima*, trans. Project Gen. San Francisco: Last Gasp, 2004.

Ostby, Marie. "Graphics and Global Dissent: Marjane Satrapi's *Persepolis*, Persian Miniatures, and the Multifaceted Power of Comic Protest." *PMLA* 132, no. 2 (2017): 558–79.

Rifas, Leonard. "From Propaganda to Real Life: A Chinese Cartoonist Draws History." *International Examiner* 40, no. 16, (September 18, 2013). https://iexaminer.org/from-propaganda-to-real-life-a-chinese-cartoonist-draws-history/.

Satrapi, Marjane. *Persepolis*. New York: Pantheon Books, 2003.

Smart, James. "*A Chinese Life* by Li Kunwu and P Ôtié—review." *The Guardian*, October 12, 2012. https://www.theguardian.com/books/2012/oct/12/chinese-life-li-kunwu-p-otie-review.

Spiegelman, Art. *The Complete Maus*. 25th anniversary edition. New York: Pantheon Books, 2011.

Stember, Nick. "Putting 25 Years of Silence in Context with Comics and Animation." *Nickstember.com*, June 1, 2014. http://www.nickstember.com/25-years-silence-context/.

Wang, Charlie. "Li Kunwu Solo Exhibition 'Storyboards.'" *Eliel Magazine*, July 8, 2017. https://elielmagazine.com/2017/07/08/li-kunwu-solo-exhibition-storyboards/.

Wang Xiaoyi 王晓易. "Yunnan Artist Li Kunwu is Awarded the Cartoon Oscar" (Yunnan huajia Li Kunwu ronghuo manhua Aosika 云南画家李昆武荣获漫画奥斯卡). *Yunwang*, November 7, 2011, https://baike.baidu.com/reference/4813795/1921U7iYUzci9vvQO7lssy1WKNVATg6Ed8lQcq3XP5qfYZB1UgAsiLZY0M4PzjhWEOwHcp6Aifb4hro2iXHmoTI6A4aEzS5ZtaTx5VJc7U26.

Yan Lianke. "On China's State-Sponsored Amnesia." *The New York Times*, April 1, 2013. https://www.nytimes.com/2013/04/02/opinion/on-chinas-state-sponsored-amnesia.html.

Yue, Ming-Bao. "Nostalgia for the Future: Cultural Revolution Memory in Two Transnational Chinese Narratives." *China Review* 5, no. 2 (2005): 43–63.

Ze Qin 泽勤. "The Chinese Version Resurrects the Legend of Bao Zheng in Red Europe: Comics Open Up Another Way of Understanding China" (Zhongguo shenfu baozheng hongbian ouzhou: manhua dakai ling yitiao renzhi zhongguo zhi lu 中国版painshen复包拯红过欧洲:漫画打开另一条认知中国之路). *Ouzhou shibao wang*, August 19, 2016. http://www.oushinet.com/ouzhong/ouzhongnews/20160819/240580.html.

Zhou Lin. "Une Vie Chinoise." *Chine-Info.com*, April 26, 2016. http://www.chine-info.com/french/look/20160426/228608.html.

CHAPTER 5

"AMERICAN GOD" TO A SOVIET SUPERMAN

Exploring the Cathartic Function of Counterfactual Narratives

AANCHAL VIJ

This chapter puts counterfactual fiction in dialogue with American exceptionalism to demonstrate the cathartic function of reparative narratives. I use two comics (one by an English and another by a Scottish author respectively)—Alan Moore's *Watchmen* (1986) and Mark Millar's *Superman Red Son* (2014)—to assert that the manifestation of a nostalgic reparation of historical events performs a cathartic function for both an individual and the collective. Both visual narratives underscore the politics, and a spectacle, of such catharsis by demonstrating the desire to repair histories in the face of the Cold War. Following a brief introduction to counterfactual fiction, I examine the suitability of counterfactual graphic narratives to host American exceptionalism within their alternate reality. At the same time, these texts challenge the cathartic release that is achieved through the reparative plot structure and demonstrate the futility of the pursuit of exceptionalism; the counterfactuals, then, underscore the stage of Freudian repetition[1] in which both texts find themselves stuck. Through a close reading of both texts, I raise larger questions about the comics form and its suitability for such catharsis, the inextricability of counterfactual fiction and catharsis, and the complexity of the Freudian repetition and "working through" in the reparative narrative form.

Paul Saint-Amour begins by describing counterfactual imagination as employed within the legal universe—beginning with the courtroom argument that uses "*ceteris paribus*"—before discussing it as a genre of fiction that "splits history in a *before*, which corresponds to real-world history, and an *after* that diverges from it" (7). Catherine Gallagher traces a history of counterfactual history through the decades from the seventeenth-century philosopher Gottfried Leibniz, who first suggested the concept of "counterfactual possible worlds" to the last few decades, in which she observes a profusion of counterfactual fictional narratives (6). Both Saint-Amour and Gallagher underscore the need to study this genre with a view that an examination of narratives that dwell on historical possibilities other than the one that actually took place allows us, as readers and critics, to question the retrospective gaze of individuals, communities, and in context of this chapter, American literature and culture. *Superman Red Son* and *Watchmen* challenge historical linearity by changing the course of events that stem from a pivotal moment or "hinge moment"—the moment that deflects the true course of history (Saint-Amour 10). *Watchmen*, with its world of costumed heroes and weaponized superhero, Dr. Manhattan, ensures that America emerges victorious in the Vietnam War and acquires the reputation of being a global threat because of its control over his actions. *Red Son*—a counterfactual to the fictional universes of American Superman—envisions a communist Superman who lands not in Kansas but in Ukraine (then Russia). Presumably, a subversion of the Superman origin story as we know it, *Red Son*'s alternate reality ultimately succeeds in bringing forth American exceptionalism despite an anti-American superhero. The premise of both texts brings forth the reparative nature of the counterfactuals and uses the hinge moments to achieve different versions of American exceptionalism even as they pretend to subvert an exceptionalist narrative at different plot points. They both lay emphasis on what Saint-Amour calls the "ethical restlessness" of narratives that aspire to create sociopolitical or cultural landscapes that are either much better or much worse in relation to the true sequence of events. This "ethical restlessness" is especially significant and foundational in the context of *Red Son* and *Watchmen* because of their specific desire to "repair" aspects of history that never took place. I call it "foundational" because it is central to my reading and analyses of the elaborate thought experiments and "what if" scenarios that both *Red Son* and *Watchmen* construct; in their history's backward glance, they make it imperative to examine the version of history that is being longed for and question who longs for it.

Richard Kearney, in "Narrating Pain: The Power of Catharsis," writes about the cathartic role of narratives for victims of trauma and the ability of "recounting of experience through the formal medium of plot to . . . *repeat the past forward*" (emphasis in original; 51). To that effect, its ability to "give a future to the past" from the very outset situates itself in counterfactual worldmaking that offers a space for the repetition of the past, albeit differently, and imagines a future for the past that did not actually take place. The trauma that this chapter examines through *Red Son* and *Watchmen* functions differently than defined by Kearney or many other trauma theorists such as Dori Laub and Shoshana Felman, Giorgio Agamben, and Judith Butler, as it is not a lived trauma but rather a manufactured one.[2] While an exploration of the individual trauma of the characters such as Rorschach, Nite Owl, or Pyotr is beyond the scope of this chapter, I choose to focus on the national or collective trauma that is created in order to justify the need for a cathartic release. In this vein, it is significant to think about the relationship between counterfactual fiction and the cathartic "recounting of experience" as both allow a retelling and reliving of the traumatic event to a certain extent, but the hinge moment leading to the alternate histories complicates the way in which repetition functions in these texts. Kearney, in the epilogue, alludes to such complexity of the narrative's cathartic function that can often "result in propaganda and distortion as in healing and release":

> Not every narrative version of the past tells it "as it actually happened"; and the inevitable temporal discrepancy between past and present usually allows for a certain conflict of interpretations . . . the question we need to constantly ask is: whose story is it anyway? Who is telling the story? To whom is it told? About what is it told? In what manner? And for what reason? (64).

Red Son and *Watchmen*, through their compelling alternate realities, concoct situations and traumatic events that pretend to transcend American exceptionalism and eradicate the need for a cathartic breakthrough but ultimately exhibit the nation's persistent fantasy of heroism. Their counterfactual worldmaking makes apparent the American tendency to forget or even misremember and urge questions about the version of history that is being told, exacerbating the necessary skepticism about the past "as it actually happened." This chapter questions how the two graphic narratives superficially "work through" a concocted traumatic event and problematize the idea of "recounting" history and "repeating" the past that is, from the very outset, constructed in order to support the national desire for exceptionalism.

The "hinge-moment" of *Red Son* is Superman's landing in Ukraine instead of Kansas in 1938 (figure 5.1) and is also the moment that deploys the schism

Figure 5.1. *Superman Red Son*

between the mainstream Superman origin story and the alternate version of it that instantly robs America of the primary superhero of its golden age.

The premise of this graphic novel, in fact, seems to probe the narrative of American exceptionalism until it quickly becomes complicit with it. For instance, Lois Lane (who in this alternate reality is married to Lex Luthor) first receives the news about a superhero embodying communist ideals right before President Hoover announces that "an alien superman . . . threatens to alter [their] position as a world superpower forever" (2). This is followed by national panic and a crippling paranoia in the face of the approaching

Cold War that America is determined not to lose; additionally, the Warsaw Pact acquires unprecedented support and power with the existence of a communist superhero. Lex Luthor, the "smartest man alive" (5), works for the American government to create several monsters to defeat Superman, including an "American Superman," and when asked about its creation, says: "Norman Rockwell, apple pie, stars and stripes and the 4th of July . . . the president asked me to design a figure that encapsulates all these things and give America back our much-needed swagger (32). Even though all the monsters or heroes developed by Luthor (including Green Lantern, Brainiac, etc., or those bred by Superman's communist ideals such as Batman) are all systematically defeated by Superman, America continues to retain a sense of superiority in the name of abiding by its capitalistic principles. In Moscow's "Superman Museum," the tour guide takes the guests and tells them that

> the Soviet Union was just a fragile assembly when Superman first came to power. Two decades later and the whole world is our ally. Only the United States and Chile choose to remain independent: the last two capitalist economies on Earth and both on the brink of fiscal and social collapse . . . Poverty, disease and ignorance have been virtually eliminated from the Warsaw Pact states . . . (54).

Keeping the principles of communism or capitalism aside, what is significant is the American defiance in the face of the world volunteering, "total control to Superman" (Millar 54). In this context, one must note Thomas Byers's apt definition of American exceptionalism as "not only the claim that America is different, but that it is unique, one of a (superior) kind—and generally that that kind carries with it a unique moral value and responsibility" (86). In the landscape of total surrender of control to a Soviet-run world, America's voluntary exclusion exemplifies this very exceptionalism that is just as much about being an "exceptional" nation as it is about being a superior one.

Despite being on the "brink of fiscal and social collapse," it refuses to ally with the Soviet Union, while the case being made here is not for America to give in to the kind of fascism that *Red Son*'s alternate reality projects onto Russia but to demonstrate the exceptionalism attached to its isolation. Its exceptionalism is inextricably attached to a sense of pride, one that Superman alludes to when Wonder Woman tells him that America is in a "disgusting state." She asks him why Kennedy still "cling[s] on to this dogma when it's quite clearly tearing his country apart," to which Superman says, "Pride, I suppose. He'll come around eventually" (65).[3] The pride that Superman attributes to Kennedy mirrors the American pride that also emanates from Luthor himself. It is especially clear in the scene where an official asks him what makes him so confident about Green Lantern's ability to defeat Superman after all the other heroes have failed, and he attributes it to his "indefatigable superiority complex" (Millar 105). These instances of American pride and exceptionalism are noteworthy because they underscore the national ability to transcend the inherent fascism of the counterfactual world that is constructed. It is in light of such a consistent thrust of exceptionalism that I situate my argument about the manufactured trauma that seeks out a kind of catharsis.

Saint-Amour writes about the fantasy of US exceptionalism as "a claim whose putative status as fact, whose facticity, inheres not in a particular timeline or world but across a constellation of actual and possible worlds" (25). This understanding of American exceptionalism as one that overcomes not just actual but also "possible" worlds informs the Soviet exceptionalism in *Red Son*'s counterfactual world that is constructed to heighten the desire for and justify the segue into American heroism. *Red Son* deliberately sets up a Soviet-run world with a communist Superman as the president as a contrast to which capitalistic and prideful America remains innocent and, of course, an exception. Luthor defeats Superman by playing on his emotional and psychological insecurities and triumphs against the superhero, and his "indefatigable superiority" culminates in a fruitful outcome for the American nation: "Lex Luthor and Jimmy Olsen won a landslide victory in 2004, re-elected to the White House with a staggering hundred and one percent of the vote . . . Within six months, Luthor was running their economy. Within a year, even Moscow had signed up with his Global United States" (Millar 135). If catharsis is "understood to refer to the "cleansing" effect of watching (or reading) a tragedy . . . [and is] linked to the peculiar fact that tragedy can give pleasure" (Royle 111), then *Red Son*'s counterfactual fiction can be seen as the tragedy that is concocted in order to "give pleasure" and soothe the exceptionalist narrative of America. The formation of the Global United States is an example of how one kind of exceptionalism is used to challenge another. Saint-Amour asks what it would mean to "feel homesick not for a different or a better exceptionalism but for an alternative to national exceptionalism altogether" (25). His question is a potent one in the context of American exceptionalism because it urges us to imagine such an alternate reality: what would catharsis be for a nation that imagines itself to be exceptionalist yet victimizes itself (both in *Red Son* and, as I will demonstrate, in *Watchmen*) look like? What is the relationship between America's oppressive past and paranoid desire to create exceptionalist narratives? Do these narratives, in fact, assert the counterfactual nature of American history rather than its exceptionalism?

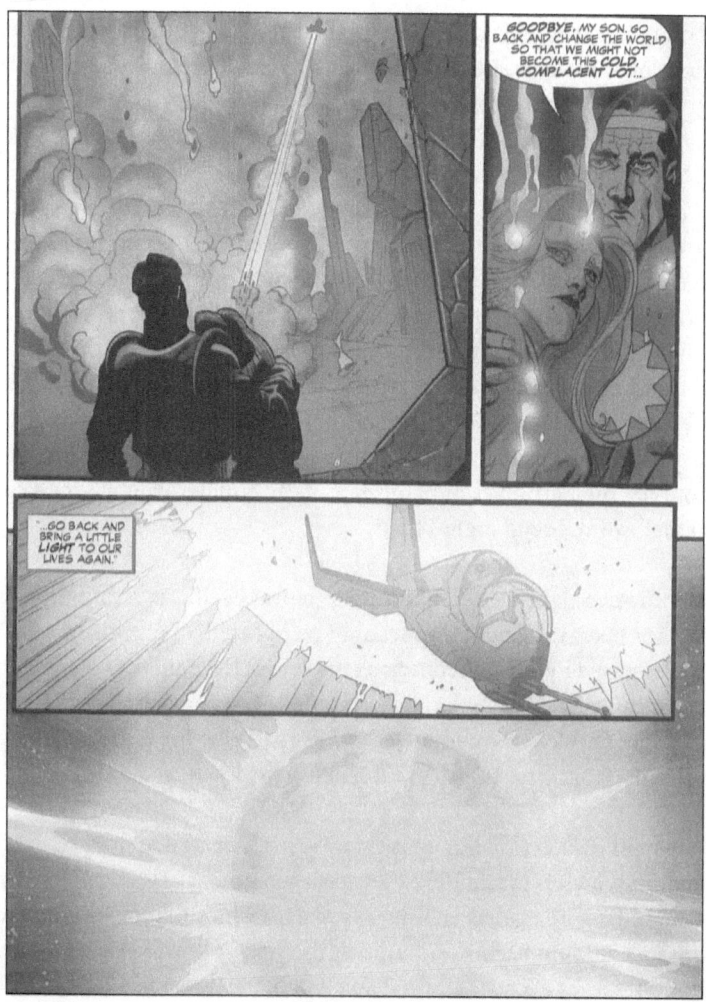

Figure 5.2. *Superman Red Son*

Red Son's ending further complicates the cathartic function of the counterfactuals by suggesting an Oedipal relationship between Superman, Lois Lane, and Lex Luthor. The timeline of predestination constructs Superman as the son of Lara and Jor-L, Jor-L being "Lex Luthor's great-grandson to the power fifty" (138). Jor-L, realizing that their world is about to be consumed by the red sun, decides to send his son back in time to save the world, with Superman landing in Ukraine in 1938 in the next and last panel (figure 5.2). This implication that Superman is the descendent of Lois Lane (his love interest in the noncounterfactual universe) and Lex Luthor (his archenemy, a man

Superman wants to kill) clearly suggests an Oedipal parallel while it gently circumvents it in its counterfactual world. The Oedipal fantasy is one that will never be realized in the counterfactual reality of *Red Son*, in which Lois Lane is married to Lex Luthor (even if it might suggest otherwise to the readers).

While the story of Oedipus offers the Aristotelian catharsis[4] to its readers, *Red Son*'s Oedipal fantasy escapes completion and hence offers no sense of release. The Oedipal ending, however, is important in the context of American heroism, whose cathartic effect is inevitable: irrespective of the counterfactual worldmaking, the nation is always expunged of its oppressive history and, in its portrayal, deserves the cathartic release.

The ending of *Red Son* also asserts the fact that it almost does not matter where Superman lands—US, Ukraine, or a different country—because the fantasy of US exceptionalism will consistently triumph, and the nation will appropriate the narratives of heroism to its advantage even within a counterfactual world. Freud argues that:

> ... whatever is repressed is bound to repeat itself ... : a thing which has not been understood inevitably reappears like an unlaid ghost ... Possessed by such unconscious mysteries, the patient is obliged to *repeat* the repressed material as a contemporary experience instead of, as the physician would prefer to see, *remembering* it as something belonging to the past (qtd. in Ellman 8).

In light of *Red Son*'s continuous time loop, it is crucial to understand how the ending, which is meant to be the ultimate moment of heroism for America, can, in fact, be read as an unresolved experience that repeats infinitely. Superman's landing back in Ukraine in the year 1938 will lead to the exact same sequence of events as in *Red Son* and make possible a Global United States over and over again. "Repeating" itself is a significant act in the realm of counterfactual fiction, where history repeats itself but imagines a different outcome or version of it. *Red Son*'s narrative, stuck in this infinite loop that creates obstructions to American exceptionalism only to overcome it, is an instance of the nation's inability to "work through" its "repressed material" or confront its past as it was. Counterfactual fiction lies at the center of this dialogue between the ability to "work through," catharsis, and reparation: it makes it imperative to ask questions about the "golden age" comics of America and their role in American history.[5] That is why *Red Son*—a comic book that inverts the expectations of exceptionalism using the origin story of the Man of Steel—is especially significant because it offers the possibility of confrontation with the past it repeatedly attempts to escape. *Watchmen*, on the other hand, uses its counterfactuals to remember and repeat in a different fashion but, as I will demonstrate, produces the same outcome of exceptionalism.

Watchmen is set in a reality where America is already a global threat due to its weaponized superheroes such as the Comedian (who plays a key role in American "victory" in the Vietnam War) and Dr. Manhattan, "an American god" (Moore 4:41). From the very outset, the graphic novel is drenched in nostalgia of different kinds. Each costumed hero feels nostalgic for a different version of history; for instance, Hollis Mason (one of the Minutemen and the original Nite Owl) for a Manichean sense of justice, Silk Spectre for her youth and "simpler times," and Rorschach for a better America that preceded its irreversible corruption. Rorschach's outlook towards the nation is significant because he is so resolutely nationalist while at the same time being immensely cynical, and while his skepticism and disgust towards the country underly the entire narrative, his nostalgia for a golden past overwhelms it. He writes in his diary about all the people of America, "They had a choice, all of them. They could have followed in the footsteps of good men or President Truman . . . Instead they followed the droppings of lechers and communists . . . now the whole world stands on the brink, staring down into bloody hell, all those liberals and intellectuals and smooth talkers . . ." (1). Rorschach's disillusionment stems from a place of hopelessness but is built on the foundation that America was once a pure and worthy nation that has degenerated over decades, justifying individual and collective longing.

At this point, I want to briefly discuss the (national) nostalgia that the counterfactuals invite by portraying America as a "beleaguered country" constantly under the imminent threat of the Cold War (Moore 275). Dr. Manhattan's superpowers are not strong enough to offer full immunity to the nation, and hence, the Cold War would imply Mutually Assured Destruction for all the countries involved. The Right Wing newspaper *New Frontiersmen* regularly attaches a great sense of nationalist pride to America and critiques anything that threatens the already sensitive "national morale" or "deride[s] the very notions that have made America what she is today" (275). The novel ends with a disclosure of Adrian Veidt's master plan to protect America from its own egotism by concocting an alien attack on New York that forces the nations at war to unite against the common threat. All the paranoia about a "Third World War," a nuclear attack, and conspiracy theories culminates into the alien attack for "humanity's salvation" (Moore 373). *Watchmen* induces longing for a "wrong" history that did not exist—one with Dr. Manhattan, an "American god" who would make the nation invincible, win the Vietnam War, and always posit America as a powerful beast—and simultaneously displays the danger of such a longing

Figure 5.3. *Watchmen*, chapter 12, page 2.

by portraying how the presence of these costumed superheroes in the day-to-day *causes* nuclear damage, in turn creating a sense of relief about not being a part of such a reality. Hence, the cathartic function of the counterfactuals lies not just in the alternate reality that they imagine but equally in the horrific ending that jolts the readers into identifying exceptionalism in the world they actually inhabit.

The alien attack conjured up by Adrian Veidt—one that even Dr. Manhattan is unable to impede—in order to end the constant threat of the looming war with Russia is the kind of preemptive move that describes American paranoia and sociopolitical insecurity despite its weaponization of Dr. Manhattan. Keeping the ethics of Veidt's plan aside, the self-caused trauma on a national scale underscores the lack of it in the real historical

Figure 5.4. *Watchmen*, chapter 12, page 3.

timeline. For instance, through associations, as evident in figure 5.3, the depiction of the alien attack on New York City (that causes half the city's population to die) invokes a sense of sympathy in us.

It shows a poster of a show titled "Pale Horse in Concert with Krystalnacht" at Madison Square Garden, suggesting an association with the genocide of the Jews in Nazi Germany in 1938. The page filled with violence, blood, and corpses immediately conjoins itself with the memory of the Jewish genocide and heightens the sense of relief about not inhabiting *Watchmen*'s alternate reality. Similarly, the subsequent page has a poster with the writing "the day the earth stood still," which, in itself, is an exceptionalist statement because of the implication that New York City's destruction somehow stands for a global meltdown (figure 5.4).

Dr. Manhattan, named after the Manhattan Project and inspiring the same fear as the atomic bomb, is able to control matter and experience time simultaneously. The simultaneity of time is in itself a significant theme in Comics Studies, beginning with Scott McCloud's theorization of comics as "sequential art" and a more recent expansion of his definition by Nick Sousanis in *Unflattening*. Sousanis, referring to Theirry Groensteen's work, writes, "while comics are read sequentially like text, the entire composition is also taken and viewed all at once . . . this spatial interplay of sequential and simultaneous imbues comics with a dual nature—both tree-like and hierarchical and rhizomatic, interwoven in a single form" (41).[6] The simultaneity of time as well as the ways in which panels and page layouts function, therefore, on the pages of *Watchmen* gather more significance because of its preoccupation with time: Jon Osterman's father's profession as a watchmaker, the repeated images of the doomsday clock, the names of both bands of superheroes (Minutemen and Watchmen), the compression and expansion of time through Dr. Manhattan's perception of time, amongst others instances, images and tropes. A closer reading of some of the images in the narrative demonstrates how it is stuck in the loop of Freudian repetition, symbolizing a microcosm of the nation's inability to "work through," as we saw in *Red Son*. This inability is relevant in the context of the catharsis that the graphic novel seems to offer through its counterfactual reality that is rendered ineffective, or at least instantly compels a remembrance (or misremembrance) and repetition engendering more counterfactual narratives, more concocted traumas, and pursuit of exceptionalism.

In the chapter "Watchmaker," Dr. Manhattan describes the accident that transformed him from Jon Osterman into a superhuman being. His narration swings back and forth in time, and every flashback or vision of the future is supported by the blue word panel that contains his narrative voice. We, as readers, inhabit his sense of time in such moments of storytelling and accept the bending of time as he does. The image of the cogs laid out on a piece of paper first appears back from 1945 when Jon was sixteen years old and his father, the watchmaker, throws out the cogs from the balcony right after he reads about the Hiroshima bombing: "They dropped the atomic bomb on Japan! A whole city gone! . . . This changes everything! There will be more bombs. They are the future . . . Professor Einstein says that time differs from place to place. Can you imagine? If time is not true, what purpose have watchmakers, hein?" (Moore 4:12). The image of these cogs, laid out on cloth and falling from the sky, appears again and again throughout the novel, reminding us of the futility of time and its linear nature (figure 5.5). *Watchmen*, of course, embodies this idea in its counterfactual fiction and demonstrates the

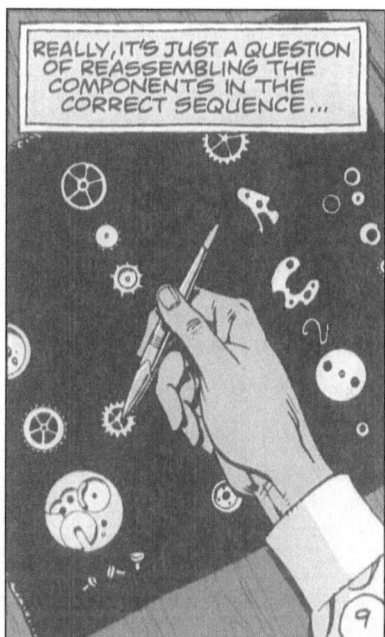

Figure 5.5. *Watchmen*, chapter 4, page 9.

failure of a "right" or "factual" perception of history. The form itself performs a similar function. The "Watchmaker" chapter's repeated imagery of the falling cogs and the photograph of him and Janey (that becomes a kind of symbol for Dr. Manhattan's tangible yet intangible past) is indicative of the many examples of repetition that transform images and words into metaphors. As Dr. Manhattan describes his process of reconstituting the atoms of his body to become the superhuman that he is, the image of the cogs on cloth appears again with his narrative voice saying, "Really, it's just a question of reassembling the components in the correct sequence . . ." (Moore 4: 9).

This "reassembling [of] the components" alludes to the counterfactual fiction of *Watchmen* (that allows a reassembly of historical events in a different order leading to hypothetical consequences) as well as perhaps to McCloud's idea of the comics as "sequential art." It is almost as if Moore urges us to take McCloud's attribution of significant importance to sequentiality with a pinch of salt by playing with the narrative style of *Watchmen* that lays emphasis on simultaneity and demonstrates the failure of sequentiality. The presence of the hand in the image notes a certain amount of agency over the order and assembly of the cogs that, too, is undercut by the image of the falling cogs that always eventually succeeds this one (figure 5.6)—bringing the narrative back to a sense of futility and the idea that "it "always will be too late" (Moore 4:28).

Figure 5.6. *Watchmen*, chapter 4, page 28.

But the return of the image as well as the desire to "piece them all together again" mirrors the desire to piece together a historical narrative that acquires a semblance of order, sequentiality, linearity, and of course—exceptionalism.

I want to dwell on *Watchmen*'s stylistic and formal use of repetition to bring together Sedgwick's ideas of reparative narrative, the Freudian idea of "repeating," "remembering," and "working through" and trauma studies. Having looked at the imagery of the cogs as one instance of repetition, another potent theme in the graphic novel that appears repeatedly is that of Veidt's perfume, "Nostalgia." The bottle of perfume becomes a metaphor for any kind of backward look, whether it is when characters are reminiscing or when we, as readers, are expected to make connections between two distinct and disconnected scenes in the story. The billboard with the brand name first appears in Chapter Three amidst Janey Slater's interview with Nova Express and Laurie walking to meet Dan Dreiberg (figure 5.7).

It is later disclosed that it was in this interview that Janey informs the interviewer about Dr. Manhattan possibly being the reason why she has lung cancer with six months to live. Her incessant coughing during the interview urges the interviewer to say, " . . . if you want, we can stop here," the words that appear along with the Nostalgia advertisement. It suggests the undesirable thrust of time and the possibility of "stopping" in that exact moment if

Figure 5.7. *Watchmen*, chapter 3, page 7.

one so desires and commodification of the sentiment that occurs throughout the graphic novel in the same vein. Similarly, the brand's tagline "Where is the essence that was so divine?" implies that the answer to that question is in the bottle of perfume itself—that it contains the "essence that was so divine." The words "treasure island" in the same panel also clearly suggest the glorified idea of New York as the treasure trove—a means to justify the desire to pause time and to allow one's nostalgic fantasies to play out in the current historical moment. Just like many other motifs in the graphic novel that problematize the idea of American exceptionalism, this too signifies the American national identification with something specious while simultaneously countering it with a deep desire to return to the "divine essence" that belongs to the past. Following this introduction to Veidt's brand, it appears over and over again, signifying different kinds of nostalgia for different individuals and, sometimes, for America.

Brandy Bell Blake in "*Watchmen*: The Graphic Novel as Trauma Fiction" argues that the *Watchmen* demonstrates post-traumatic stress primarily because of Jon Osterman's own traumatic accident that alienates him socially and leaves him with an inescapable sense of temporal impotence. Blake uses trauma theory by Felman and Laub, Cathy Caruth, and Ann Whitehead to tease out examples of fragmented narrative voice, repetition, and intertextuality to support her argument. However, I want to build on the idea of repetition alone in relation to the Freudian "repetition" as a symptom of the traumatized narrative of *Watchmen* (that I do not specifically attribute to Osterman's PTSD). To that effect, chapter 9 of *Watchmen* especially engages with the motif of the "Nostalgia" brand and throbs with the suffocation of being stuck in a temporal and narrative loop. The bottle of perfume appears in and out of frames almost like a curtain change to take the readers between the past, present, and future. In this chapter, Laurie and Dr. Manhattan have a conversation on Mars about the future of humanity, Dr. Manhattan's perception of time, and most importantly, Laurie's childhood. It is during this correspondence that she, much to her shock, discovers that the Comedian was, in fact, her father. Dr. Manhattan asks her about her earliest memory, which she revisits using a snow globe—"a toy, one of those snowstorm balls" (Moore 9:6)—as a totem that she associates with her parents' separation. The snow globe undeniably resembles the Nostalgia perfume bottle, and together, their imagery reinstates the cyclicity of time: the snow globe first appears at the beginning of the chapter (figure 5.8) and then returns towards the end in the form of the perfume (figure 5.9). In the meantime, Laurie realizes that the Comedian is her father and, in her anger, breaks the bottle of perfume. *Watchmen* deliberately uses the images that have come to signify the contingent nature of narrative time in a cyclical fashion to assert the loop of remembering and repeating a traumatic event in a similar fashion.[7]

The exact repetition of the images—first of the snow globe and then of the bottle of perfume—with the same text accompanying it, "I figured inside the ball was some different sort of time. Slow time" (Moore 9:7), underscores *Watchmen*'s reliance on repetition as a stylistic tool. On repetition and trauma fiction, Whitehead writes, "One of the key literary strategies in trauma fiction is the device of repetition, which can act at the levels of language, imagery, or plot. Repetition mimics the effects of trauma, for it suggests the insistent return of the event and the disruption of narrative chronology or progression" (qtd. in Blake 86). Such "insistent return" is mirrored in the repetition of imagery as I have demonstrated through that of the perfume bottle, falling cogs of the watch, or the snow globe, as well as through innumerable other such symbols that interrupt the narrative time of the graphic novel. Thus, the remembering (or misremembering) and relentless repeating of the images and plot points in this graphic novel are symptomatic of a kind of trauma. Shoshana Felman and Dori Laub, in their theorizing of Holocaust trauma, attach significance to ellipticity and circularity (Blake 29), and Dominick LaCapra defines *Erlebnis* trauma as one that "may be acted out or compulsively repeated in so-called traumatic

Figure 5.8. *Watchmen*, chapter 9, page 7.

Figure 5.9. *Watchmen*, chapter 9, page 24.

memory" (117). To that effect, I argue that such narratological trauma is entirely manufactured and embodies the tension between the alternate reality's ability to offer catharsis and the superficiality of it.

The repeated images of the perfume bottle signify fragility (even clearly suggesting it, as in figure 5.10) and a sense of anxiety since the bottle is always in a state of almost crashing until it does crash towards the end of the chapter (figure 5.9). The anxiety mirrors the national anxiety leading up to the Cold War and is all-pervasive and subtextually omnipresent until the alien attack in the end. However, both crashes do not put an end to the cycle of Freudian repetition, offering no sense of closure or "working through." "And inside there was only water" is the text accompanying the broken glass bottle, implying the façade of, and disappointment with,

Figure 5.10. *Watchmen*, chapter 9, page 8.

the reality of the nostalgic remembrance that breaks only to disclose the never-ending loop of repetition in which the nation is stuck (Moore 9:4). To that effect, the ending of *Watchmen* offers no sense of closure despite Veidt's masterplan as is apparent through the last exchange between Veidt and Dr. Manhattan:

> "Jon, wait, before you leave . . . I did the right thing, didn't I? It all worked out in the end."
> "In the end?" Nothing ends, Adrian. Nothing ever ends" (Moore 12:27)

This ending, just like *Red Son*'s, suggests the idea of repetition ("nothing ever ends") as well as the futility of the alternate reality that promises a cathartic outcome as well as a space to "work through" the constructed trauma but ultimately underscores the ineffectuality of the pursuit of national exceptionalism.

I previously discussed the paranoia of American exceptionalism that overrides the pretense of a reparative reading through the use of counterfactuals in both works. I briefly want to return to Sedgwick's framework of the reparative position to which she ascribes the necessary experience of being "surprised":

to read from a reparative position is to surrender to the knowing, anxious paranoid determination that no horror, however apparently unthinkable, shall ever come to the reader as new ... Hope, often a fracturing, even a traumatic thing to experience, is among the energies by which the reparatively positioned reader tries to organize the fragments and part-objects she encounters or creates. Because the reader has room to realize that the future may be different from the present, it is also possible for her to entertain such profoundly painful, profoundly relieving, ethically crucial possibilities as that the past, in turn, could have happened differently from the way it actually did (146).

While Sedgwick's framework makes clear that there needs to be a confrontation with the fact that the past "could have happened differently from the way it actually did," *Watchmen* demonstrates the danger of America's defiant belief that the past *actually* did happen differently: in the American imagination and denial of its oppressive past, there is no possibility of a "bad surprise." Such defiance, I assert, ends all possibilities of "working through" or being "surprised," and thus, the nation, just like *Watchmen*'s and *Red Son*'s America, remains rooted in the cyclical and paranoid pursuit of exceptionalism. The nation, then, never experiences the "profoundly painful" possibility that it is indeed counterfactual and ordinary. At the same time, *Watchmen* refuses to offer it the "profoundly relieving" possibility of inhabiting a past that is as golden as it imagines it to be—it not only demonstrates the failure of a counterfeit reparative project, but its form also resists the thrust of exceptionalism (even though it is inextricable in the very fabric of its counterfactual fiction).

In conclusion, the counterfactual narratives of *Red Son* and *Watchmen* play a crucial role in opening up a dialogue between the ability of a reparative narrative to offer catharsis and simultaneously demonstrate the futility of it—in the context of American exceptionalism or, as Saint-Amour puts it, "exceptionalism of any kind." It must be noted that while this chapter extensively ascribes the cathartic role to the counterfactual nature of both texts, their graphic form is equally potent in the discussion. But the alternate realities that are specifically inhabited by superhumans are a great starting point to question the suitability of such heroic tropes within the comics space: the way in which the panel structures exhibit fluidity of time, the silent space of the gutters, the nostalgia attached with the form (that mirrors the nostalgia backward glance of the individual or the nation), the form's rootedness in the migrant American communities (for instance, the relationship between the form and Jewishness), among many other aspects. This chapter provides a starting point to identify the role of "hinge-moments" in counterfactual fiction such as *Watchmen* and *Superman Red Son*: while they may be constructed to justify a cathartic function for the (national) exceptionalist narratives, their study can often reveal the inherently counterfactual nature of American history itself.

NOTES

1. Sigmund Freud's ideas on "repetition" are closely explored further in this chapter.
2. Felman and Laub (in *Testimony: Crises of Witnessing in Literature, Psychoanalysis and History*), Agamben (in *Homo Sacer*), and Judith Butler (in *Precarious Life*) write about lived trauma, but their theoretical frameworks can be used to read the kind of manufactured trauma that these counterfactual works deal with.
3. The chronology in this alternate reality is deliberately different. In the novel, Kennedy is in power in 1978 and Nixon is assassinated in 1963, whereas, in real time, it was the other way around.
4. The catharsis is achieved through Oedipus's "tragic flaw" and his self-punishment (by blinding himself) after his self-fulfilling prophecy comes full circle.
5. The idea that the birth of the golden age superheroes (Batman, Superman, Captain America) during the Depression years is not a coincidence—these superhero comics were perhaps a way of coping with the real-time sociopolitical and economic changes and boosting the morale of the nation.
6. This takes into account the valuable concepts such as "braiding" and "cohesion" that Groensteen theorizes within the Francophone tradition of visual forms.
7. According to Freud, "the patient does not *remember* anything of what he has forgotten and repressed but *acts* it out. He reproduces it not as a memory but as an action; he *repeats* it, without, of course, knowing that he is repeating it" (Ellman 150).

WORKS CITED

Ellman, Maud. *Psychoanalytic Literary Criticism*. New York: Routledge, 1994.
Gallagher, Catherine. *Telling It Like It Wasn't: The Counterfactual Imagination in History and Fiction*. Chicago: U of Chicago P, 2018.
Kearney, Richard. "Narrating Pain: The Power of Catharsis." *Paragraph* 30.1 (2007): 51–66. JSTOR, www.jstor.org/stable/43152699.
McCloud, Scott. *The Invisible Art: Understanding Comics*. New York: William Morrow, 1994.
Miller, Mark, et al. *Superman Red Son*. DC Comics, 2014.
Moore, Alan, and Dave Gibbons. *Watchmen*. New York: Warner Books, 1987.
Royle, Nicholas, and Andrew Bennett. *An Introduction to Literature, Criticism and Theory*. London: Taylor and Francis Ltd., 2004.
Saint-Amour, Paul. "Counterfactual States of America: On Parallel Worlds and Longing for the Law." *Post45* 20 (Sept. 2011): np.

Sedgwick, Eve. "Paranoid Reading and Reparative Reading, or, You're so Paranoid, You Probably Think This Essay Is about You." *Touching Feeling: Affect, Pedagogy and Performativity*. Durham: Duke UP, 2003.

Sigmund Freud, "Remembering, Repeating and Working-Through," 1914, in *The Standard Edition of the Complete Psychological Works of Sigmund Freud*, trans. Joan Riviere. London: Vintage, Hogarth Press, 2001. 12:145–56.

Sousanis, Nick. *Unflattening*. Cambridge: Harvard University Press, 2015.

CHAPTER 6

RE-FRAMING (POST-)SOVIET UKRAINIAN HISTORY

Walter Duranty, Igort's *The Ukrainian Notebooks*, and the Ethics of Graphic Reportage

ANASTASIA ULANOWICZ

When, in 2010, the internationally acclaimed Italian comics producer and journalist Igort (born Igor Tuveri) published his work of graphic reportage, *The Ukrainian Notebooks (Quaderni ucraini)*, very few readers within or beyond Europe had much interest in his book's depiction of twentieth- and early twenty-first-century Ukrainian history. Shortly thereafter, however, a series of dramatic historical events—beginning with Ukraine's 2014 Revolution of Dignity, followed shortly thereafter by Russia's preliminary invasion of Ukraine and seizure of Crimea; the first impeachment of US President Donald Trump on the grounds of "abuse of power" for withholding US military aid to Ukraine in exchange for information about his political rival's son; and finally, the Russian full-scale invasion beginning in February 2022—propelled Ukraine into the global spotlight and in turn ignited popular interest in Igort's graphic narrative. Indeed, *The Ukrainian Notebooks*—available in English translation in 2016 along with Igort's subsequently published *Russian Notebooks (Quaderni russi,* 2011)—became a regular staple on Internet "must-read" lists following Russia's full-scale invasion, alongside historian Serhii Ploky's *The Gates of Europe: A History of Ukraine* (2015) and translations of Romana Romanyshyn and Andriy Lesiv's internationally-acclaimed picture book, *How War Changed Rondo (Viyna, shto zminila rondo* 2015).

If *The Ukrainian Notebooks* has become a "go-to" source for international readers curious to discover the history of a long-neglected nation, this is in part because its author/narrator—a Western European of Ukrainian and Russian heritage—begins his work by humbly admitting his own ignorance of Ukraine. Indeed, in the first two panels of his text—which effectively frame its narrative trajectory—he depicts a cloud whose shape resembles the contours of the present nation-state of Ukraine, followed by a precise map of the country that bears its name in Cyrillic: УКРАИНА.[1] Read together, these panels foreground the two-year process by which the celebrated Italian comics producer moved from perceiving Ukraine as "a hazy thing, a cloud in the Soviet firmament" to a distinct historical, cultural, and political entity (5). Indeed, the collage-like character of Igort's text—an assemblage of vignettes, testimonies by Ukrainian citizens, profiles of historical personages, and facsimiles of archival documents—invites readers with little previous acquaintance with Ukrainian history and culture to share in the author's practice of critically piecing together sources from a former Soviet republic in order to recognize it as a nation-state as diverse and complex as any other.

Significantly, Igort's graphic narrative is particularly concerned with how the Stalinist-engineered famine of the 1930s—the *Holodomor*, or literally "death by hunger" in Ukrainian—not only claimed the lives of at least four million Ukrainian peasants but also traumatized their descendants, including each of the post-Soviet Ukrainian interviewees whose oral histories he illustrates in the course of his text. To this end, he is preoccupied with critiquing and ultimately countering the fabricated reports offered by the Pulitzer Prize-winning *New York Times* correspondent, Walter Duranty, whose infamously spirited denial of the Holodomor ultimately led to the Roosevelt administration's recognition of the Soviet Union. Indeed, it is notable that Igort places a hand-drawn replica of Duranty's portrait squarely at the midpoint of his narrative (104)—and that the facing page offers a facsimile of Duranty's September 18 1933 *Times*: "BIG UKRAINE CROP TAXES HARVESTERS, Talk of Famine Now Is Called Ridiculous After Auto Trip Through the Heart of Region, PEOPLE WELL NOURISHED" (105). Here, Igort's juxtaposition of a portrait of a celebrity journalist and an example of one of his most blatant fabrications prompts readers to question how their own perception of Ukrainian history has been mediated, if not distorted, by institutions such as Western print journalism.

In this essay, I argue that Igort's exposure and disputation of Duranty's journalistic accounts of the Holodomor function as the ethical heart of the project he undertakes in *The Ukrainian Notebooks*. Not only does Igort attempt to fill in the gaps left conspicuously open by Duranty's obfuscating coverage of the Ukrainian famine, but he also does so by offering visual and verbal renditions of direct testimonies offered by famine survivors. In this way, he constructs his graphic narrative as a counterpoint to Duranty's own dispatches, which privileged the journalist's claims of objective observation over the voices of Ukrainian peasants he encountered. Furthermore, precisely by representing his research odyssey within a graphic narrative—a medium which, as Hillary Chute argues, is a "conspicuously artificial form"—Igort calls attention to the necessary mediation and "made-ness" of his depictions of Ukraine in ways that Duranty refused (17). Indeed, by deliberately employing the "spatial syntax" (4) of the graphic narrative in order to subvert narrative conventions that subtend notions of history as linear, progressive, closed, and otherwise limited to the rarefied domain of "experts," Igort presents a nonchronological and multiply-mediated account that beckons readers to engage with a rich, complex, and unresolved history.

"THE PRESENT DIFFICULTIES WILL BE SPEEDILY FORGOTTEN"

In order to appreciate how *The Ukrainian Notebooks* offers an implicit rejoinder not only to Duranty's reports but also, more broadly, to the purportedly objective, "hardboiled" style of Western journalism he represented, it is first necessary to account for Duranty's career within its historical context. Born near Liverpool in 1884, Duranty emigrated to the United States following his graduation from Cambridge and was swiftly hired by the *New York Times* as a junior correspondent in First-World-War-era Paris; during his time in France, he built his reputation as both a war reporter and a *bon vivant* whose entourage included the likes of notorious occultist Alastair Crowley. Following his celebrated coverage of the Paris Peace Conference of 1919, he was assigned to a position in Riga in the newly established republic of Latvia and then to Moscow in 1922, where he would live for twelve years. There, his coverage of the Volga famine of 1921–1922,[2] Lenin's New Economic Policy (NEP) of 1922,[3] and Stalin's eventual accession to the leadership of the Soviet Union following Lenin's death in 1924 won him the respect of Stalin, who granted him a coveted series of interviews.[4] In turn, Duranty's audiences with Stalin, as well as the rare glimpses into everyday Soviet life he granted to curious Westerners, rendered him an international celebrity. In 1933, he drew on his reputation to broker President Franklin D. Roosevelt's official recognition of the USSR.

Although Duranty repeatedly insisted that he was "no Marxist" and that his meetings with Stalin did not influence his coverage of Soviet policy and practice, his subsequent reports nevertheless communicated a clear admiration for Stalin's First Five Year Plan: a set of sweeping measures instituted in 1928 to mobilize urban industry; "liquidate" the kulaks, or wealthier land-holding peasants, and organize remaining peasants into mass collective farms envisioned as rural factories. Although Duranty was aware that this massive undertaking involved the conscription of urban workers to backbreaking labor, the deportation and execution of poor farmers misnamed "kulaks," and the forced collectivization of peasants who still preserved a collective memory of serfdom, his editorial asides communicated approbation, if not justification, of Stalin's plan. For example, in an article published on November 30, 1932, the journalist stated, with characteristic flourish, that the "whole Soviet history is one of storms and the emergencies of battles, of expedients and sacrifices, but throughout it runs the same red cord of purpose, the same iron determination to spare no effort or face any danger or hardship to attain their goal." Moreover, in an earlier piece published on December 5, 1932, the former English schoolboy, raised during the heyday of British imperialism, quoted Kipling in order to assert that the "blood" shed at the hands of the "Bolsheviki" was the evidence of the necessary price paid by an emerging empire.

Duranty's self-professed begrudging respect for violent Stalinist measures was tested, however, in early 1933, when the Welsh journalist Gareth Jones detached himself from his state handlers in Kharkiv[5] and reported mass starvation, as well as instances of nécrophagie and cannibalism, throughout the central Ukrainian countryside as a direct result of Stalinist measures of dekulakization and mass collectivization. In response, Duranty published an article on March 31, 1933 entitled "Russians [sic][6] Hungry But Not Starving." Less a news report than a scathing rejoinder to a rival journalist's breaking scoop, this piece dismissed Jones' eyewitness report and interviews with Ukrainian peasants as a "big scare story" and instead drew on testimonies offered by Soviet "commissariats" and "personal connections" in Moscow to claim that collectivized peasants in Ukraine were simply suffering from temporary "malnourishment" occasioned by bureaucratic "mismanagement." Although, as Duranty admitted in a characteristic editorial aside, such incidences of want were certainly unfortunate, they were nevertheless necessary sacrifices made toward the greater glory of an emerging empire: "to put it brutally," the self-professed hardboiled journalist contended, "you can't make an omelette without breaking eggs, and the Bolshevist leaders are just as indifferent to the casualties that may be involved in their drive toward socialization as any General during the World War who ordered a costly attack in order to show his superiors that he and his division possessed the proper soldierly spirit." In any case, he concluded, "the present difficulties will be speedily forgotten." Later, on September 18 1933, Duranty published a particularly ebullient piece in which he categorically stated that the difficulties of the earlier year were not only forgotten but simply did not exist in the first place: reporting at the conclusion of an automobile journey through the Ukrainian countryside, he maintained that "the harvest is splendid and all talk of famine now is ridiculous."

Ultimately, however, the "talk of famine" which Duranty so glibly derided was not only proven to be *not* "ridiculous" but, in fact, a matter of historical record. As early as 1953, the Polish-Jewish intellectual Rafael Lemkin made use of his newly coined term, "genocide," by stating that the widespread hunger in Ukraine between 1932–1933 was not only a famine but also one that was artificially engineered by the Soviet state to literally starve off the Ukrainian peasantry in an effort to ensure the "destruction of the Ukrainian nation" (80). Years later, immediately before and after the collapse of the Soviet empire, scholars and journalists such as Anne Applebaum, Robert Conquest, Andrea Graziozi, Stanislaw Kulchinksy, and James Mace have corroborated Lemkin's initial claims by offering concrete evidence that widespread hunger throughout Ukraine in the early thirties was not merely the result of bureaucratic mismanagement—or even the sacrifice of a few casualties on behalf of a larger utopian "omelette"—but rather an intentional effort to starve into submission an ethnic and national minority whose not-so-distant memory of serfdom under Russian imperial rule impelled it to resist collectivization under the new Soviet empire. Today, the Ukrainian famine (formerly "the Great Famine") is recognized by a specific name, "Holodomor"—literally, in Ukrainian, "murder by starvation"—and it has been officially recognized as genocide by a growing number of nations such as Canada, Denmark, France, Israel, Mexico, and the United States.

In the past quarter century, Duranty's legacy has been met with censure. In 2003, following the publication of S.J. Taylor's exhaustive biography of the journalist *Stalin's Apologist* (1990)—which reveals Duranty's private confession to members of the British embassy that Ukraine was being "bled white" by famine even at the moment he publicly and vociferously denied reports of mass starvation in the republic (Taylor 221)—the *New York Times* commissioned a Columbia University historian, Mark von Hagen, to make an independent assessment of Duranty's career. In response, von Hagen concluded that Duranty was a "disgrace in the history" of the newspaper and recommended that his 1932 Pulitzer Prize be rescinded (Steinberg A29). Shortly thereafter, Karl E. Meyer, a member of the *Times* editorial board, stated that Duranty's dispatches from the Soviet Union constituted "some of the worst reporting to appear in this newspaper." Likewise, the *Times* publisher, Arthur

Sulzberger Jr., corroborated von Hagen's and Meyer's responses by pronouncing Duranty's journalistic work "slovenly"—but nevertheless recommended that his Pulitzer not be rescinded, lest the *Times* be accused of the same methods of censorship and historical erasure practiced by the journalist's apparent hero, Stalin (Kirkpatrick A13).

Certainly, these individuals' damning assessments of Duranty's career demonstrate a good faith effort to discredit his reports and to justify the integrity of a periodical long committed to disseminating "all the news that's fit to print." And yet, to Holodomor survivors and their descendants, such belated responses offer little more than cold comfort. After all, Duranty's glib denials of the famine, as well as its precise occurrence in the culturally and politically distinct republic of Soviet Ukraine, all but ensured that generations of global readers would remain ignorant of the long and vexed history of an entity called "Ukraine."

"I HAVE LEARNED, OVER TIME, TO LISTEN AND NOT JUDGE"

Following the Chornobyl disaster of 1986, the subsequent periods of *glasnost* and *perestroika*, and the ultimate fragmentation of the Soviet Union—not to mention the triumphs of Ukrainian athletes at the 1994 Winter Olympics in Lillehammer—the global community began to perceive Ukraine as a distinct entity and thus started to express interest in its history. Certainly, popular histories and travelogues responded to such newly founded curiosity: for example, journalist Anna Reid's masterful *Borderland* (1997) offered a concise history of Ukraine from the founding of Kyivan Rus' in the ninth century to its roles in the twentieth-century world wars through a virtual tour of its discrete regions.[7] Crucially, texts such as Reid's not only cited Duranty and redressed his obfuscations but also strenuously countered his most egregious depictions of citizens of the (former) Soviet Union as either "dumb cattle" patiently resigned to life in "dirt and ignorance" or as an "Asiatic race" instinctively inclined to violence (*I Write*, 287, 288, 151). However, as necessary as these verbal texts might have been in correcting the historical record and counteracting harmful Western stereotypes, they nevertheless could not adequately communicate cultural and historical nuances that might only be best conveyed through the effect of visual imagery: for example, the sublime expanse of the Ukrainian steppe, or how a *divan* overhung by a *kilim* functions as the heart of both urban and rural households, or how the sight of pyres of corpses terrorized Soviet Ukrainian citizens during both the Holodomor and the Second World War.

Enter Igor Tuveri, an Italian comics artist best known by his penname, Igort. Unlike Duranty, Igort is not a journalist; nor is he, like Reid, a travel writer. Rather, he is a critically acclaimed comics artist who, in 2000, founded Coconino Press, Italy's premier publishing house for graphic narratives. Even so, as the son of a Russophilic family and the spouse of a Ukrainian national, he drew on his international reputation as a prodigious graphic narrativist to chart his immersive two-year-long odyssey in the eastern provinces of Ukraine to publish *The Ukrainian Notebooks* in 2010. As its title suggests, this text is not so much intended as a conventional travel narrative that charts a writer's closely managed itinerary as it is a loose compendium of sketches, notes, and research sources compiled in the midst of travel. As such, it testifies to the process of Igort's gradual assimilation of Ukrainian culture and history, as well as his recognition of this newly sovereign nation's fraught relationship with its recent Soviet past.

The Ukrainian Notebooks is constituted by three distinct narrative modes, each of which appears intermittently throughout the body of the text. The first involves vignettes and reflections, often offered in page-long mini-comics rendered in shades of red and black. Here, Igort directly employs the first-person in his verbal text and occasionally draws himself into visual sequences in order to reflect on how the "roots of the former Soviet Union—the *Sovetsky Soyuz*—are still pulsating with life" in the sociopolitical climate of present-day Ukraine (15). For instance, he depicts his consternation during an interview with a fireworks factory employee who jollily predicts Putin's imminent invasion of Ukraine (12). Likewise, he considers how his acquisition of new Russian and Ukrainian terms such as *avaria* (or "accident") is enhanced by regular radio reports of assassinations and suspicious disappearances. Unlike these more self-referential sequences—which resemble the comics reportage of such celebrated authors as Joe Sacco and Guy Delisle—the second major component of Igort's text involves cross-hatched black and white sketches that illustrate earlier Soviet-era traumas such as dekulakization, collectivization, the Holodomor, and the Stalinist purges.[8] Here, Igort refrains from the use of first-person and rather deploys a detached scholarly tone as he explicates 1930s-era Soviet policies, profiles major historical personages such as Stalin, Vyacheslav Menzhinsky,[9] and Vsevolod Balitsky,[10] and recites statistics regarding kulak deportations and the death toll of the Holodomor. Occasionally, Igort absents his own voice entirely and allows the archival sources he has encountered to speak in his stead: for instance, his line drawing of an emaciated widow and her two naked children leaning over a bloated corpse is accompanied by a direct quotation from an OGPU[11] regional department chief's report of nécrophagie in the Vysokopolsk district of Ukraine (47). Once read in relation to the confessional red-tinted "mini-comics" that precede and follow them, these verbally and visually stark sequences suggest how instances of violence and paranoia in contemporary Ukraine are not mere anomalies but rather are intimately bound up with unresolved Soviet-era traumas.

Certainly, *The Ukrainian Notebooks* would be powerful enough if it relied simply on Igort's personal encounters and reflections and his scrupulously researched reports of Ukraine's Stalinist past. And yet, it is the third component of his text—four separate illustrated transcriptions of testimonies offered by elderly Ukrainians—that ultimately broadens and enriches the scope of his entire work. As Igort states in the expositional passages of his narrative, his quest to discern Ukraine as a distinct national entity and to understand its long entanglement with Soviet history led him to "chance" encounters with everyday citizens of the city of Dnipropetrovsk and its rural environs (16). Although some of these meetings were relatively brief ones that Igort highlights in his more confessional mini-comics, others were the result of relationships forged over time and through the gradual establishment of mutual trust (55). From these latter conversations, Igort constructs "faithful transcription[s]" (55) of testimonies offered by Serafima Andreyevna,[12] a cancer patient whose first memories were of near-starvation in the early 1930s; Nikolay Vasilievich, a luckless indigent who was forced into hard labor during the Nazi occupation of Soviet Ukraine; Maria Ivanovna, a pensioner who supports her disabled daughter by begging in a popular shopping district; and Nikolay Ivanovich, a former collective farmer who, with his wife, Emilia Vasilievna, laments the fallow fields he once tilled. These testimonial sequences are visually and formally distinguished from the other material in Igort's book. For instance, unlike the "first-person" and "historical" sequences—most of which take the form of either page-length mini-comics or a succession of full-page spreads, respectively—these four testimonies are tightly rendered in a grid of three-panel rows per page, each comprised of either two small frames or one elongated one. Every panel includes both a text box featuring a direct passage seized from the respective interviewee's first-person narrative as well as an accompanying illustration that offers Igort's visual interpretation of that passage. Moreover, unlike the other sequences in *The Ukrainian Notebooks* that are rendered either in glaring red or impressionistic black and white, these testimonial sections are colored in earth tones that convey the concrete but otherwise unremarkable existence of witnesses to history—individuals whose lives, much like sepia-toned photographs, have long been consigned to the musty archives of collective memory. They also function to connote the constricted, colorless, anemic, airless reality of Soviet existence in its multiform brutality.

Ultimately, the integrity of Igort's graphic narrative inheres in its implicit insistence that the testimonies offered by these four humble interviewees might function as the crucial link between the historical record he excavates and the present sociopolitical realities he surveys. Indeed, these four individuals, born between 1926 and 1939, bear witness to a string of historical events—from the Holodomor to the Second World War, from Khruschev-era "thaw" to Brezhnev-era "stagnation," and from the Chornobyl crisis to the final disintegration of the Soviet Union leading to post-communist-era economic "free fall"—which continue to haunt Ukrainian collective memory. Not insignificantly, the Holodomor is a recurring theme in most of these testimonies; indeed, this seems to be the reason why Igort's third-person "historical" section dwells so heavily on the causes and consequences of this artificial famine. Serafima Andreyevna's witness narrative, for example, is entirely concerned with the events of 1932: here, she describes hunting at midnight for hedgehogs, snakes, and roots (24);[13] chewing on raw horsehide and branches to stem her hunger (25); and steering clear of neighbors who, having gone mad from starvation, were known to have abducted and consumed children and other weakened villagers (26–27). Likewise, Maria Ivanovna's testimony, although it addresses her later life during the Khrushchev and Brezhnev eras, returns intermittently to her childhood during the Holodomor: she recalls, for instance, seeing live bodies being deposited in mass graves, and she credits her survival to the mere fact that her mother was able to draw on her status as the collective farm's bookkeeper to retain a milk-cow.

In order to place into relief these harrowing accounts of near-starvation and brushes with mortality, Igort renders them in shades of blue and violet that contrast dramatically with the earth-tones he generally uses in his testimonial sections. Although such cool colors conventionally signify peace and reassurance, their use here conveys frozenness, sterility, and an ultimate evacuation of any sense of warmth or hope. For instance, he depicts Serafima Andreyeva's memory of illicit hunts for snakes in a chilly blue that conveys the desperation involved in extracting lethargic reptiles from layers of "ice and snow" (24). Similarly, he casts Maria Ivanovna's memory of discovering living corpses in purple tones that suggest the interior of a violent storm (122–23). In perhaps one of the most haunting images of panels of the entire book, Igort interprets Serafima Andreyevna's contention that "cannibalism became commonplace" in her village by depicting a wild-eyed man in a violet cloak strangling a child who strains against his deadly embrace, their mortal dance is set against a deep blue sky, and the motion lines that wave about them suggest not only their mutual desperation but also a cold and blustery setting emptied of the last traces of mutual human self-regard. Inserted into a sequence of otherwise brown- and red-toned panels, this one immediately arrests the reader's attention and thus reminds them of how a human-engineered famine ultimately starved individuals' ability to maintain their humanity.

Igort's highlighting of his interlocutors' particularly traumatic memories of famine, however, is not merely concerned with abstract questions about the impact of violence on the individual psyche or the limits of definitions of the human. They also place into dramatic relief discrete experiences of a mass traumatic event that would radically alter Ukrainian history. After all, as Igort suggests in the "historical" sections of *The Ukrainian Notebooks*, the decimation of the Ukrainian peasantry during the Holodomor effectively weakened a major labor force in the proverbial "breadbasket of Europe" and thus necessitated the forced migration of ethnic Russians into Soviet territories once dominated by fiercely independent Ukrainians.[14] Thus, he suggests, any Western attempt to understand the internecine violence currently being fought (in 2014) between Ukrainian nationalists and Russian sympathizers in eastern Ukraine is incomplete without a recognition of the earlier historically traumatic events that precipitated them in the first place. Here, as elsewhere, Igort draws on the witness testimonies offered by elderly Ukrainians in order to expose the entangled "roots" of Soviet-era trauma in contemporary events—and thus to call attention to the "residue of a past that doesn't want to die out" (15).

Crucially, however, Igort does not blame his Western audience for their ignorance of such "roots" and "residue." Rather, as he makes clear in his brief but strategically placed exposé of Walter Duranty's infamous career, he holds self-assured and purportedly objective Western journalists especially accountable for denying a disastrous politically engineered event whose consequences would ripple through decades of Eastern European history. To this end, Igort's effort to offer "faithful transcriptions" of elderly Ukrainians' testimonies takes on particular significance. First and foremost, his diligent recording and expressive illustration of accounts of the Holodomor offered by such first-hand witnesses as Serafima Andreyevna and Maria Ivanovna fills in a gap—if only belatedly—left open by journalists such as Duranty and other literary luminaries such as George Bernard Shaw, H. G. Wells, and Beatrice Webb who vehemently denied the existence of famine during their respective visits to the Soviet Union in the early 1930s.[15] Indeed, these two women are about the same age as famine orphans who once swarmed visiting Western dignitaries in an effort to secure bread and tell their stories—or, who, more often than not, were forcibly prohibited from contact with Westerners for the precise reason that their mere bedraggled presence might betray evidence of mass starvation in the cosmopolitan city of Kharkiv and the surrounding eastern provinces of Ukraine.[16]

Moreover, and perhaps more crucially, Igort's willingness to enter into mutual relationships of trust with his Ukrainian interviewees runs entirely counter to the *modus operandi* of earlier twentieth-century journalists such as Duranty. It is not significant, for example, that Duranty's now infamous March 1933 dispatch categorically dismissed Gareth Jones' (later corroborated) interviews with starving Ukrainian villagers by stating that the Welsh journalist's illicit three-week sojourn in the Soviet interior was "hasty" and did not support the official findings of both Soviet state representatives and "specialists" employed by Western consuls. Indeed, Duranty not only distrusted Soviet citizens who were not official state representatives but went so far as to dismiss them outright as liars. In his first memoir, unironically titled *I Write As I Please* (1935), Duranty categorically states that "Russians"—a term he uses to refer to Soviet citizens, no matter their ethnic identity—are a "romantic folk whose innate sense of drama is stronger than their regard for truth" (125). The "average Russian," he avows, "would sooner tell you what you want to hear, especially if he suspects you want to hear something lurid, than any plain, unvarnished fact" (125). Such prevarication, he goes on to explain, is not indicative of a conscious effort to deceive, but rather a feature of an essentially underdeveloped ethical sensibility: the "division in [the "Russian's] mind between romance and reality," he states, "is more nebulous than with Western nations" (125). To this end, Duranty volunteers himself as an expert who might offer an "interpretation" (164) of such a "nebulous" people to naïve "foreigners" who may not understand "this quirk of the Russian character" (125) and who thus might "take home from Russia what they went to find there" (126). Thus, not unlike the white hero of early twentieth century Hollywood Westerns whose claim to "know Indians" establishes his mastery over them, Duranty asserts himself as, in effect, a "man who knows Russians." Defending his position as both a polyglot insider and a "self-respecting reporter" who "tries to write the truth as he sees it" (105), he thereby implies that he, as a purportedly objective and cosmopolitan Western journalist, is better qualified to report the "facts" of Soviet reality than Soviet citizens are themselves. In the final analysis, however, Duranty's confidence in his own authority and privileged perspective contributed to his eventual downfall. As the *Times* editor Karl E. Meyer noted in an "editorial notebook" piece published on June 24, 1990, the correspondent's confusion of an internalized "thesis" propagated by Soviet state officials with his own purportedly objective observations ultimately led him to report "what he wanted to see."

By contrast, Igort actively resists not only Duranty's faulty claims to mastery of "Russian" culture but also the correspondent's willingness to mask his reliance on dubious state sources with cocky expressions of Western exceptionalism. For instance, whereas Duranty privileged sources from the upper echelons of Soviet administration and elite diplomatic corps, Igort deliberately seeks out interviews with indigents who were marginalized in the old Soviet system and continue to be neglected after its disintegration. In this way, his text resembles Joe Sacco's comics dispatches from Palestine, the former Yugoslavia, and the US Appalachians—which, as Chute observes, focus on the "lives that get left out, obviated, or ignored by mainstream and institutional narratives of history across (and enforced by) conventional narratives and disciplines" (199). Moreover, whereas Duranty could hardly tolerate, much less respect, first-hand accounts from humble Soviet citizens, Igort not only entertains but diligently records even the most long-winded of testimonies. For example, he precedes his visual rendition of Nikolay Ivanovich's meandering narrative of a life wasted by war, disease, and crass opportunism by admitting that it constitutes an "undigested mass"; even so, he respects the integrity of his interlocutor's account by offering a "faithful transcription" of it. At other moments, Igort expresses initial skepticism at his interlocutors' claims but nevertheless withholds judgment. For instance, he confesses to being "taken aback" when Maria Ivanovna states that she begs on the street in sub-zero temperatures to earn a few kopeks for an adult daughter who "doesn't work" (115). However, when he allows the woman to spin out her narrative, he soon learns that she does so because her daughter, a former engineer once commissioned to work on a "secret nuclear project" in North Korea, is now disabled by a thyroid condition (136). As Igort states in his prologue to Maria Ivanovna's testimonial transcript, he has "learned, over time, to listen and not judge" (115). In this way, he counters Duranty's naïve credence in both state sources and his own objective capacities with a comparatively more constructive expression of naïveté: that is, with an admission that he is *not* by any means an expert on (post-)Soviet culture, and thus that he is most capable of understanding it by standing back and allowing others to speak to the truth of their own experiences.

Of course, as a graphic narrativist, Igort possesses the ability not only to listen, transcribe, and translate verbal narratives but also to illustrate them. As the author/artist states in the introductory passages of *The Ukrainian Notebooks*, he "simply could not keep" his interlocutors' stories "inside" and thus was compelled to "draw" them (16). Certainly, Igort's visual renditions of these stories, as well as of the people who recount them, convey a degree of immediacy that a purely verbal text may not. Although Western readers who are little acquainted with (post-) Soviet Ukrainian history and culture might well garner both information and affect from a written text—especially if it demonstrates particular attention to detail and lyrical style—they nevertheless may project their own culturally specific assumptions and experiences onto the mental images they produce through their reading. Igort's drawings, however, so capture the nuances of daily life during discrete moments in Ukrainian history that they thwart readers' inclination, as unconscious as they might be, to enmesh their own expectations and sensibilities within the narrative. Notably, Igort resists the effort to exoticize his Eastern European subjects and settings: he does not, like Duranty, depict (post-) Soviet Ukrainian life as so inscrutable or otherwise "nebulous" that it demands his expert "interpretation." Rather, he fills each of his frames with rich visual details—changing hairstyles and winter-wear, the presence of "wall rugs" or *kilims* within living rooms (68), spotted birches and white-painted tree trunks, the exteriors of peasant homes decorated with floral designs (22) and even Krushchev-era eyeglasses—that remind readers of their temporal and cultural distance from his subject matter. In this way, he beckons his readers to assume an ethical position he himself occupied during his two-year stay in Ukraine: one that involves an open engagement with witnesses that is nonetheless predicated on an acknowledgment of their cultural and historical differences.

Igort's concern for such an ethical relationship is particularly demonstrated in his illustrations of his interlocutors' faces. As Chute argues, through an appeal to philosophers Emmanuel Levinas and Judith Butler, hand-drawn images of human faces not only acknowledge the "particularity of the other" but also call viewers to confront, or otherwise *face*, the "frailty and precariousness" embodied by the other—a condition so inherently shared by humans that it prompts both a responsiveness to and a "responsibility for" the other (249). The work of the graphic narrativist, she continues, is comprised of "*giving face* through drawing" (249). It involves, in other words, calling attention to—or drawing out—the most unique features of a human subject in a way that provokes viewers to acknowledge both their ineluctable distance from any one individual and the vulnerable human condition they nevertheless share (249). Such a process of "giving face" to the other—and the invitation to critical facing it invites—is especially evident in the watercolor portraits of his elderly interviewees that Igort inserts into the introduction to each of their testimonies. These portraits, much like photographic headshots, effectively capture their subjects' distinct personae: Serafima Andreyevna meets the illustrator's (and reader's) gaze with a direct and defiant one of her own (19); the world-worn dreamer Nikolay Vasilievich directs his glance rightward toward an object beyond the audience's vision (55); Maria Ivanovna, an indigent mother of a disabled nuclear physicist, hunches over to refuse eye-contact (115); and the balding former farmer Nikolay Ivanovich likewise looks downward, as though he is meditating over dispossessed land. Insofar as these images establish the concrete specificity of these witnesses' existence—as witnessed or otherwise "drawn out" by Igort—they also demand, *pace* Judith Butler, that viewers reevaluate how they "determine what will and will not be a grievable life" (Chute, 249). It is not insignificant, after all, that Stalin allegedly justified his bloody regime by avowing that "one death is a tragedy, a million deaths a statistic"—or, for that matter, his *Times* apologist rationalized genocide by stating that "you can't make an omelette without breaking eggs." If both of these notorious claims were intended to erase from collective memory the discrete experiences of countless Soviet citizens, Igort's portraits of four unmistakable human faces not only restore their effaced integrity but also gesture indexically to countless other victims of Stalinism whose lives cannot, or should not, be "speedily forgotten."

A "CONSPICUOUSLY ARTIFICIAL FORM"

Crucially, even as Igort attempts to draw out his subjects and thus draw his readers nearer to their respective experiences and historical realities, he actively resists making any claims to an objective or definitive account of Ukrainian history. Indeed, he foregrounds such resistance precisely by depicting his two-year stay in Ukraine within the "conspicuously artificial form" of the graphic narrative: one which involves the spatial arrangement of hand-drawn, and thus undeniably mediated images (Chute, *Disaster* 17). As Kate Polak observes, readers' "awareness of the graphic narrative as something *produced* is embedded in the form, which gives comics the possibility of engaging in commentary on the production of history and its violences" (11). As a collage of testimonies, archival excerpts, and personal reflections arranged more or less thematically rather than in chronological order, *The Ukrainian Notebooks* invites readers not only to analyze its deliberate organization but also to posit questions in response to the narrative gaps it allows to remain.

As noted above, Igort periodically inserts images of himself into the narrative: for example, walking along the banks of the Dnieper River (9) or "racing in a sidecar through farmland as far as the eye could see" (145). Such veritable cameos function similarly to moments in Art Spiegelman's *Maus*, in which the author occasionally interrupts his visual representation of his father Vladek's Holocaust testimony in order to depict the contemporary, quotidian conditions in which their interviews take place: for instance, Vladek's exercise room or park paths. In both cases, these moments thwart readers' immersion in the narrative and thereby remind them that they are not immediately witnessing events as they unfold but are rather engaging with a representation of them produced by a specific creator through the duration of a professionally and emotionally intense research period. Moreover, much like Spiegelman, Igort variously gestures to his mediating presence even when he does not directly feature his visual avatar. For example, he follows a sequence in Serafima Andreyevna's testimony regarding her childhood forays for roots and snakes with a frame featuring the present-day subject pouring tea from a kettle (25). Although Igort (or his avatar) is not explicitly present in the scene, the reader recognizes that the woman is framed from his point of view; in turn, the reader is prompted to acknowledge how the preceding sequence, though it may be based on a transcription of the elder's narrative, is likewise illustrated from Igort's perspective. Although the author may have drawn extensively on research materials, as well as the environmental and cultural nuances he registered during his immersive journey, in order to offer an informed and convincing image of childhood in famine-stricken Ukraine, his depiction of Serafima Andreyevna's experiences is ultimately at least twice-removed: it is an imaginative reconstruction of an octogenarian's already distant memories.

Furthermore, Igort emphasizes the "conspicuously artificial form" of *The Ukrainian Notebooks*, even in those sections that document his archival research of Stalinist-era traumas. Certainly, he could have included iconic photographs of the famine, such as those taken by Alexander Weinberger,[17] to accompany the official documents from which he quotes periodically in his text. After all, he reproduces original photographic portraits of his final set of witnesses, Nikolay Ivanovich and Emilia Vasilievna (160–61). His decision instead to juxtapose passages excerpted from archival sources with deliberately rough, cross-hatched line drawings thus places into relief his acknowledged distance from his subject matter. Ultimately, these illustrations do not so much offer concrete, definitive corroboration of the events documented in these sources as they convey the nightmarish, if not apocalyptic, images they inspire in the imagination of the twenty-first-century Italian author. Indeed, in an effort to gesture toward the contemporary reproduction of his historical images, Igort preserves certain blemishes—either coffee stains or water stains—that testify to the materiality of his work and text, as well as the passage of time. Moreover, some of Igort's black-and-white illustrations, such as one of an emaciated figure driving a scraggy horse over a barren field (48), are evocative of the expressionist lithographs of Käthe Kollwitz—whereas others, particularly one of a cannibal with wide, sunken eyes (49) rhyme uncannily with the terrifying visions of Edvard Munch. Such allusions to iconic artworks (Picasso's *Guernica*, 248) are not uncoincidental; rather, they signal Igort's having been influenced by, and his indebtedness to, earlier aesthetic traditions that posit the artist as a witness to the ravages of modernity. Indeed, it is not insignificant that the "new category of the artist-reporter essentially developed" during the Crimean War of 1853–1856—in precisely that region of the world in which Igort produced *The Ukrainian Notebooks* (Chute 10). In this way, his graphic novel attests not only to visual traditions of bearing witness established by other artists before him but also to the potential of a contemporary form that opens up new ways of seeing the present and the past and resonates powerfully within literary and visual practices of testifying to atrocities.

As Chute maintains, the form of graphic narrative is one that, through "its spatial syntax [. . .] offers opportunities to place pressure on traditional modes of chronology, linearity, and causality—as well as on the idea that 'history' can ever be a closed discourse, or simply a progressive one" (4). Certainly, Igort's text thwarts readers' expectations for a linear explanatory narrative, not least because its various "notebook entries" juxtapose discrete historical events—for example, the capitalist "free fall" of the early 2000s and the Holodomor, or the plight of post-Soviet collective farms and the Chornobyl disaster of 1986—in ways that leave the audience responsible for making critical connections between them. In this way, as Elisa Briccio argues, *The Ukrainian Notebooks* resembles a "mosaic" wherein heterogeneous narrative forms and fragmentary stories, once read together, produce a composite impression of Ukrainian history. Crucially, however, the book produces *only* an impression: it resists, that is, any effort to depict this history as complete or "closed." This is especially evident in the final witness narrative Igort transcribes and illustrates: that of Nikolay Ivanovich, a former collective farmer. In his testimony, Nikolay Ivanovich proudly reports how, at the conclusion of the Second World War, he received gainful employment as a tractor operator at a *kolhoz*, or collective farm, and how under Communism, he and his comrades "felt like people" (154). Subsequently, he decries the new era of capitalism, in which "people thought only of themselves," and laments how former state-owned lands now "lie abandoned" (157). If Nikolay Ivanovich's testimony is jarring, this is in part because it contrasts so dramatically with previous testimonies that depict collective farming in the 1930s as a failed endeavor resulting only in famine and desolation: indeed, the farmer avows that, after the war, "people quickly forgot hunger and famine" (154). The reader is thus left with an ethical and historical conundrum: On the one hand, as Nikolay Ivanovich contends, Stalin's project of collectivization eventually did produce relative prosperity and contentment; on the other hand, as the earlier passages in Igort's text make abundantly clear, such success was built on the untold misery—if not state-sanctioned murder—of millions of people whose suffering cannot be rationalized by smug platitudes such as "you can't make an omelet without breaking eggs."

Likewise, Igort's inclusion of Nikolay Ivanovich's testimony near the end of his text effectively shuts down any expectation that Ukrainian history—or history more generally—proceeds progressively according to a clear narrative trajectory. In a letter, Nikolay Ivanovich gives to Igort in anticipation of the author's departure from rural Ukraine—a photographed version of which Igort reproduces and translates—he bluntly states that "fifty two million people lived in Ukraine, but since Ukraine became independent eighteen years ago, seven million people have died" (162). Here, he implicitly holds the capitalist nation-state accountable for mass suffering in ways that his compatriots hold the Soviet state responsible for an earlier engineered famine. For all the differences between these ideological perspectives, one insight becomes evident: neither the utopian ideals of Communism nor those of capitalism have neatly ushered Ukraine into a brave new era—at least, not without considerable cost. Certainly, such an insight contrasts dramatically with the pragmatic assumptions of earlier Westerners such as Duranty, who was assured that Stalin's Five Year Plan would effectively script the proceedings of a dawning imperial history (or, for that matter, Western pundits who were convinced that the collapse of the Soviet Union would herald the emergence of a capitalist New World Order.[18] Moreover, Igort's presentation of the various contradictions and fissures within the past century of Ukrainian history demonstrates the preposterousness of claims made by Western journalists such as Duranty to authorize categorical "interpretations" of Soviet (or "Russian") culture and history—since, as Igort makes abundantly clear, post-Soviet Ukrainians themselves are still struggling to articulate such history themselves. Ultimately, if there is one outstanding feature of *The Ukrainian Notebooks*, it is its author's willingness to present Ukrainian history, much like Nikolay Vassilievich's testimony, as an "undigested mass." The ongoing task of "digesting" such a history, Igort implies, is one that must be taken up by Ukrainians and their Western neighbors alike.

NOTES

1. Specifically, this is the Russian word for Ukraine: the Ukrainian word is slightly different—"Україна." On the one hand, it is curious that Igort does not use the Ukrainian term—not only because it was spoken by most victims of the Ukrainian famine but also because, upon independence in 1991, it became the nation's official language. On the other hand, Igort may use the Russian term because he is a Russian speaker, and most

Ukrainians in the eastern provinces he visited (e.g., Dnipropetrovsk) still speak Russian even though they may identify as Ukrainian. Indeed, most Ukrainians are bilingual in Ukrainian and Russian, and many speak a combination of both, known as *surzhyk*. One might also speculate that Igort's decision to overlay an image of the contemporary Ukrainian nation with its Russian name suggests historical and contemporary Russian claims on this former imperial/Soviet colony—certainly, claims he addresses in both *The Ukrainian Notebooks* and *The Russian Notebooks*.

2. Like the Ukrainian famine of 1931–1933, the Volga famine—which affected regions in central Russia—was precipitated by state efforts of collectivization. However, unlike the later famine, this one was also exacerbated by natural environmental conditions such as drought; additionally, unlike the later famine, it received worldwide press coverage that resulted in international aid efforts. In the later famine, the Soviet Regime did not allow any international aid that was offered. Although, as I note below, Duranty remained suspicious of eyewitness accounts of this famine, he nevertheless acknowledged it and expressed sympathy for its victims. Indeed, in his memoirs, he wrote that, despite his feelings of helplessness in the face of the "ugly nakedness" of the famine, he hoped his dispatches would "move people in America and hurry their promised aid" (132). Evidently, he had lost this sense of sympathy and advocacy by the time of the second, and much more devastating, Soviet famine of the early thirties.

3. Lenin's New Economic Policy was designed as a temporary respite from the previous, violent measures undertaken by the Bolshevik state; this program ensured, among other things, private local entrepreneurship and the development of arts and culture within distinct Soviet republics. According to then-official Soviet history—as well as Duranty's reports—it was ultimately dismantled under Stalin because it enabled the emergence of a predatory *nouveau riche* class. However, as historians such as Anne Applebaum have recently argued, the NEP also enabled distinctly regional and national expressions of communism that threatened Stalin's interpretation of a centrist, Russophilic state.

4. As Duranty proudly reports in his 1935 memoir, *I Write As I Please*, Stalin praised him on "Christmas day, 1933" by saying, "You have done a good job in your reporting of the U.S.S.R although you are not a Marxist, because you tried to tell the truth about our country and to understand it and explain it to your readers. I might say that you bet on our horse to win when others thought it had no chance, and I am sure you have not lost by it" (166–67).

5. Throughout this essay, I will use contemporary transliterations of Ukrainian names, words, and cities (e.g., "Kharkiv" and "Chornobyl") but will retain their earlier Russian transliterations (e.g., "Kharkov," "Chernobyl") when they are used in direct quotations from Soviet-era sources.

6. Here, as elsewhere, Duranty referred to all Soviet citizens—even Caucasian nomads and ethnic Ukrainians or Belarusians—as "Russians." This is a generalization that even many contemporary scholars continue to make. Although the Russian city of Moscow was the capital of the Soviet empire and Soviet policy was Russo-centric, it is crucial to remember that although all Russians were Soviets, not all Soviets were Russian.

7. In 2015, Reid published an expanded edition of *Borderland* that accounts for the Orange Revolution of 2004, the Maidan Revolution—or "Revolution of Dignity"—of 2014, the Russian seizure of Crimea in 2014, and the ongoing war between Ukraine and Russia

in eastern Ukrainian provinces. These latter events coincided with Igort's travels within Ukraine and Russia and—as I discuss below—are addressed in the postscript of his subsequent graphic narrative, *The Russian Notebooks*.

8. Igort stops short of documenting the infamous show trials and purges that followed the assassination of Sergei Kirov in 1934—or, for that matter, the purges of the Ukrainian Communist Party that occurred, not coincidentally, during the height of the Holodomor. Even so, he does note the sensational case of Pavel ("Pavlik") Trofimovich Morozov, a Young Pioneer from the eastern provinces of Soviet Russia who so stridently ascribed to utopian visions of collective farming that he named his father as an "enemy of the State." Shortly thereafter, he was murdered by his grandparents and cousins—not, as Igort states, "his own parents" (111)—and was swiftly enshrined as a Soviet martyr. Igort's minor mistake notwithstanding, Pavlik's sensational case places into relief countless instances in which Soviet citizens betrayed family members as "kulaks" and/or "enemies of the state" either voluntarily or under force.

9. The chair of the Soviet secret police (OGPU) during the height of the Ukrainian famine.

10. Menzhinsky's "Ukrainian equivalent" (39) in the OGPU who assisted in supervising the artificial famine.

11. Soviet secret police (*Obyedinyonnoye gosudarstvennoye politicheskoye upravleniye*)—successor to the Leninist Cheka and predecessor of the NKVD and KGB.

12. Notably, Igort identifies his interviewees by their first names and patronymics but withholds their surnames—perhaps in an effort to protect their privacy and full identities.

13. Serafima Andreyevna's mention of illicit midnight hunts is not insignificant since Ukrainian peasants could receive capital sentences for poaching on land seized by the Soviet state. Miron Dolot's witness narrative, *Execution By Hunger* (1987), offers a particularly detailed account of the gradual process by which Ukrainian peasants were alienated from communally shared wilderness.

14. Curiously, Igort merely gestures toward this conclusion in *The Ukrainian Notebooks* but makes it explicitly clear in the postscript to his subsequent book, *The Russian Notebooks* (2011). Here, he states that the "tensions" occasioned by post-famine Russian migration lately have been "spurred on by the Kremlin" and have brought on "pain and suffering to a Ukrainian population that is already worn down by poverty" (351). "Today," he continues, "the tragedy is going on under the nose of an inert Europe, hostage to Russian gas and oil, that pretends not to see the extent of an absolute tragedy, just like in the Thirties" (351). Here, Igort's reference to "the Thirties" and Western European moral inertia not only continues his project of linking together the Soviet past and the post-Soviet present but also subtly reflects back on his exposé of ethically slovenly Western journalism. It is not insignificant, for example, that *The Russian Notebooks* hinges on the investigative work of the Russian journalist and "beacon of consciousness" Anna Politkovskaya, who was assassinated in 2006 for her coverage of human rights abuses in the Chechnyan war (181). Here, Poliktovskaya's uncompromising commitment to reporting the truth contrasts dramatically with Duranty's aforementioned willingness to tow the Party line.

15. As Anne Applebaum reports in her history, *Red Famine: Stalin's War on Ukraine* (2017), George Bernard Shaw was so convinced that reports of starvation in Ukraine

were invented by "anti-Soviet rumour-mongers" that on a train journey from Poland to the Soviet Union in 1931, he demonstratively threw gifted cans of food "out the window" before reaching the Soviet border (307). Such insouciance, Applebaum claims, was performed equally by visiting "true believers," celebrities flattered by the "pomp and favour that the USSR could shower upon them," and state representatives eager to confirm their vision of a socialist utopia (307–8).

16. Visiting Western dignitaries to 1930s-era Soviet Ukraine—including, presumably, Duranty himself—were ushered through veritable Potemkin villages. For instance, Applebaum accounts for how Édouard Herriot, "a French Radical politician and former prime minister who was invited to Ukraine at the end of August 1933," visited "a model children's colony, saw shops whose shelves had been hastily stocked in advance, rode down the Dnieper River on a boat and met enthusiastic peasants and workers coached especially for the occasion" (308). Subsequently, Herriot pronounced that his travels across Ukraine had exposed him to a "garden in full bloom" (308). Curiously, in his memoirs, Duranty expresses suspicion that the worst consequences of the 1921 Volga famine were disguised by similar "Potemkin villages" (127)—but does not consider how his own 1933 "automobile journey" through famine-ravaged regions of Ukraine might have been similarly constructed.

17. Alexander Weinerberger was a Jewish Austrian engineer whose position in a Kharkiv factory allowed him to take surreptitious photographs of famine victims; according to Applebaum, "these are still the only verified photographs taken in Ukraine of famine victims in 1933" (304). Weinerberger's photographs variously capture curious city-dwellers poised over dead bodies, escaped peasants dying in the middle of city streets, Soviet agents seizing bags of grain, and mass gravesites.

18. See, for example, Francis Fukuyama's contention that the collapse of the Soviet Union heralded the triumph of capitalism and, thus an "end of history" that overrides other possible socio-economic arrangements. Despite its apocalyptic overtones, Fukuyama's concept of the "end of history" was largely utopian; indeed, he was a signatory to the Project for the New American Century, which envisioned the United States' global promulgation of capitalist democracy.

WORKS CITED

Applebaum, Anne. *Red Famine: Stalin's War on Ukraine*. New York: Doubleday, 2017.
Bricco, Elisa. "Le Roman graphique et l'Histoire: Pour un récit engagé" *Cahiers de Narratologie* 26 (2014).
Chute, Hillary L. *Disaster Drawn: Visual Witness, Comics, and Documentary Form*. Cambridge: Belknap Press of Harvard University Press, 2016.
Dolot, Miron. *Execution By Hunger: The Hidden Holocaust*. New York: W.W. Norton & Co, 1987.
Duranty, Walter. "Big Ukraine Crop Taxes Harvesters." *New York Times*, September 18, 1933, 8. Accessed May 14, 2019.
Duranty, Walter. "Bolsheviki United on Socialist Goal." *New York Times*, November 30, 1932, 4. Accessed May 14, 2019.

Duranty, Walter. *I Write As I Please* New York: Simon & Schuster, 1935.
Duranty, Walter. "Russians Hungry But Not Starving." *New York Times*, March 31, 1933, 13. Accessed May 14, 2019.
Duranty, Walter. "Soviet Will Strive in New Plan to Lift Burden of the People." *New York Times*, December 5, 1931, 1. Accessed May 14, 2019.
Fukuyama, Francis. *The End of History and The Last Man* New York: Free Press, 1992.
Igort. *The Ukrainian and Russian Notebooks*, trans. Jamie Richards. New York: Simon & Schuster, 2016.
Kirkpatrick, David D. "Pulitzer Board Won't Void '32 Award to Times Writer." *New York Times*, November 22, 2003, E20. Accessed May 14, 2019.
Lemkin, Raphael. "Soviet Genocide in Ukraine." In *The Holodomor Reader: A Sourcebook on the Famine of 1932–1933 in Ukraine*, ed. Bohdan Klid and Alexander J. Motyl, 124–30. Edmonton: Canadian Institute of Ukranian Studies Press, 2012.
Meyer. Karl E. "Trenchcoats, Then and Now: The Correspondent Who Liked Stalin." *New York Times*, June 24, 1990, E20. Accessed May 14, 2019.
Polak, Kate. *Ethics in the Gutter: Empathy and Historical Fiction in Comics* Columbus: Ohio State University Press, 2017.
Reid, Anna. *Borderland: A Journey Through the History of Ukraine*. 2nd ed. New York: Basic Books, 2015.
Spiegelman, Art. *Maus: A Survivor's Tale. Volume I: My Father Bleeds History*. New York: Pantheon, 1991.
Steinberg, Jacques. "*Times* Should Lose Pulitzer From 30's, Consultant Says." *New York Times*, October 23, 2003, A29. Accessed May 19, 2019.
Taylor, S.J. *Stalin's Apologist: Walter Duranty, the New York Times Man in Moscow*. New York: Oxford University Press, 1990.

IV. DRAWING CLOSE:
INDIVIDUAL, INTIMATE, AND TRAUMATIC

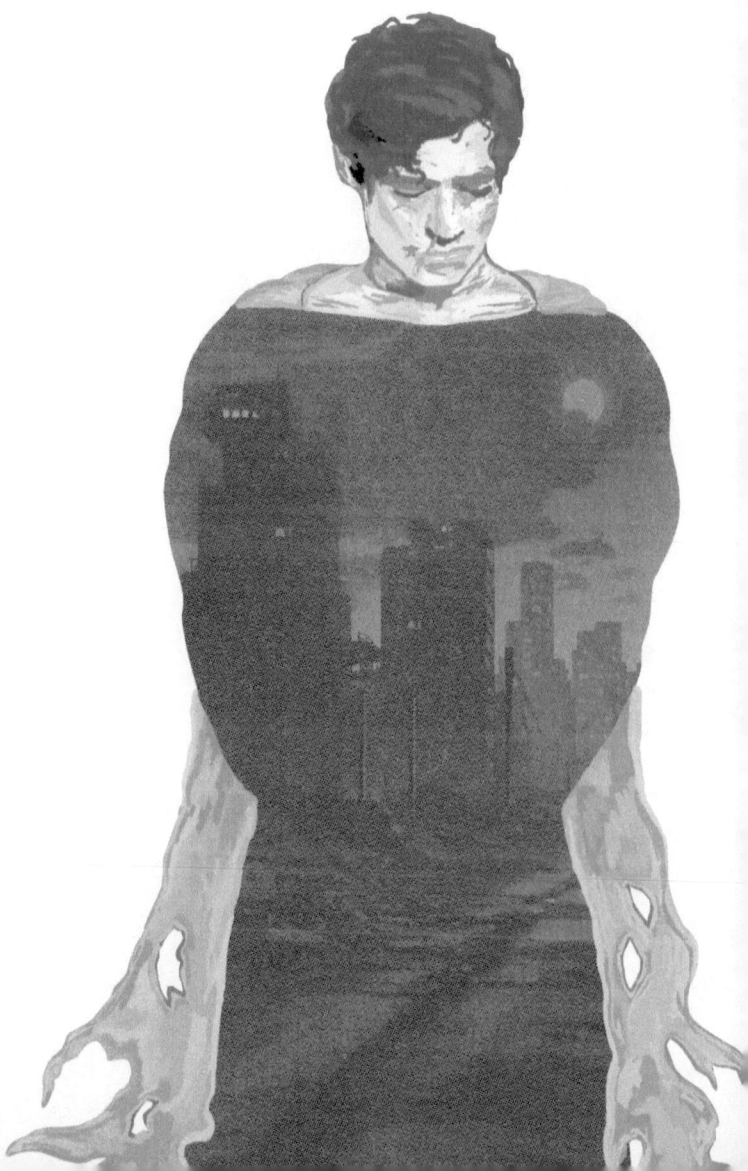

CHAPTER 7

ALISON BECHDEL'S *FUN HOME* AND THE IMPOSSIBILITY OF TESTIMONY

KELLY BARON

There is an insistence on fidelity in Alison Bechdel's *Fun Home* (2006) that is impossible to ignore. Perhaps developed in contrast to her father's "skillful artifice" used "not to make things, but to make things appear to be what they were not" (16), Bechdel is open about her anxiety towards rendering her early memories faithfully. A chapter devoted primarily to her childhood bout of Obsessive-Compulsive Disorder details the insertion of the words "I think" into her journal entries, a precursor to her "epistemological crisis" in which she began representing those words with a squiggly circumflex meant to designate an uncertainty of knowledge (141–42). This anxiety over-representation, made further evident in her meticulous writing process, seems out-of-place for a memoir negotiating the author's relationship with her father, a man who she presumes to have committed suicide while she was still at college. Specifically, this attention to fidelity or faithfulness—her anxiety over representing her father, his life, their relationship, and his death—writes against the typical understanding of the impossibility of testimony, an ongoing debate in trauma theory. This concept, initially developed from Elaine Scarry's (1987) idea that pain is an affective response without a referent, rendering it near impossible to convey in literary form, was popularized by Shoshana Felman and Dori Laub in 1992 as the difficulty of communicating experiences of trauma. The impossibility of testimony is not meant to imply that narratives have been falsified or cannot be communicated—indeed, the historical precedent of Holocaust literature precludes such a claim—but instead considers the compulsion of survivors to rely on clichés and narrative structures that are episodic and repetitive rather than linear, lending an unreal quality to the narrative. As such, narratives of trauma appear fragmented, with certain smaller details missing or factually incorrect, while other details appear magnified, reliant on clichés or euphemisms in order to communicate an event as being in the past, although it is not yet in the past for the survivor. Exploring the testimonial response to Bechdel's father's suicide in the graphic novel form, however, presents a unique case study in explicating the impossibility of testimony: what does it mean to convey trauma in a medium that combines the textual with the visual, consequently allowing for a more literal transmission of the experience to the page?

This study explores Alison Bechdel's iconic work through a theoretical lens of the impossibility of testimony, building from the previously mentioned theories of Scarry and Felman and Laub on the topic, but also from more recent studies, such as Jane Robinett's (2007) investigation into the narrative structure of trauma. Bechdel's work is particularly appropriate for a study into representations of traumatic experiences in comics; as the repetitive drive to convey traumatic experiences in literature is frequently due to anxiety surrounding the need to provide an accurate depiction of the experience, Bechdel's dedication to rendering her experiences faithfully is of great significance for this study. Having spent seven years on the project, Bechdel is well-known for her dedication and attention to detail in the work; beyond drawing her family photos as the chapter headings, she created hundreds of "reference shots," or photographs of herself doing the movements she wanted each of the characters to make in the panels to ensure her drawings would be accurate.[1] I use the term faithful here in distinction to the anxiety surrounding what Felman and Laub refer to as the "impossibility of testimony," a concept that emphasizes the difficulty in conveying traumatic experiences in literary form. Faithful, then, is defined as "true to the fact" or "accurate," a definition which has roots in Thomas More's (1529) *Dialogue Heresyes* and continues to be used in this context (OED, "Faithful"). Her commitment to rendering her father faithfully went beyond photographic evidence, with Bechdel acknowledging in a 2006 interview with Hillary Chute that she used the letters between her mother and father, her diaries for references on specific dates, along with the "detective work" (1006) of finding his university transcripts and police record to inform her writing of *Fun Home*. Her research also included rereading many of her father's favorite books, resulting in each of the chapters having a different literary focus, presumably to be able to better understand her father's psyche (Chute 1005).

What this means is that Bechdel's graphic memoir is uniquely situated to overcome the so-called impossibility of testimony; with an anxious commitment to rendering the experiences faithfully resulting in a seven-year project, there is no doubt of her dedication to detail. What is unique about Bechdel's project, however, is that she maintains many of the central components of the narrative structure of trauma that typically would lead to a depiction of the impossibility of testimony without resulting in the traumatic disjuncture inherent in reading narrative examples of the form. My interest is then not in determining the ability of her experiences to have been rendered faithfully into a graphic memoir; instead, I am interested in understanding how the form of a graphic memoir facilitates a faithful testimonial response to trauma while maintaining elements of trauma narratives that typically would support the impossibility of testimony or develop an almost unreal depiction of the traumatic event. Specifically, what elements remain the same in a narrative structure of trauma in the graphic novel, and how does the medium impact a depiction of the impossibility of testimony? I address these questions by analyzing key scenes of trauma in Bechdel's graphic memoir, looking to understand how the integration of both the visual and the textual presents a faithful rendering of a traumatic event.

TRAUMA, THE IMPOSSIBILITY OF TESTIMONY, AND GRAPHIC NOVELS

Broadly speaking, the rise in trauma studies can be divided into two ongoing theoretical areas of debate: work focused on understanding a traumatic experience and work that considers the representation of traumatic experiences in art and literature. The first of these two debates owes a great debt to Freud's *Beyond the Pleasure Principle*, responsible for developing the repetition compulsion, or the compulsion to repeat a traumatic event.[2] Popularized in 1996 by Cathy Caruth in her seminal *Unclaimed Experience,* Caruth connects the Freudian repetition compulsion to contemporary understandings of Post-Traumatic Stress Disorder, or PTSD, which she describes as an "overwhelming experience of sudden or catastrophic events in which the response to the event occurs in the often uncontrolled, repetitive appearances of hallucinations and other intrusive phenomena" (60). It is useful to note that even in the naming of PTSD, trauma is a belated experience; PTSD is, quite literally, the *post*-traumatic stress disorder, a disorder that intends to understand the impact of a traumatic experience on the psyche in its aftermath. In this belatedness, the nature of the traumatic experience is made evident: it is one experienced simultaneously too soon and too late; too soon, in that it is best characterized as "unmasterable stimuli on an unprepared psyche" (Forter 269); too late, in that it is only through the continual repetition of the event that the experience can finally be understood.

This definition of trauma, in which the focus is on the repetition compulsion, has been critiqued in recent years, specifically as it supports the idea that traumatic experiences are viewed as unrepresentable (Cvetkovich 121). This is, perhaps, a misreading of Caruth's work; Caruth's insistence on the repetition compulsion as central to understanding trauma does not imply that the event would be continually repeated without further understanding or without resolution; indeed, Caruth notes the importance of the act of leaving in Freud's articulation of trauma. Freud looks to understand why it is that someone who gets away, or *die Städte verlässt*, quite literally one "leaving the site," experiences the reprisal of traumatic events in much the same way as someone who may have been harmed; in this sense, the act of leaving becomes a departure that, "in the full force of its historicity, remains at the same time in some sense absolutely opaque, [. . .] linked to the sufferer in his attempt to bring the experience to light" (Caruth 23). This is useful in understanding Bechdel's work; the traumatic experience at the center of the text is not her own or even one she witnessed, and so the continual repetition of her father's death is one in which she attempts to understand her relationship with him after his death. In this, the repetition of trauma is not one that is unrepresentable but is instead a repetition that inspires difference; the repetition compulsion can most accurately be understood as "the very attempt to claim one's own survival" (Caruth 66). As Caruth poignantly notes, "if history is to be understood as the history of trauma, it is a history that is experienced as the endless attempt to assume one's survival as one's own" (66).

Survival and trauma, as the two sides of the repetition compulsion, are still, however, difficult to represent. It is perhaps the anxiety over representing these two experiences that results in the epistemological crisis in the memoir. This anxiety of representation gestures toward the other broad category of theory that trauma studies aims to understand, known as the impossibility of testimony. Initially popularized by Elaine Scarry's (1987) *The Body in Pain*, the impossibility of testimony is most associated with Shoshana Felman and Dori Laub's (1992) *Testimony: Crises of Witnessing in Literature, Psychoanalysis, and History*. Felman and Laub define testimony as the act of giving witness, or retelling a traumatic event, with an early passage explicating well how testimony becomes impossible:

> This imperative to tell and to be heard can become itself an all-consuming life task. Yet no amount of telling seems ever to do justice

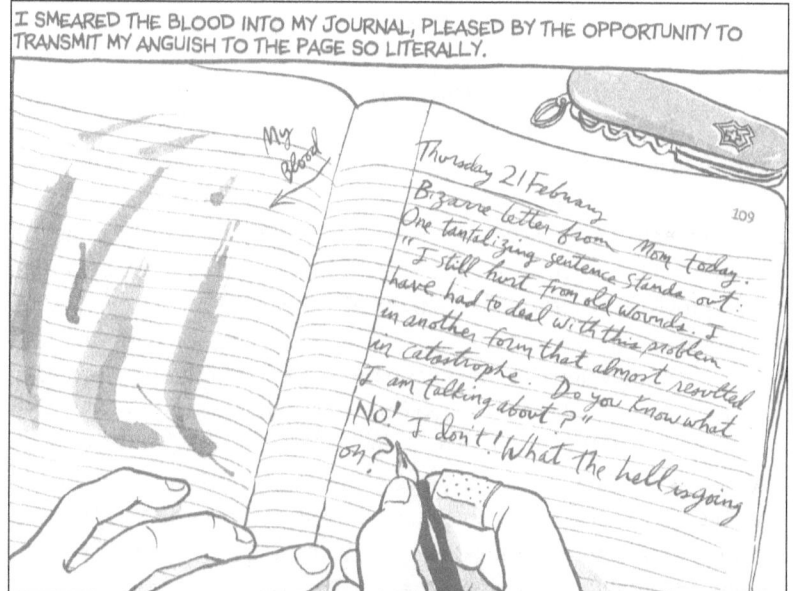

Figure 7.1. Alison Bechdel, *Fun Home*, 78.

to this inner compulsion. There are never enough words or the right words, there is never enough time or the right time, and never enough listening or the right listening to articulate the story that cannot be fully captured in thought, memory and speech. The pressure thus continues unremittingly, and if words are not trustworthy or adequate, the life that is chosen can become the vehicle by which the struggle to tell continues. (58)

Felman and Laub's words, although written fourteen years prior to the publication of Bechdel's *Fun Home*, provide a great insight into Bechdel's process. The book was all-consuming for seven years of her life; part of the length of the project was quite literally the anxiety over finding the right words. Bechdel noted in her interview with Hillary Chute that she needed to learn how to write and that she "struggle[d] to get to a point where [she] trusted [her]self enough to commit things to a page" (1008). And yet, that anxiety reads as honest and genuine; Bechdel's insertions of "I think" and the curvy circumflex signifying her epistemological crisis in the aforementioned chapter on her OCD render what reads like an honest investigation into her relationship with her father.

An early panel in the memoir conveys this well. Accompanied by a drawing of a blood-smeared journal, the caption "I smeared the blood into my journal, pleased by the opportunity to transmit my anguish so literally" (78), given in response to her mother's rejection of her sexuality, is contrasted with a journal entry.[3] "Bizarre letter from Mom today. One tantalizing sentence stands out: 'I still hurt from old wounds. I have had to deal with this problem in another form that almost resulted in catastrophe. Do you know what I am taking about?' No! I don't! What the hell is going on?" (78). The contrast between Alison's blood and her mother's words describing anguish is profound.[4] For past-Alison, smearing the blood from accidentally cutting herself provides an image of the pain she felt at being rejected by her mother; if, following Scarry's articulation, pain is an emotional response without a referent, then, of course, it could not be communicated with words, and so present-Alison, who narrates, emphasizes this with taking pleasure in being able to accurately communicate such an emotion. It is not through words that pain is communicated, she suggests, but instead with an image, in this case, the image of her blood. In contrast, her mother's words, communicating a very real emotive response of pain, confuses past-Alison, who hasn't yet been made aware of her father's sexuality. Instead, all she can interpret from her mother's letter is that her mother is rejecting her sexuality and is unaware that her mother is viewing her coming out as a repetition of her father. Alison's depiction of pain is easier to interpret than her mother's letter, specifically because it is not communicated in words.

This contrast begins to address the impossibility of testimony: words fail when communicating traumatic experiences. Felman and Laub address this concern in their initial articulations of testimony; testimony does not offer "a completed statement, a totalizable account of events" (5), they write. "In the testimony, language is in process and in trial, it does not possess itself as a conclusion, as the constatation of a verdict or the self-transparency of knowledge" (5), later suggesting that testimony will not be understood as a "*statement of*, but rather as a mode of *access to*, truth" (16, emphasis in original). The impossibility of testimony is not meant to imply that it is impossible to give testimony on traumatic events, nor is it meant to imply that the testimony given is false or inaccurate; rather, it simply implies that the words cannot possibly communicate an experience such as trauma, one that could not be assimilated as it was experienced. In this, Felman and Laub's articulation of testimony as a distinctly performative statement rings true; it is through the act of giving testimony that an event can be experienced, processed, and understood. What this means is that Bechdel, in conveying her traumatic experiences in the graphic memoir, is simultaneously experiencing her trauma as she depicts it; if trauma is a belated event that cannot be assimilated as experienced, then the creative depictions of traumatic events can be equally traumatic, resulting in the survivor to process what they have experienced. In other words, when Bechdel draws her anguish, she re-experiences it, and the repetition is one which inspires difference, in which her later insight into her father's life helps her to understand the "old wounds" referenced in her mother's letter. The repetition compulsion, then, is not simply a compulsion to repeat but is instead a compulsion to repeat with a difference, allowing a survivor to understand a traumatic event and gain insight into an experience that could not be assimilated as it occurred.

Later articulations of the impossibility of testimony moved beyond this initial theoretical discussion. Felman and Laub's ideas would remain influential in the years that followed, resulting in a recognition of trauma not as unnarrativizable, but simply as adhering to a different set of narrative conventions—resulting in a traumatic event becoming unrepresentable in a typical narrative structure. Resulting from this was Robinett's discussion of the narrative structure of traumatic experience, in which she investigated variations from typical narrative structures to those more consistent with narratives of trauma. Specifically taking the position that the "fundamental inaccessibility of trauma" developed by Caruth and others fails to explain the narratives that illustrate a close relationship to the writer's lived experience, Robinett suggests that narratives of trauma are representable in a different form (290). Elements of this form, among others, are subtle shifts of tense; repetitive syntax that stalls anticipated narrative moments; fragmentary narrative structures with a linearity that is typically not present in the text as a whole; flatness of tone; unmarked transitions; inclusion of intrusive memories; variations in depictions of time; and, finally, a minute attention to detail that lends an unrealistic sense to the narrative (297, 298, 300, 302). These are elements that are, I'd like to suggest, easily incorporated into a graphic novel due to the unique form characterized by a cross-discursiveness of image and text. What this means is that many of the elements outlined by Robinett would, as she notes, leave "the reader stunned not only at the incidents themselves but also at the recognition of the state out of which the narrator is speaking" (300) can easily be incorporated into the graphic novel form without the degree of traumatic disjunction consistent with Robinett's analysis.

It is in this recognition—that the elements noted by Robinett can easily be included in graphic novels without traumatic disjunction—that Alison Bechdel's *Fun Home* becomes particularly insightful as a memoir of trauma. Although the graphic memoir details much more than just her father's presumed suicide—it is, notably, a coming-out memoir that negotiates her relationship with her father and his complicated past—it continually returns to her father's death, referencing it in every chapter of the text. In her graphic

Figure 7.2. Alison Bechdel, *Fun Home*, 232.

depictions of her father's suicide, the form of the content is able to emphasize many of the elements that would be jarring in the typical narrative form—namely, the shift between tenses, variations in time, fragmentary narrative structures, and minute attention to detail—without detracting from the central narrative, and without emphasizing the traumatic disjunction that Robinett notes in the readers of these stories of trauma.

FUN HOME AND THE FORM OF TRAUMA

Given the centrality of the Freudian repetition compulsion in trauma theory, the role of repetition in *Fun Home* is important to note. The repetition of elements in *Fun Home* is vast; perhaps playing on Bechdel's own childhood obsessive-compulsive disorder, she repeats a number of themes throughout the graphic memoir.[5] In a review of just the first three chapters, for instance, Icarus is repeated three times, the ornate details of the house five times, Camus appears eleven times, and Fitzgerald more than eight. The most visibly repeated element of the memoir, of course, is her father's death; his presumed suicide provides a distinctive narrative framing to the work. The first reference to Bruce's death appears almost nonchalant in manner: "It's true that he didn't kill himself until I was nearly twenty" (23), and the repetitions of his death are vast, either in terms of content matter or visuals, of which the most prominently repeated image is of the truck that killed him.

The visual of the truck is repeated throughout the memoir until its final appearance in the second last panel, which features only a close-up of the truck as Bruce would have seen it had he turned in time to see the vehicle

Figure 7.3. Alison Bechdel, *Fun Home*, 89.

approaching.[6] The contrast between the first, casual reference to his death, given as the caption to a panel that had Alison sitting on her father's lap as a child, driving a riding lawnmower, and this final repetition of the truck is profound. In the first panel, the fact of his death is remarked casually and without pause; it startles the reader, particularly one unaware that the portrait of her father that she has been developing for the first twenty pages is going to end in his early death. In this last panel, although the reader is now well-accustomed to the details of Bruce Bechdel's presumed suicide, it is the figure of the truck that looms forward, giving a sense of an impending death, and the final reference to Icarus hurtling into the sea looms large, emphasizing the affective tense of the panel.[7] The position from which the reader views the image also changes; from looking above at an image of young Alison and her father on the riding lawnmower, the impression is one of an omniscient viewer from on high; in this last panel, the reader takes the place of Bruce in the final moments of his life, staring down a truck about to kill him. If these images represent the repetition compulsion in Bechdel's narrative, they are repetitions that inspire difference, emphasizing the insight that Bechdel has gained in reflecting upon her father's life.

Figure 7.4. Alison Bechdel, *Fun Home*, 120.

Another distinctive moment of repetition is that of the family photo of Bruce cross-dressing in a woman's swimsuit. Initially given at the beginning of chapter four, the family photo makes it unclear that Bruce is the subject of the photograph. Later, repeated on the last page of the chapter, the photograph is clarified to address that Bruce is the subject of the image. The repetition of this image is complex.

The first repetition shown to the reader in the chapter heading is that of the family photo, found in the same box as the memoir's centerfold, an image of Roy, Alison's childhood babysitter, in jockey shorts on a bed, presumed to have been taken by her father. This image has been frequently commented upon in the scholarly literature, typically used as the center of analysis for works on *Fun Home*.[8] Of note in these analyses is Sam McBean's work on seeing in Bechdel's graphic memoir; in his discussion of the centerfold, he focuses on the reproduction of Alison's hand, frequently visible in *Fun Home* when she reproduces family photographs. This, he suggests, "invites the reader to see as Alison sees, to witness her own witnessing of the photographs" (116), later noting that the inclusion of her hand "references Bechdel's hand as the reproducer of the photographs—they are drawn rather than directly inserted into the narrative as photos, reminding readers that we are not seeing the photos themselves but Bechdel's careful and intricate reproductions of them" (117).[9]

McBean's analysis complicates the repetition of the family photo. The initial drawing is itself a repetition, as the second instance of the photo suggests by the inclusion of Alison's hand; the photo itself is recalling the oft-commented-upon centerfold, reminding the reader of Bechdel's own discovery of the picture of Roy, later acknowledged by Bechdel as the spark behind the book, found in the same box as the photo of her father in women's

Figure 7.5. Alison Bechdel, *Fun Home*, 60.

swimwear. In finding the photo about a year after her father's death, she acknowledged a kinship with Bruce, recognizing the similarities between herself and her father as she was coming out as a lesbian. And, finally, the variation between the two images in the memoir—between a simple reproduction as the chapter title and the repetition of the image with the context of knowing the subject to be Bruce and to see Alison's hand holding the photo—addresses once again a repetition which inspires difference, in this scenario, one of knowledge, as her father's private life becomes public with her discovery of the photograph.

Beyond the repetition of compulsion, Jane Robinett details a number of elements of traumatic disjunction that can be found in narratives of trauma. The elements that frequently leave the reader stunned, as Robinett writes, are the variation in time, the sharp shifts between tenses, and the minute attention to detail (300). Bechdel's attention to detail is well-documented and obvious in nearly any panel of the memoir.[10] An early review from Sean Wilsey at the *New York Times* acknowledges that the maps in her memoir are accurate, having taken an odometer reading to confirm that Bechdel's assertion that her father's grave, where he died, her childhood home, and the farm where her father was born were within a mile and a half of each other, giving the declarative statement of "true" in response, enthusiastically acknowledging that *Fun Home* is "a memoir you can navigate by!" (2006). Bechdel, in her interview with Chute, addresses her "mistake" in omitting the photo corners for one of the images (1010) and that she didn't get the wallpaper pattern for the book cover right, having only used five different shades of green, when William Morris's "Chrysanthemums" uses eleven—details that seem laughably insignificant to the reader. But Bechdel's careful attention to detail ensures that elements that would appear out-of-place for typical memories of traumatic experiences—specifying the company brand of the truck that killed her father, for example, or the news headlines the day he died—appear perfectly in line with the rest of the narrative. Considering her development of the details in the Fun Home, she spends a number of panels explaining the interior decoration, along with her father's attention to updating the Victorian home. Panels such as the one outlining the interior decorations of the library are commonplace, and the cross-discursiveness of the text and image allows for significant attention to detail to emerge without appearing out of place. In the description of the library, William Morris's "Chrysanthemum" wallpaper emerges as a squiggly backdrop, identified as a "flocked" wallpaper; the curtains are velvet, Bechdel notes, with an ornate gilt decorating the windows and lamps with busts of Don Quixote and Mephistopheles as their stands. Artwork lines the walls, high-backed chairs are positioned around a coffee table, and a table beside the wall has an open book. A Tiffany lamp sits on her father's mahogany desk, and a mirror is hung opposite the entire scene, reflecting just a corner of the Don Quixote lamp on the side. The cross-discursiveness of an image with text is essential for depicting this level of detail; in a typical memoir without graphic novel elements, such descriptions of place would impede the development of the narrative, resulting in a slow or dragging reading experience. Detailed descriptions of the setting would also lend a level of unreality to a narrative of traumatic events, contributing to arguments supporting the impossibility of testimony. In Bechdel's graphic memoir, it is the cross-discursiveness of text and image that allows this distinct attention to detail to appear natural and perfectly in line with the development of her relationship with her father and his presumed suicide.

Another central element of narratives of trauma is the variation in time. Traumatic events typically are characterized as having a continuous present through the repetition compulsion; in its continual repetition, a traumatic event is unable to be relegated to the past and instead remains in the

Figure 7.6. Alison Bechdel, *Fun Home*, 220.

day-to-day of the individual. This inability to leave the event in the past defies the typical chronological narrative structure, contributing again to the depiction of the impossibility of testimony. In a graphic novel, however, variation in panel size allows for the variation of time consistent with the continuous present inherent in the depiction of traumatic experiences. As McBean argues, the architecture of the page is a space to play with "chronology, sequence, and narrative time" (106). McBean quotes McCloud in suggesting that the "panel is the comic medium's most important icon" by providing an indication that time or space is being divided, later suggesting that the panels be seen as "boxes of time" (105–6). Bechdel, in her drawing process, would begin from a standard page of three tiers, two panels across, but acknowledged in

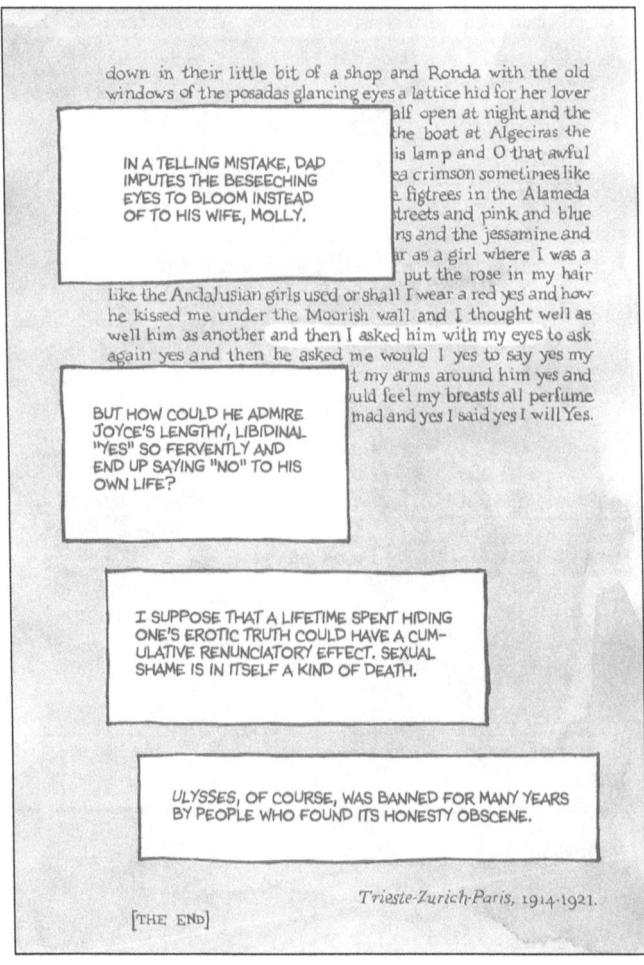

Figure 7.7. Alison Bechdel, *Fun Home*, 228.

her interview with Chute that the page could be broken down in a number of ways (1011), resulting in a varied depiction of time in the memoir. A huge range in variation can be found just within the last chapter of *Fun Home*. About halfway through the chapter is a spread of two pages with twelve panels each (220), a breakdown that cannot be found anywhere else in the memoir.

Michael Kelley looks to film theory to explain the quickening pace of time in these pages: "the design would suggest, in cinematographic terms, a decrease in average shot length, in other words, a quickening pace. This technique is frequently, if not always, used when the action picks up, in a car chase scene, for example. We cannot be sure that Bechdel is looking to speed up the reading process here physically, but the rhetorical choice is poignant: as the action of the entire 24 panels occurs in one car ride, we do feel a building suspense" (48). In these panels, while the pace quickens, time slows down; in comparison, the page that features Alison learning of her father's death only has five panels, covering the phone call of the event, her two minutes of grief with her girlfriend, and the trip home from college (46). To have spent the same page length on a car ride with her father, dividing the page into twelve panels instead of her typical six, quickens the suspense for the reader while letting time slow down, resulting in the variation of the depiction of time consistent with a narrative of trauma.

Of course, it is not just that the formal elements of a panel breakdown can quicken time while simultaneously slowing it down; by experimenting with a full-page panel, Bechdel also forces the reader to slow down and pause, contemplating the text and ideas of the page in more detail. The panel featured to the right appears shortly after the 24-panel spread; in this panel, Bechdel provides a reprinted page from *Ulysses* to note her father's mistake when complimenting her mother's prose: "In a telling mistake, Dad imputes the beseeching eyes to Bloom instead of to his wife, Molly" (228). She provides four text boxes in this panel, implying a development in thought as she considers her father's love for *Ulysses*, looking to reconcile his predilection for Joyce with his decision to commit suicide, suggesting that a lifetime of sexual shame is akin to a kind of death. In the development of these text boxes, Bechdel achieves her goal of not overshadowing the image; the cross-discursiveness of the drawn last page of *Ulysses* with the imposed text boxes ensures that the context of "Joyce's lengthy, libidinal 'Yes'" (220) is still evident—the reader can identify the last few lines of the novel of *Ulysses*, seeing the "yes I said yes I will Yes" beside the text box addressing the theme. By breaking apart the ideas into multiple boxes, there is the implication of a thought in development, one that asks the reader to slow down and think. Whereas the reader can speed through the earlier 24-panel spread quite quickly, this page requires pause, slowing down the tempo of the text.

Finally, the variation in time and the continuous presence of the traumatic event are reinforced by the shifting of tenses that appear in the graphic memoir. Throughout the memoir, there are at least two versions of Alison Bechdel that appear: past-Alison, depicted in the images and diary entries but not in the captions of the panels, and present-Alison, the author and artist behind the graphic memoir, commenting on the events of her childhood with her father. What this means is that without actually shifting tenses, Bechdel is able to provide the variation in tense throughout the work; she attains this through the cross-discursiveness of present-text and past-image that characterize her memoir. This contributes to the variation in time throughout

Figure 7.8. Alison Bechdel, *Fun Home*, 232.

the work, resulting in the ability to cover a huge amount of time in a single page. The last page is an excellent example of this.

The page begins with the aforementioned visual of the truck from her father's point-of-view before his death, which, by the end of the memoir, we know to have occurred when Alison was close to twenty years old; then, the next panel is of past-Alison, jumping into her father's arms in a pool. The caption on the two panels is clearly present-Alison, giving a degree of insight that would only time could provide: "He did hurtle into the sea, of course. But in the tricky reverse narration that impels our entwined stories, he was there to catch me when I leapt" (232). What this means is that three points in Alison's life are represented: her childhood, her father's death in early adulthood, and present-Alison, able to reflect upon her father being there for her, in his own unique way, when she was coming out. The variation in time, here, does not have the same jarring impact of shifting verb tenses, resulting in a diminished traumatic disjunction from the formal element. It is through the cross-discursiveness of the text and image from the graphic novel medium that this can be achieved, much like with the other elements of a narrative of trauma naturalized within Bechdel's memoir.

HURTLING INTO THE SEA: CONCLUSIONS

Past scholarship on *Fun Home*, when addressing the theme of trauma, has focused on the role that the graphic memoir plays in demonstrating witnessing, primarily in relation to Marianne Hirsch's concept of postmemory.[11] Ann Cvetkovich, in an influential article drawing comparisons among Alison Bechdel's *Fun Home*, Art Spiegelman's *Maus*, and Marjane Satrapi's *Persepolis*, explores the role of past-Alison as a child witness to intergenerational trauma. Her focus is on Alison and her father's queerness, looking to place Bruce's past and Alison's coming-out narrative alongside the Stonewall Riots, referenced in *Fun Home* as having occurred between Bruce's time in and Alison's move to New York City. In this, Cvetkovich's conclusion is that Alison adds a queer dimension to the narratives of intergenerational trauma, such as Art Spiegelman's (1980) *Maus*, analyzed by Hirsch; in complicating the story of her father to be neither hero nor victim, Cvetkovich suggests, Bechdel "keeps history indeterminate" (125–26). Cvetkovich comes to an insightful conclusion, looking beyond *Fun Home* in the ending lines of her article: "Perhaps we can look to graphic narrative and other new genres of public feeling that shape personal witness into historical commentary to renew both queer politics and public cultures" (126). Jennifer Lemberg continues this analysis; again, considering Marianne Hirsch's postmemory, Lemberg differs from Cvektovich in her focus on the formal elements of graphic novels, considering the impact of the interplay of image and text in the memoir. While I am less convinced of Lemberg's enthusiastic connections made between Marianne Hirsch and *Fun Home*—indeed, Cvetkovich addresses the main failing in including *Fun Home* into the category of postmemory when addressing that Bechdel had no overt connection with her father, given that he did not tell her about his sexual life—I find Lemberg's conclusion compelling: that *Fun Home* "asserts the value of comics as a medium for bearing witness" (139). I aim to have extended these conclusions, working to specify exactly what value the graphic memoir plays in literary witnessing; specifically, the formal elements of the graphic memoir are able to seamlessly integrate elements of the narrative shape of trauma without the traumatic disjuncture that typically results in an unreal depiction of very real traumatic events, referred to now as the impossibility of testimony. Bechdel integrates variations in time by varying her panel size and by the integration of her past self in panels while her present-self narrates. The minute attention to detail is believable through the cross-discursiveness of image and text, and the repetition compulsion becomes less jarring with the repetition of images instead of just scenes and references. Here, Bechdel's form reinforces its function; if her memoir is one of witnessing, then it is one that achieves its goal through the unique graphic form.

NOTES

1. Although Bechdel herself has recorded many YouTube videos detailing this process, Cynthia Barounis's 2016 article "Alison Bechdel and crip-feminist autobiography" provides a thorough explanation of her attention to detail: "she digitally photograph[ed] herself in every single pose she depicte[d]—props included—before committing the image to paper. Even then, she meticulously scrutinized the drawings for erroneous details and painstakingly corrected them through an elaborate system of erasure and revision" (146). Barounis concludes, quite convincingly, that *Fun Home* "performs the very compulsions that it thematizes" (146).

2. In this work, Freud theorized what would become the fort-da game after watching his grandson throw a toy onto the ground with the expectation that it would be returned to him. The words—fort, or gone, and da, or here—were meant to symbolize the child's most traumatic experience: the loss and return of his mother. This laid the theoretical groundwork for the repetition compulsion, or the compulsion to repeat the traumatic experience.

3. Bechdel depicted her mother's rejection of her lesbian identity in *Fun Home*, an element of the narrative that would later become a focus in her follow-up memoir, *Are You My Mother?* (2012). In the later work, Bechdel's mother would explicitly tell her that she wasn't "comfortable" with Bechdel's lesbianism in a scene during which she critiqued her comic strip, *Dykes to Watch Out For* (228). See Heike Bauer's (2014) "Vital lines drawn from books: difficult feelings in Alison's Bechdel's *Fun Home* and *Are You My Mother?* for a more in-depth analysis of the topic.

4. I use "Alison" to refer to Alison Bechdel, the character in *Fun Home*; Bechdel is used to refer to Alison Bechdel, the graphic memoirist.

5. For a more in-depth discussion of the repetitions within the memoir, see Hélène Tison's "Loss Revision, Translation: Re-Membering the Father's Fragmented Self in Alison Bechdel's Graphic Memoir *Fun Home: A Family Tragicomic*. Tison suggests that the repetitions can be divided into two main modes: a cumulative and recursive mode, in which specific events, scenes, and references are repeated, and a metonymic mode, in which the repetition of a scene or theme is established by association, resulting in themes flowing into each other (346).

6. All images from *Fun Home*.

7. As Sam McBean notes, the narrative repeats the scenes of his death "multiple times to fill out the details, depicting the truck that hit him and the road on which he was killed in many different panels" (105).

8. For example, Hélène Tison uses the centerfold for her 2015 article, and Sam McBean uses the image to create a theory of seeing and of the hand, noting that the image in the centerfold is held in Alison's hand, among others.

9. In the 2006 interview with Hillary Chute, Bechdel acknowledges the image: "In fact the whole story was spawned by a snapshot I found of our old babysitter lying on a hotel bed in his Jockey shorts. This photo was from a vacation when I was eight when Dad took my brothers and me to the beach with our male babysitter in tow. About a year after Dad died, right after I got out of college, I was at home, sort of organizing all my stuff. That's when I ran across this photograph. It was a stunning glimpse into my father's hidden life, this life that was apparently running parallel to our regular everyday existence. And it was particularly compelling to me at the time because I was just coming out myself. I felt this sort of posthumous bond with my father, like I shared this thing with him like we were comrades. I didn't start working on the book then, but over the years that picture persisted in my memory. It's literally the core of the book, the centerfold" (1005–6).

10. For a more in-depth discussion of Bechdel's attention to detail and methodology in drawing *Fun Home*, see Cynthia Barounis's (2016) "Alison Bechdel and crip-feminist autobiography."

11. It is worth noting here that Ann Cvetkovich acknowledges limitations in *Fun Home* working within the concept of postmemory; without access to her father, Alison's second-generation witnessing is from documents and photographs, not familial stories. Jennifer Lemberg, taking up Cvetkovich's initial comparisons between *Fun Home* and *Maus*, as explained through postmemory, develops a much more enthusiastic argument for the graphic memory fitting within this theoretical paradigm.

WORKS CITED

Barounis, Cynthia. "Alison Bechdel and Crip-Feminist Autobiography." *Journal of Modern Literature* 39, no. 4 (2016): 139–61.
Bauer, Heike. "Vital Lines Drawn from Books: Difficult Feelings in Alison Bechdel's *Fun Home* and *Are You My Mother*?" *Journal of Lesbian Studies* 18, no. 3 (2014): 266–81.
Bechdel, Alison. *Are You My Mother?* Boston: Houghton Mifflin Harcourt, 2012.
Bechdel, Alison. *Fun Home: A Family Tragicomic*. Boston: Houghton Mifflin Harcourt, 2007.
Caruth, Cathy. *Unclaimed Experience: Trauma, Narrative, and History*. Baltimore: Johns Hopkins University Press, 2016.
Chute, Hillary L., and Alison Bechdel. "An Interview with Alison Bechdel." *MFS Modern Fiction Studies* 52, no. 4 (2006): 1004–1013.
Cvetkovich, Ann. "Drawing the Archive in Alison Bechdel's *Fun Home*." *Women's Studies Quarterly* 36, no.1/2 (2008): 111–28.
"Faithful, n.5." *OED Online*, Oxford University Press, June 2014. Accessed October 21, 2019.

Felman, Shoshana, and Dori Laub. *Testimony: Crises of Witnessing in Literature, Psychoanalysis, and History*. Taylor & Francis, 1992.

Forter, Greg. "Freud, Faulkner, Caruth: Trauma and the Politics of Literary Form." *Narrative* 15, no. 3 (2007): 259–85.

Freud, Sigmund. *Beyond the Pleasure Principle*, trans. James Strachey. New York: W. W. Norton & Company, 1920.

Kelley, Michael J. "Mirrored discourse in Alison Bechdel's *Fun Home*." *Journal of Graphic Novels and Comics* 5, no. 1 (2014): 42–57.

Lemberg, Jennifer. "Closing the Gap in Alison Bechdel's *Fun Home*." *Women's Studies Quarterly* 36, no. 1/2 (2008): 129–40.

McBean, Sam. "Seeing in Alison Bechdel's *Fun Home*." *Camera Obscura: Feminism, Culture, and Media Studies* 28, no. 3 (84) (2013): 103–23.

Robinett, Jane. "The Narrative Shape of Traumatic Experience." *Literature and Medicine* 26, no. 2 (2007): 290–311.

Scarry, Elaine. *The Body in Pain: The Making and Unmaking of the World*. Oxford: Oxford University Press, 1987.

Tison, Hélène. "Loss, Revision, Translation: Re-Membering the Father's Fragmented Self in Alison Bechdel's Graphic Memoir *Fun Home*: A Family Tragicomic." *Studies in the Novel* 47, no. 3 (2015): 346–64.

Wilsey, Sean. "The Things They Buried." *The New York Times*, June 18, 2006, www.nytimes.com/2006/06/18/books/review/the-things-they-buried.html.

CHAPTER 8

GRAPHIC NOVELS AND SEXUAL TRAUMA
Processing Sexual Trauma Through Creative Expression

LEE OKAN

Comics provide creators with a medium to portray, simultaneously, image and text-based narratives, the interplay of which provides a rich experience for readers. In recent years, graphic novels have become particularly well-suited in exploring personal stories as creators mine their own personal struggles, such as immigration, coming of age, family strife, and trauma (and of particular interest for this chapter, sexual trauma) as catharsis.[1] That catharsis is the processing of emotions, as well as the experience. An expression of pain through any art seeks connection and acknowledgment. In this process of creation, emotions are externalized and can be potentially received by others. In other words, art wants validation and a response. In the context of traumatic experience, the response that is asked of the viewer is one of empathy and compassion.

In trauma narratives portrayed through the graphic novel, it is the interplay of text and image that has the potential to tap into subconscious memory and serve at both individual and collective levels to process traumatic experiences. In this chapter, I explore, more specifically, sexual trauma narratives in graphic novels and such narratives' relationship with memory and catharsis.

An aspect of graphic novels that makes this medium fitting for a subject like sexual trauma is the sense of agency the medium gives the viewer. There is ownership in the reading process of the graphic narrative. As readers can choose to see (or not see), to read (or not read), the graphic narrative engages readers to participate and, through their participation, become a part of the

Figure 8.1. "Chapter 6: At the Bust Stop." Stoian, Maria (2015). *Take it as a Compliment*. Philadelphia: Singing Dragon. Page 29.

narrative. This engagement is in part because of the temporal duration that graphic narrative offers. As the author of *American Born Chinese* (2006), Gene Lang Yuen observes, past, present, and future "sit side by side on the same page [. . .] This means that the rate of information flow is firmly in the hands of the reader" (5:10—5:20). Since graphic narratives have two sources of information—text and image—the reader has agency in the duration of processing and how they process the information from both text and image. As so much of the experience of sexual trauma is about the loss of control, reading such narratives, wherein the visual nature of the text can make such topics more approachable (comic illustrations add universality), and the texts' temporal duration offers multiple entry points for reader engagement.

For the creators, relating a traumatic experience through both a graphic novel gives them ownership in the experience: in memoir or memoir-like narratives where the character represents (or closely represents the artist), the creator can determine the structure of the narrative in terms of text and image, and most importantly, how the story is told. Whether the character of the story is the creator or only resembles the creator, the fictional "space" gives an opportunity for writers to cast off traumatic experiences onto the character to take on, live through, and process. As a narrative, readers can connect to cast off their own traumatic experiences onto these characters. And as a comic narrative, when the images are less vivid or realistic, the figure of the narrative is more universal for others to attach (see Figure 1). Scott McCloud writes in *Understanding Comics*, "The cartoon is a vacuum into which our identity and awareness are pulled ... an empty shell that we inhabit which enables us to travel into another realm. We don't just observe the cartoon, we become it" (36).

Thus, because graphic novels have so much potential for both creators and readers to project experiences, we can become part of an experience. We recognize the narratives portrayed are fiction boundaries, which provide a shelter of control. Thus, even the process of creating graphic novels can be a form of expressive therapy, wherein the creator can use a graphic novel to delve into traumatic experiences in a safe place. According to Dr. Natalie Carlton, art therapist and professor of therapy at Drexel University, the graphic novel lends itself as a medium to examine trauma as its imagery permits connection to a character, "while photos may have more specific associations, with the mixed text and image relationship found in graphic novels, it pushes sensory responses, and pushes a person to better interact with the art and form a more direct conversation with memory experience" (Carlton, interview). It is closure, the process in which part of an image or images are open so that the viewer can fill in the missing information, which allows the viewer to create a unified and continuous reality, and that unified and continuous reality for the reader becomes memory and experience. As closure is a necessary aspect of communication for the medium, it relies on the viewers' investment of imagination. As McCloud claims, "closure in comics fosters an intimacy surpassed only by the written word, a silent, secret contract between creator and audience" (69). Graphic novels are like memories in that they are "polysemiotic," composed of images and words. Golnar Nabizadeh writes in the introduction of *Representation and Memory in Graphic Novels* that "comic panels can perhaps be regarded as sites of remembrance placed within the gutters (the spaces between the panels) as a 'sea of forgetting' or at least of unconscious memory" (4). For the graphic novel, these "spaces between" can help to process memory, process emotions, and an experience of catharsis, a resolution of the pain.

Because these stories are so intimate and relatable, readers may become empathetic with the characters/creator. Regardless of whether the reader has experienced a traumatic experience or not, they now "live through" the experience with the character as they journey through the process. Creators can give voice to their own individual experiences to connect to the community of collective trauma. Memory is a painful experience for victims and part of the long-lasting effects of the trauma. However, as Kelvin Ramirez, art therapist and professor of expressive therapies at Lesley University, observes, by rendering pain through compelling, visual stories, the reader can both understand and process the experience with the creator/character. For both the reader and creator, the experience is a mechanism of release, providing victims who search in the pages for commonalities in experiences, as well as educating others on how to manage traumatic experiences (Ramirez).

Using the works of *Ghost Stories* (Whit Taylor, 2018), *Lighter Than My Shadow* (Katie Green, 2013), and *Becoming Unbecoming* (Una, 2016), this essay will examine how each of the creators explores experiences of sexual trauma as well as how they processed their own personal experiences through creative expression. *Take It as a Compliment* (Maria Stoian, 2016) and *The Courage to Be Me* (Dr. Nina Burrowes, 2018), on the other hand, address sexual trauma not as personal experiences of the authors, but rather as a collective experience. These two graphic novels aim to educate the larger public about support for victims of sexual abuse, as well as begin a discourse on ways to identify abuse and confront it. *The Courage to Be Me* takes a unique approach in that the narrative is not written from the perspective of an abused victim but from the point of view of a therapist (Dr. Nina Borrowes) with the goal of giving the victim's perspective on their recovery process. These two graphic novels move beyond individual pain to address social and cultural trauma, confronting sexual trauma at a public level. It is not enough to resolve this one individual at a time; it is an issue that we all need to comprehend and liberate from its long-kept silence. Through analyzing examples from the graphic novels, the essay will identify connecting themes of sexual trauma, specifically how the graphic novelist uses the medium to delve through their memories to process their personal traumas.

GHOST STORIES, WHIT TAYLOR

Ghost Stories by Whit Taylor is a graphic novel memoir collection. The author's comic self has been granted the chance to meet with three of her dead idols, and each story transitions through a journey of self-discovery. In "Ghost," for instance, the author transverses through past relationships that are examined internally before the character feels that she can move on, spiritually reborn. In the final pages of "Ghost," the author's wish to meet with her idol Marilyn Monroe is instead greeted by her past self. The author hints at sexual trauma by starting her story with, "Who are these idiots that think the Bill Cosby accusers are in it for the money? There's no f*****g money or protection for them! They just wanna be heard!" (47) (see figure 8.2). The following panels sequence the character's evolution over time, looking frazzled, then lethargic, as she processes her experience of trauma, which is not explicitly seen by the reader but at which it is hinted. The author uses temporality to explore how

Figure 8.2. "Ghost." Whit Taylor (2018). *Ghost Stories*. Page 47.

the character transitions through recovery, that recovery which is oftentimes interrupted by a memory of the traumatic experience.

Retelling the story of how and when Taylor's character was abused is not what is important here. Rather, over the next several pages, the reader experiences Taylor's character's examination of her world before and after the assault, "Up until my assault, much of my sense of self was based on what I did or had achieved" (49). As Taylor's character and her past self go for a walk, they discuss the effects she experienced after the assault, of being scared, being alone, and going out into public. She describes the experience as if she "had been traveling for months in [what] felt like no man's land. I felt lost, and I couldn't find you, and I didn't know if I could make it" (48). The "you" used in the quotation refers to herself, Taylor's character. As a result of the trauma, she has lost her sense of self. Taylor uses the temporality to not only explore memory, but the fractured self. Throughout the narrative, the character has conversations with another "self." This fracturing is examined in the layout of the narrative, images that are portrayed without a panel, at times overlapping with one another as they sometimes do to reflect overlapping time. It is only at the end of the story where one "self" says to another, "So yeah, I was thinking that finding meaning in just being is hard as hell, but vital in being, well . . . vital [. . .] I'm not out of the woods yet, but I'm not scared. I—" (62). The character breaks off, and one of the selves disappears, and the character is singular, waving away the ghosts that had visited her.

In the event of a trauma, victims may feel as if they have no sense of self, as if the structures of who they have come undone (RAINN). In "Ghost," Taylor chronicles the journey of post-traumatic stress disorder[2], the ups and downs that follow, of feeling like one can manage one's own life, followed by panic and anxiety. As the reader follows Taylor through her post-traumatic experience, the reader watches the character visit a clinic, "The place you disappear to that you're not supposed to talk about" (63). The character pointedly says, "I've also never felt so alone in my life. People want to support sexual assault survivors but have no clue how to. You see the pained look on their faces when you talk about it, so you just stop mentioning it. You want to get over it for everyone's sake" (63). Taylor addresses both a common sentiment that sexual trauma victims feel as well as directing her commentary in both cultural and societal contexts. Diagnosis of post-traumatic stress disorder by sexual abuse victims often overemphasizes the survivor's role in recovery rather than acknowledging the role that social support can provide (RAINN). Society and culture need to adjust their thinking of how sexually abused victims deal with their trauma and how support can be better provided through the community.

Victims' inability to express an experience of trauma may isolate them from their community, further making them feel as if they are to carry the "burden" of the experience (RAINN). Taylor, however, in "Ghosts," strives to free herself from this burden, as well as other victims, through the retelling of her experience. "Through groups, through meals, and through impromptu chats, I heard stories and shared my own. Because regardless of what you assume, everyone has a story" (64). Art is part of the recovery process for the character, and there is a scene in which the character is part of a group art therapy session. The character is given a postcard and asked to write a story about it, a story which becomes an earlier part of "Ghost" as the character digs through unconnected memories until the memory of her traumatic experience resurfaces. The act of creation becomes the point of release of those memories. The story follows as the character first tries to open herself up to others, finding value in herself through their validation. But it is not enough to overcome the effects of her experiences. The character finds a closed room and cries, "It was the first time I felt safe crying in months," she writes. "I can't say that it completely fixed everything, but perhaps it made me realize, at the end of the day, what mattered most was my humanity" (66).

It is a cathartic release, and the character finds some hope in being, a resolve in who she is, and the experience that has shaped her. The story, obliquely told through Whit Taylor's character, focuses on a story of hope and recovery, managing little by little, day by day, efforts to overcome an experience. Taylor uses temporality to explore memory and self, specifically the fracturing of self because of sexual trauma. It isn't until the third ghost visits that the previous two ghosts and their visits can be comprehended more completely. While the character of Taylor understands the importance of being, and of her own being, and that is very much of a release for her, the story also recognizes the importance of process: while such a cathartic release is essential to the recovery process, it is only part of it.

LIGHTER THAN MY SHADOW, KATIE GREEN

In another graphic novel, *Lighter Than My Shadow*, creator Katie Green tells the story of her personal struggle with anorexia, exacerbated by a sexual trauma she experienced as an adolescent. She begins the graphic novel with a letter to the reader:

> You are holding a book I wish had been there for me [. . .] I wanted to be honest about how hard recovery is, and how long it takes, at the same time proving that it is possible [. . .] I hope that sharing my experience, my choices—good and bad—that I might reach out to someone struggling on their own journey. (1)

After seeking alternative therapy from a healer named Jake, Green's character is at first charmed by Jake's charisma. However, it becomes clear that Jake is using therapy to emotionally abuse Katie's character, and as the graphic novel develops, the emotional abuse becomes physical abuse, which isn't immediately revealed to the reader (Smith and Fitzpatrick). She turns to Jake to help her overcome her issues with anxiety, but Jake takes advantage of her. Jake begins texting her often, conversing with her familiarly, and certainly violating a therapist-patient relationship boundary. Green portrays a scene in which, while conversing with her mother over the phone, she

Figure 8.3. Green, Katie (2013). *Lighter than My Shadow*. Page 277.

simultaneously texts Jake. Green's character responds indignantly to her mother, "He's not trying to push you [her mother] away. I just want a bit more independence... You don't understand" (281). For victims of emotional abuse, as well as those aware of the red flags, the scene is a strong indicator of the relationship the character of Green and Jake have, as well as Jake's dominance over her: pushing away family members and friends, isolating the victim to further assert power.

In another scene, the character of Green has a near-sexual experience with her boyfriend. The boyfriend, Ed, is portrayed as sweet and patient, but as the two begin to engage in intercourse, she breaks down. Instead, the two go to sleep, but she cannot: her mind begins to obsess, throwing her into turmoil. Green portrays this scene—and relative scenes where the character battles internally with herself—as a state of powerlessness. This is visually conveyed to the readers as chaotic scribbles that begin as a small cloud over Green's character, manifesting into a more ominous cloud as she loses control. In these moments, Green portrays the anorexic and bulimic victim's inner conflict to suppress negative feelings, manifesting in the relationship with food (see Figure 8.3). The character is unable to cope and leaves her boyfriend in bed to consume large amounts of food, continuing the cycle of shame, guilt, fear, and anxiety, all like victims of sexual violence (RAINN).

In this scene, the reader does not yet know that Green's anxious relationship with sex—as well as using food consumption and abstention as a coping mechanism—stems from Jake's abusive control over her mind and body. Later in the story, Green's character spends the summer with Jake and his family camping at a festival. The reader senses Jake's deception in the way he expresses to her, "I promise I'll keep you safe" (299). He pressures her to drink a tea made of psychedelic mushrooms. Under the influence of the drug, Jake isolates Green's character and takes her to a tent where he forces himself onto her. Green's character runs out of the tent and into the woods and has an epiphany when she considers that "My whole recovery is based on this . . . on him . . . (313). Overwhelmed by the experience, Green depicts the scene by symbolically burying her experience into the ground while thinking, "This didn't happen. This didn't happen. This. Didn't. Happen" (314–15).

The character's recovery is long and slow, and this release of this trauma becomes first expressed in her eating disorder. Because her symptoms of the sexual trauma manifest in an eating disorder, over time, she has periods of rehabilitation followed by triggering experiences that push her back to anorexia. She finds physicians unable to help her. A doctor once tells her, "We all comfort eat from time to time. I'd take it as a sign of your recovery. At least you're eating, eh?" (359). Without realizing the root of the issue, the doctor further triggers her response to the trauma. Green writes that for several months, she struggled with the memories of the trauma, her eating disorder, and the stress and anxiety from both, culminating in a decision to take her life. She writes:

> The months around that turning point are a muddle in my memory. Looking back, it's easy to think that things changed in that single moment. Certainly, it's more dramatic to tell it that way. Through I don't remember much of when or how. I knew I had to make that decision more than once, more than a few times. In truth it was a process of gently reminding myself, every time I was drawn to the medicine cabinet, to sharp objects or high places: no, this is not what I want. Sometimes the decision came easily, even with laughter: Oh, here we

are again. No, not today thank you. Other times it took every strength I had left. Clutching on, telling myself over and over and over the only things I could hold on to. I want to live. I want to draw. (403)

The story is powerful in that it does not obscure the truth of the trauma. The reader follows the character through the process of recovery: the pain and isolation of finding herself again, and—perhaps a desire that many victims may feel—standing up to their abuser and coming out on top.

What is most intriguing about the story of the character of Katie is that she recognizes her anorexia as a symptom of sexual trauma and begins to process her processes her grief and anger through art; the graphic novel that we read is the author's own process of grief and recovery. Through the symbolic and indirect application of lived experiences, traumatic experiences can be released through art. According to art therapist and Lesley University professor Kelvin Ramirez, there is power in expressive therapy. For instance, in the example of the graphic novel, the medium "in essence, allows for processing of traumatic [experiences]," patients are able to "reflect on [traumatic experiences] with some distance, with the purpose of healing." As a tangible product, the patient can "refer back to what they went through." As such, the graphic novel is "very reflective and dynamic," and for both the patient and the clinician, the graphic novel provides a record or document as a guide to addressing the trauma (Ramirez). As Kathleen Nader writes in *Honoring Differences: Cultural Issues in the Treatment of Trauma and Loss*, "recovery from trauma and loss requires the reconstruction of meaning, the rebuilding of hope, and the sense of empowerment needed to regain control of one's being and life" (xvii). The graphic novel mediates represented life through the symbolic. Wherein, releasing life's experiences into the represented form, we can begin to explore and understand memory in relation to the self and begin.

Green examines in her memoir trauma as a process. Coupled with therapy and support from family and friends, victims can find methods to give compassion to themselves, allowing themselves to not be defined by a moment out of their control. Like the characters in *Ghost Stories*, Green uses the notion of expression in two approaches: 1) There is the act of expression in how Green's character articulates her experience verbally, sharing it with others, which allows her to process and heal; 2) Additionally, Green, like Taylor's character in "Ghost," uses creative expression to manifest trauma, using art as a method to process, to reflect, and to understand experience. In a scene from the graphic novel, Green uses creative expression as an exercise to learn how to be kind to herself. She starts taking art classes at her college, where she learns that creating is not about accuracy or perfection, but as her professor tells her, "You have to let yourself make mistakes if you want to learn from them" (444).

Ramirez recounts that the creative process, as used in expressive therapy, allows the "artist to see the process and to engage in" the experience. The patient can "gain access to content that is very volatile and toxic." Releasing such volatile and toxic experiences into the fictional world contains and allows both creator and viewer to navigate on their own terms. Creative expression can allow victims to feel a sense of empowerment and control, all of which are taken away during a sexual abuse experience (Ferguson 4).

The graphic novel serves as a cathartic release of experiences, not only in the culmination and collaboration of text and image but because, as an artifact, the product of the graphic novel can be used to address traumatic memories, which will allow for reflection. Carlton, an art therapist and artist, examined how she used graphic novels in her practice with patients, as well as for her own personal work; she noted "how my reflecting mind often lags many steps behind the creating body that forms, shapes, and collages shadows into whole obfuscated truths, only made clearer through time and process" (Carlton, personal interview).

Addressing memories abstractly and indirectly through characters on a page, artists, writers, and patients can give up ownership of the experience; in doing so, understanding personal moments of powerlessness can, in turn, reinstate power. As Nabizadeh writes, art and literature, including graphic novels, "hinging as they do on the act of representation, offer an invaluable scaffold through which to explore the theme of memory" (4). The graphic narrative has become the medium in which to explore the traumatized mind because of how it can represent temporality through image and text. The medium works through memory, and as such, memory has become, particularly in the trauma genre of graphic narratives, its subject. In *The Trauma Graphic Novel*, Andrés Romero-Jódar writes that creators who are interested in memory as a subject "delve into the possibilities of the language of comic books and graph novels in order to depict, as realistically as possible, the mental processes happening within a traumatized psyche" (2).

In her graphic novel, Green creates psychological distance from her experiences through the creation of a character version of herself. She observes the symptoms of the trauma (anorexia) outside herself to identify the event of the trauma. Through this process of reflection, she can begin to understand and move through the process of recovery. Like Whit Taylor, Green uses art as an expression of that pain, allowing her to cast off the experience onto a character that can take on the ownership of that trauma. And like Taylor, Green acknowledges that "Things are not perfect," she writes, "but I'm OK with that" (498). Healing is a process; while the graphic novel may be a product of traumatic catharsis, it does not stop but continues with the sharing of her story.

BECOMING UNBECOMING, UNA

Becoming Unbecoming by Una takes another approach to telling the story of sexual trauma. The first page of the narrative opens with an image of a girl carrying what appears to be a heavy burden while climbing a steep hill. *Becoming Unbecoming* is a personal experience that centers on victim-blaming and a more holistic perspective of violence against women within the backdrop of the 1977 Yorkshire Ripper serial murders.[3] Una connects with readers through her personal story, as well as reaches out to a community of victims of sexual abuse.

The creator, Una, begins the narrative by framing the reader on the elements of her early childhood: how her mother had her older sister out of wedlock before marrying and having Una, and how this framed the respectability of her mother and similar women in her position. The illustrations are hauntingly beautiful in black and white (with some touches of other colors now and again). And in other cases, women are drawn like paper dolls, framed singularly in roles that can be intermittently changed: mother, nurse, daughter (see figure 8.4).

Una molds her story around the frame of the Yorkshire murders: while telling her own story of assault, she examines the lives and circumstances of the women who were attacked and/or murdered by the Yorkshire Ripper, using the case as an example of misogyny and victim blaming, which was not only prevalent in the 1970s and 1980s but continues to persist in today's cultural understanding of sexual assault and trauma. She mirrors the accounts of her traumatic experiences, and she reflects, "And still no one knew, or guessed what had happened to me . . . in fact, I didn't know what had happened to me! People didn't talk about adults who use and exploit children. There were some vague warnings about strangers and puppies that weren't much use to me . . . It's become hard to avoid talking about it. But it's still not easy" (37).

She illustrates the results of her trauma: the fear of being alone and obsessive-compulsive symptoms. She writes:

> Something under the bed or in the wardrobe. Soon I took to checking these places every couple of minutes. I had to keep checking because I couldn't trust my own eyes and I couldn't feel safe. When I understood my precautions were inadequate, I started sleeping with a pair

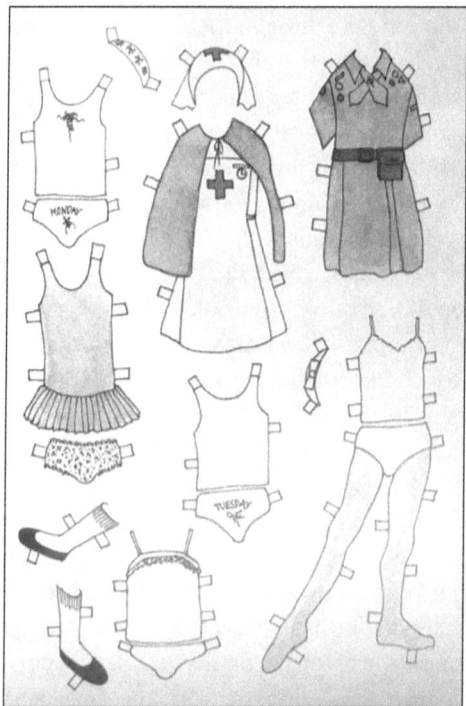

Figure 8.4. *Una* (2016). Becoming Unbecoming. Page 33.

of scissors under my pillow . . . I continued doing this into my early twenties when a boyfriend pointed out it wasn't quite the norm (42).

Throughout the narrative, Una's character is rarely seen with other individuals; she is often depicted alone, or distanced from others, or contrasted from others with the use of shaded coloration. Even more so, Una's character is depicted in the shape of a paper doll: roundish and girl-like, the paper doll theme becomes prevalent, and in some cases, a single page of cut-out clothing separates sections (33). While making her own story universal through the simplicity of the illustration, Una's purpose is to also indicate the various roles women are expected to play, as if shifting between them as easily as changing a paper doll's clothing; her meaning goes much deeper, however, suggesting that just as easily, women must mask the experience they suffer.

The reader experiences the images of assault indirectly from the perspective of Una as a young child. The young child version of Una questions why an adult may say something strange such as " . . . then [he] asked me questions I didn't understand, as he thought I was much older than I was . . .

He practised at soothing me through the shock of what he did next" (44). Una's retrospection layers the text and defines the experiences that she had.

The narrator examines how girls and women are given reputations and how any sexual conduct connotates low morals in the eyes of society. She juxtaposes this to the victims of the Yorkshire murders: "Two of these women were described by police as having loose morals" (62). The narrator then counters obvious victim blaming[4] with "Even if every one of them had been walking down the street stark naked, shouting, 'A tenner to touch my beautiful arse' at the top of her voice, this wouldn't be a reason to attack her—of course" (63). Una examines the word "slut" (a word that appears large and bold in contrast to other content, for example, on page 69) and how it is used to demean women, silence women, shame them, using her graphic novel to explore rape culture and victim blaming.[5] For example, in the case of the Yorkshire Ripper, the victims were often derided by the press as having loose morals; had these women been more righteous, such instances of murder and assault would not have happened to them (64). Una cites a police statement made by the West Yorkshire detective, Jim Hobson, in 1989: "He has made it clear it clear that he hates prostitutes. Many people do . . ." (quoted in Una 68). In a montage of images on the next page: a curvaceous woman, a couple within a heart, Una's character—looking small and girlish beneath different sets of texts which declaim: "Some girls get called sluts because they *won't* give it away! Or Because they only give it to girls," as well as "If you're female and someone wants to show how much they hate you, you're likely to be called a slut or something similar" (69).

How society treated these murder victims' murder manifests in the character so that, when raped, Una finds that she cannot express or even report what has been done to her. Una uses two scenes to capture her experience: the first from a bird's-eye-view, the second in extreme close-ups, and then text. She writes:

> That dull ache . . . raw, breathless horror. My first response was to try to pretend it hadn't happened. It can't have been noticeable—no one noticed anything. I noticed something. A torrent of wretchedness, a great wall of hefty space I had to push through each day . . . every minute. A deafening silence, ringing in my ears as I lurched forward, onward, one foot in front of the other. (88)

Becoming Unbecoming transitions back and forth from the stories of the murders and Una's experience, interjecting, at times, criticisms at society and culture in how it handles sexual abuse and the treatment of women. Visually, and what makes this topic so potent in the medium of the graphic novel, is that just as *Becoming Unbecoming* transitions between Una's experience and the story of the Yorkshire Ripper, Una also visually alternates the narrative between comic illustrations in contrasting black and white (and occasional touches of green, yellow, blue, and red to make more striking and symbolic emphasis) with realistic images, photographs that have been adapted as illustrations, and reproductions of newspaper clippings, or visually represented statistics that give clearer meaning to the figures (114). From abstract to simple comic illustrations, to realistic renderings, Una uses the realistic imagery tactfully to shock the reader with the importance of the information, but also knows when to pull back with more "comic" illustrations to make the information more approachable.

Like Whit Taylor, Una does not confine her narrative to frames or panels, and this allows her to transition nimbly from simpler drawings to more realistic images. However, what is most striking about how Una delivers the narrative is that text can function in tandem with the images. For example, on page 125, in an image depicting from above a figure rowing a boat, Una writes, "Then there is the ocean of sexual crime that goes unreported." The "ocean" is depicted with numbers in blue to represent the enormity of unreported sexual assaults, becoming at once text and image. Una uses the shifts between the styles of how images are drawn, from realistic to simple, the dynamic between text and image, and the contrasts between black and white and color to demand attention to the issues she is presenting.

While Una uses her experience as an avenue to broach the deeper issue at hand with regard to sexual trauma, she begins to narrow her focus on trauma itself and support. "Trauma is not easy to deal with, even when support is available. Unfortunately, a lack of support from family and community can worsen the effects of trauma" (108). She describes her process of the experience using therapy and drugs:

> There were many wasted days . . . unable to focus . . . or to stay calm . . . small inconveniences left me beside myself with frustration and despair. In between times I functioned well enough to keep plodding on, one foot in front of the other . . . But occasionally I'd find myself standing on the edge of the platform, thinking. There were times I was so crippled with anxiety and panic, I just had to lie on the floor . . . There were days I only felt ok if I was submerged in water, in the bath . . . (111)

In *Becoming Unbecoming* Una dissects her process of healing as a means to broaden her message to not just how victims process trauma but the lack of support, especially in light of a culture and social system that continues to victim blame, as if to ask: how can a victim even begin to process trauma when our systems inherently fail to support victims of sexual trauma? With the backdrop of the Yorkshire serial murders, Una sets the tone for the progress women have achieved in breaking the silence, and yet, she also notes the continued need for support. While movements like Time's Up[6] and #metoo[7] have ushered in a new wave of feminism that encourages women to speak up and out against sexual assault, she writes, " . . . Despite much work towards improvements to the criminal justice system, some judges and jury members still need persuading that rape and sexual assault are not trivial issues that are at least partly the woman's fault. This attitude infects the system and leads to many acquittals" (Una 123). Because the justice system—worldwide—does not usually advocate for the rights of women or the rights of sexual abuse victims, it further perpetuates behavior of abuse (131). Moreover, because of the confusion about sex, consent, and what constitutes sexual assault allows for predators to continue their behavior, and unfortunately, to get away with it. Una later counters that "There's no doubt that we need a reliable system of justice, but we can't blame the justice system for the things it thinks and does if it just thinks and does the same things as everyone else" (167).

In her graphic novel, Una tackles the hostility that often silences women: shame, isolation, disbelief, ridicule. While the Internet has allowed for anonymity that may intensify misogynistic behavior, "it's also easier for women to find each other and give support. Sharing experiences on the web means we can organise against the silence, the shame, the dismissal . . . so the digital revolution is a solution as well as the problem" (117). By comparing the 1970s and now, Una observes how far women's rights have come and the gaps that need to be addressed. Una writes:

> It's good to talk, but action is better. In the UK and around the world, the bulk of this work is done by groups of women, who scrape together the funds and goodwill to run rape crisis cent[res], refugees and advocacy services. They have to fight to be funded but they still manage to consistently provide much-need access to justice, along with practical and emotional support. (131)

She points out how women have for so long been objects of sexual desire rather than viewed as autonomous beings with human desires and needs. The inability of society to promote women as such, and moreover, to examine sexual consent—especially to define it within legal terms—makes it even murkier for women to understand their rights and to feel confident in making their voices heard.

Victims of abuse—a majority of whom are women—find it difficult to discuss the experience. They suffer not only from fear of castigation by peers, colleagues, and family members but also the fear of revealing that they were victims of sexual abuse, a stigma that traces deep into cultural and societal norms. It can seem impossible to be first listened to and then believed. It is only when many victims can come together that steps to a resolution seem possible. Una cites examples of Jimmy Saville and Bill Cosby, like Whit Taylor. "The culture within which all of this was possible relied on silence . . . relied on shame . . . The truth is awful but we must all learn to leave with it" (130).

Just like Whit Taylor points out in *Ghost Stories*, Una too acknowledges that most rape crisis centers and resources that have been created by groups of women are largely underfunded. She cites how, after an assault, most women and girls cannot rely on their own families for support, "Appropriate support after being attacked reduces trauma and helps victims of violent crime to recover, so funding women's services properly would save money in the long run" (131). Una discusses her own recovery and acknowledges that therapy never accommodated her process. "Some people use humour as a defense mechanism," she writes, "It strikes me as odd that under those circumstances they felt a need to direct me to take my experiences more seriously. Surely mental health professionals realise how serious humour can be?" (139).

Like Katie Green's *Lighter Than My Shadow*, Una's idea coincides with using expression as therapy and connects to the use of graphic novels and comics in their treatment of serious themes and topics. Knowing the gravity of the topic, Una transitions back and forth in her narrative, telling her personal story of abuse, the story of the Yorkshire Ripper, and focusing on the victims, as well as revealing startling statistics around the world and the UK. The structure of the graphic novel is like a memory, swirling and shifting between her childhood memories, recounting the story of the Yorkshire serial killer, and elevating the two together to comment on misogyny and explore how sexual trauma is handled by both the victim and society. In sparse black-and-white imagery, which includes representations of herself (as a paper doll figure), Una uses text as part of the image, playing with the structure of the layout to depict a victim's isolation. Through the dearth of text in several potent layouts, Una makes an overwhelming critique of society in their failings to serve sexual abuse victims. The most compelling scenes of the narrative are in its final pages when Una draws each of the murdered victims of the Yorkshire Ripper, "Thirteen women lost their lives to one man while I was growing up. There is no memorial to them. They exist only in the memories of their loved ones . . . I wonder what they would be doing now?" (Una 171). A series of full-body portraits follow, depicting the women almost fifty years later after their murders, living seemingly normal, happy lives as women they could have been. The images, in black and white, and a faint background sketched in blue, and each portrait spans two pages. Throughout the graphic novel, the viewer has been bombarded with textual information, yet in these final pages, there is no text. We confront the faces of these women as Una imagines they might be fifty years later if they had survived. Again, Una is using contrast, which before had been so concentrated visually through black and white imagery or realistic versus "comic" illustration, but now becomes concentrated in the absence of text, just as we feel the absence of these individuals. The power of the images and the lack of text culminates in the final point Una strives to make: these are the lives lost, these are the lives that can be saved. Depicted as these victims are doing mundane things like washing windows, holding a baby, cooking, walking a dog, etc., we see faces that could be our friends, our family, our neighbors, ourselves. With each flip of the page, the reader has an intimate moment with each woman, reflecting on their loss and the awful cause that prematurely ended their lives (171–99).

The balance of the themes is held in the images: simplified, revealing only what needs to be shown, while the text itself is conversational: the creator makes the subject manageable for the reader. And although at times intense, Una moves the viewer back and forth through her memory and reported statistics and news, transitioning from simple to realistic images; our cathartic moment as readers is in those last few pages when we come to understand this issue more completely. This issue is important, Una seems to say, because it affects us all.

COMIC THERAPY

As with *Ghost Stories* and *Becoming Unbecoming*, the creators suggest that giving voice to the issues of sexual violence and abuse can help victims process their experiences. Writing, reading, and illustrating graphic novels can be used successfully to help victims of sexual abuse through comic therapy (Carlton and Ramirez, personal interview). Graphic novel creators can push boundaries, using layout as an organizing principle in processing their emotions and memories (Carlton 3). As such, image and text are key ingredients in processing trauma because of the symbolic and temporal nature of image

Figure 8.5. "I should know better." Stoian, Maria (2015). *Take It as a Compliment*. Page 51.

and text; creators and readers alike can address memories on their terms, thus re-establishing control and self-empowerment.

Creator Maria Stoian wrote *Take It as a Compliment* as a collection of stories (based on anonymous online submissions) to give perspective to different accounts of abuse. She writes, "It is both distressing (that these stories are so common) and provides hope that in sharing, we can make it easier for survivors to deal with their experiences and create a society that does not tolerate sexual violence" (94). At the end of the collection, she provides useful information to both survivors and what others can do to support survivors:

> Listen to what survivors have to say. It's often difficult to discuss, so be patient and attentive. Do not be dismissive of their experiences. Survivors' stories are too often unheard and unbelieved, and this keeps people from speaking out. Survivors can feel safe to talk about their experiences, whether they are seeking comfort or justice, and this starts with one pair of ears at a time. (95)

The role of *Take It as a Compliment* is as much a graphic novel for other victims to relate to as it is for others to learn how to respond to victims, as well as stand up against abusers. Stoian's collection ranges from stories of child abuse to adult abuse, domestic abuse, and public harassment and includes stories told from the female and male perspective and heterosexual and homosexual relationships. Each story is told in a different artistic style to illuminate the unique voice of the story and give emphasis to the individual and the story. This is important to note, as each vignette was based on actual interviews.

As the book provides actionable recommendations to survivors and their supports, the book positions itself as a beginning point for discussions about forms of sexual assault, how it can be both nonconsensual verbal, or physical, and emotional abuse. The diversity of the experiences gives breadth of relativity for the reader, as well as highlights that sexual abuse is not only limited to women but can affect anyone. Several stories note systematic factors that are somewhat responsible for these situations, such as gaslighting, objectification, apathy, and poorly educating people on how to be aware of abuse and what to do when confronted with it. Readers can point to an image or refer to a story as a shared experience, as well as use the graphic novel to facilitate discussions on sexual trauma.

Using the graphic novel as its medium, *Take It as a Compliment*, alternates between a free-flowing layout style (absent of frames and panels) to the more traditional frames and panel layout. Some stories use black-and-white coloring, while others are quite colorful or fall somewhere in between. While the artistic stylings vary, the focus is clearly on the protagonists of the story, and all imagery is in a "comic" or "cartoonish" style—the lack of realism in the nature of the illustrations, as noted before, removes the images from reality to place them firmly in fiction. This has two outcomes: 1) the images and the characters are more "universal," meaning we as readers can project ourselves onto the characters and their experiences; 2) while these stories may be based on actual accounts, rendered as they are in this graphic novel, we can situate them in the secure boundaries of fiction. The consequence of this for viewers is that we feel safe approaching these topics because we are not immersed in the actual reality. *Take It as a Compliment* opens us up to this topic and serves to release this topic from silence into a more open cultural and social dialogue.

While *Take It as a Compliment* serves to examine the spectrum of sexual assault and trauma as a means to broaden the conversation around these topics, another contemporary graphic novel, *The Courage to be Me*, was created with the purpose of helping victims. The graphic novel began as a free online work created by Dr. Nina Burrowes, a London-based psychologist interested in helping people understand cases of sexual exploitation, harassment, assault, rape, and domestic abuse. On her website, she writes: "This book has been posted on my website in full for free for the person who can't afford to buy it; for the person who is still living in an abusive relationship and is too afraid to have a book on abuse in their home; and for the person who simply isn't ready to walk into a bookshop and buy a book like this" (Burrows, *The Courage to be Me: Why is this book available online for free?*).

The narrative, illustrated by five comic creators—including Dr. Burrowes herself, as well as Katie Green, author of *Lighter Than My Shadow*—navigates stories of sexual abuse and trauma, much like *Take It as a Compliment*: however, with the added professional approach and perspective of Dr. Burrowes. She writes: "... The book only tells the story of *beginning* to rebuild your life after abuse. Life after abuse *can* be wonderful—but it's a long journey. There are no easy solutions in this book..." (Burrows 5). With the knowledge that a victim of abuse may be reading her book, Dr. Burrowes suggests that the reader consider if this is the right time to be reading the book, suggesting that they may be triggered by any of the stories in the graphic novel, it may not yet be the best time for them to read it. She further suggests that the reader take their time in reading and processing the information of the book, as well as finding a space that feels safe to read the book. Throughout the narrative, cats will often appear, and Dr. Burrowes reminds the reader that "When you see a cat it's a reminder to take a break if you need it" (8). While many graphic novels that touch upon themes of sexual abuse and trauma are from the perspective of the victim, *Courage to be Me* takes the perspective of the therapist, her experiences in working with patients to process their experiences and move towards recovery, as well as her insights and advice to other victims.

Dr. Burrowes infuses the narrative, not only with her perspective as a professional and the stories of her patients (not based on any single individual), but also explains why victims, after assault, react on a neurological and biological level. She explains how when encountering a dangerous situation, most human responses are fight, flight, and freeze. While most people would like to think that they might fight or flee a situation, it is more likely that a person will freeze (38–41). "My instinctive brain knows that as a human being I am weaker and slower than my natural predators ... I'm even less likely to fight or run away from someone I trust ..." (42–43). She addresses victim's sense of guilt, inability to process emotions and thoughts, and shame, and how they can manage their feelings to move on with their lives.

One chapter of the graphic novel, "Along Came Hope," captures through metaphor how victims can feel both in control and out of control simultaneously, expending enormous efforts to bottle up and silence emotions. The artist Jade Sarson depicts a character on a sailboat on a wide ocean, alone and clutching jars that hold symbols of her memory. The character narrates that compartmentalizing her pain was "a way of containing my past. Containing my pain" (89). As the story continues, the character navigates a storm, and, in the process, goes overboard with her jars of memories. She reboards her boat, and the storm dissipates, and she opens the jars, a symbolic representation of her process of vocalizing and sharing her experiences with others. The character learns, rather than containing her past to herself, by confronting her past and sharing it in group therapy; she was able to learn how to manage her experiences and move on towards her future.

The titular chapter, "The Courage to be Me," illustrated by Katie Green, tells the story of a character reflecting on the journey she took towards recovery, as well as acceptance and compassion for herself. She analyzes how, because of the trauma, she felt herself schism, losing a sense of her former self before the trauma. Yet, she is still and has always been that person. The chapter emphasizes that regardless of the experience, like sexual violence, victims still have the free will to decide who they want to be. "But there is more to me than my past. I'm the woman who experienced something horrible . . . who still carries it with her. But I want to be so much more than that (122–23).

While the focus of the narrative primarily illustrated the perspective of sexual abuse victims and a therapist, Dr. Burrowes concludes the narrative by acknowledging volunteers and charity organizers who support and run groups for victims of sexual abuse. She recognizes, just like Una mentions in *Becoming Unbecoming,* that trauma abuse clinics and organizations are severely underfunded financially and with staff. In "Kim: Epilogue," Dr. Burrowes urges readers to support local organizations and charities, pointing out that because of the lack of resources, organizations are paralyzed to adequately provide resources. As the artist, Dr. Burrowes draws simply and clearly, using black and white to create a sharp contrast between images and the sparsity of the text. Rather than portraying her narration as a disembodied voice, Dr. Burrowes portrays herself, often in a long-shot format; the impression is that behind the advice of the narrative, there is an actual person that the reader can identify with.

As much as giving "voice" to the traumatic experience through shared support groups or therapy, alternatively, creative expression can provide an outlet to articulate emotions or thoughts that may not yet have words for victims of sexual abuse. It can be a struggle to find the right words to express painful thoughts, as much as it can be a struggle to articulate an experience the victim may not want to acknowledge having. Visual expression can be used to tap into those emotions. Because art creation can be a solitary endeavor, it may also afford victims the opportunity to reflect and meditate on their experiences first by themselves before reaching out to a larger community. In its own way, creative expression can "speak" for the victim when they are not yet ready to share, as well as "speak" for them through "alter egos" or alternative personalities that can take over ownership of the experience. Creators (and readers) can cast trauma onto characters in a fictionalized world—which, as a fictionalized world, invites a sense of control—to mitigate the negative emotions of the real traumatizing experience.

The Courage to Be Me is novel in its approach because it serves as an illustrated self-help book for victims. The therapy is accessible through the narratives combined with the images, which, again, because of their "comic" style, make the topic more approachable. As McCloud writes, "by de-emphasizing the appearance of the physical world in favor of the idea of form, the cartoon places itself in the world of concepts" (41). This is to mean that while our means of approaching this topic might appear "softer," culling from our familiarity with cartoons as comics as children, the message behind the stories and images is no less potent. Moreover, Dr. Burrowes is likely aware of and uses "viewer-identification" through the imagery to connect with viewers of the graphic novel (McCloud 59). Images demand our participation "to make them work. There is no life here except that which you give to it," as McCloud writes (59). Our participation with comics, what we fill in the "spaces between," is filled with what we ourselves project into the comic from our memories.

Many of the creators, like Katie Green and Whit Taylor, comment on how they felt an "otherness" after their traumatic experience, a separation of self. What victims face, however, is the deterioration of their ability to communicate with others because the experience now divides who they are and how they interact with others (RAINN). Creative expression can assist in re-establishing that sense of connection through public displays or performances, which attribute a sense of empowerment to the survivor (Hennig).

As the graphic novels in this essay explore, creative expression can provide cohesion and insight, as well as a cathartic release from the experiences. Perhaps what graphic novels can do—because we are invited, at a foundational level of this medium, to participate, either through viewer-identification with characters or through the projection of our memories in the "spaces between," and especially with regards to the sexual trauma—is to help viewers "re-unite" with themselves, much as Whit Taylor's character does in "Ghosts." Through the graphic novel medium, these sexual trauma narratives can become part of and projections of our memories; with two sources of information working complementarily, or like Una's *Becoming Unbecoming*, contrastingly, the narratives can tap into us and compel an emotional release, at an individual or collective level.

CONCLUSION

Expression through art, in the context of graphic novel and comic creation, affords the creator and the reader an indirectness to the subject matter so that it can be more accessible and more manageable than reality. The simulation of reality, by representing real experiences in the fictional world, creates boundaries around our subjects that enable us to approach difficult subjects more easily. By casting off these experiences to characters, creators and readers give the characters ownership of their roles as victims so that they no longer carry them on their own. Victims of sexual abuse have been silent, needlessly, for so long. The collective voices of these creators' resonant themes that have already emerged in research on victims of sexual abuse (Ramirez, personal interview). Using image and text, an artifact exists for both creator, clinician, and reader, which explores the effects of trauma with the purpose and intent of spreading a message of healing. When these difficult narratives can be shared together, the trauma itself can be shared; these stories are important because of their power to create community (Carlton, personal interview).

The creators' portrayal in the graphic novel and comic form can give perspective to many different experiences and provide an opportunity to explore other solutions. In each graphic novel and comic reviewed, the current methods of recovery have been criticized as inefficient, and yet, each creator provides hope that in expressing, in voicing, and naming the trauma, a cathartic release can be found.

NOTES

1. See *The Trauma Graphic Novel* by Andrés Romero-Jódar (2017), who analyzes the rise of the trauma genre within the graphic novel in Western culture. For example, in *Maus* by Art Spiegelman (1991), Spiegelman explores the relationship between father and son within the context of a larger narrative about his father's experience during the Holocaust (Spiegelman). Spiegelman made use of psychological distance from the reality of the subject through the medium of the graphic novel. His characters do not look like their real human depictions but rather as anthropomorphized animals, like pigs, frogs, cats, and mice.

2. Post-traumatic stress disorder is "a disorder that develops in some people who have experienced a shocking, scary, or dangerous event" (National Institute of Mental Health). For more information about post-traumatic stress disorder, see the National Institute of Mental Health.

3. The Yorkshire Ripper, Peter Sutcliffe, murdered thirteen women between 1975 and 1980 in Northern England. Of the women murdered, seven were sex workers; he also attacked eight other women who survived. The case has become infamous for its victim blaming in the press, as well as the associated misogyny and failures of the police.

4. Victim blaming (or victim shaming) occurs when the victim of a violent scenario is questioned about what they could have done to avoid the crime committed against them rather than questioning the perpetrator. Victim blaming shifts the focus and the fault of the assault from the person who committed the act to the survivor.

5. Rape culture refers to stereotyped or false beliefs that trivialize sexual violence and in which sexual violence against women is normalized and excused in popular culture and the media.

6. Time's Up is a social welfare organization that addresses changes in company policies and laws "to increase women's safety, equity, and power at work" (Time's Up Now).

7. #metoo is an organization that addresses sexual assault and raises awareness on the dialogue of survivor healing. The movement went viral with the hashtag #metoo in October 2017, following the Harvey Weinstein, a Hollywood producer, sex scandal (Me Too Movement).

WORKS CITED

Burrowes, Nina. *The Courage to be Me*. London: NB Research Ltd., 2014.
Burrowes, Nina. *The Courage to be Me: Why is this book available online for free?*, Nina Burrowes, 2018, https://ninaburrowes.com/books/the-courage-to-beme/preface/. Accessed May 28, 2019.
Carlton, Natalie. Personal interview. October 23, 2019.
Carlton, Natalie. "Chapter 7: Illustrating Stories: Using Graphic Novels in Art Therapy Research and Practice." *Psychology's New Design Science and the Reflective Practitioner*, ed. S. Imholz and J. Sachter. River Bend, NC: LibraLab Press, 2018, 110–29.
Chute, Hillary. *Why Comics? From Underground to Everywhere*. New York: Harper Collins, 2017.
Ferguson, Cherie. *Art Therapy for Adult Survivors of Child Sexual Abuse*. California State University, San Bernardino, 2014. CSUSB ScholarWorks, https://pdfs.semanticscholar.org/da6a/d8a7687c52f76e4381abb47be3a422275e2d.pdf. Accessed May 25, 2019.
Green, Katie. *Lighter Than My Shadow*. China: Jonathan Cape, 2013.
Hennig, Christine. "Art Therapy Benefits for Sexually Abused Adults." Resources. *Art Therapy*. 2004. http://www.arttherapyblog.com/sexual-abuse/benefits-for-sexually-abused-adult-survivors/#.XPFUOy2ZNN0. Accessed May 25, 2019.
Johnson, David Read. "The role of the creative arts therapies in the diagnosis and treatment of psychological trauma." *The Arts in Psychotherapy* 14 (1987): 7–13. https://www.sciencedirect.com/sdfe/pdf/download/eid/1-s2.0-019745568790030X/first-page-pdf. Accessed May 25, 2019.
Laub, Dori, and Daniel Podell. "Art and trauma." *International Journal of Psychoanalysis*, 76 (1995): 991–1005. https://pep-web.org/browse/document/IJP.076.0991A. Accessed May 25, 2019.
Me Too Movement. "About: History and Vision, Me Too Movement," https://metoomvmt.org/about/#history. Accessed October 25, 2019.
Nabizadeh, Golnar. *Representation and Memory in Graphic Novels*. New York: Routledge, 2019.

Nader, Kathleen. *Honoring Differences: Cultural Issues in the Treatment of Trauma and Loss*, ed. Nancy Dubrow and Hudnall B. Stamm. London: Brunner/Mazel, 1999.

National Institute of Mental Health. "Post-Traumatic Stress Disorder." National Institute of Mental Health, 2019. https://www.nimh.nih.gov/health/topics/post-traumatic-stress-disorder-ptsd/index.shtml. Accessed October 15, 2019.

RAINN. "National Resources for Sexual Assault Survivors and their Loved Ones." Rape, Abuse & Incest National Network. https://www.rainn.org/national-resources-sexual-assault-survivors-and-their-loved-ones. Accessed May 25, 2019.

Ramirez, Kelvin. Personal interview. Accessed October 2, 2019.

Romero-Jódar, Andrés. *The Trauma Graphic Novel*. New York: Routledge, 2017.

Smith, David, and Marilyn Fitzpatrick. "Patient–Therapist Boundary Issues: An Integrative Review of Theory and Research." *Professional Psychology: Research and Practice* 26, no. 5 (1995): 499–506.

Spiegelman, Art. *Maus*. New York: Pantheon Books, 1991.

Stoian, Maria. *Take It as a Compliment*. London: Singing Dragon, 2016.

Taylor, Whit. *Ghost Stories*. Greenbelt: Rosarium Publishing, 2018.

Time's Up Now. "About TIME'S UP," https://www.timesupnow.com/about_times_up. Accessed October 25, 2019.

Una. *Becoming Unbecoming*. Vancouver: Arsenal Pulp Press, 2016.

Unnamed Student Work. Simmons University, Comm120: Digital Media and Communications, Spring 2019.

Wattis, Louise. "Revisiting the Yorkshire Ripper Murders: Interrogating Gender Violence, Sex Work, and Justice." *Feminist Criminology* 12, no. 1 (2017): 3–21.

Yuan, Nicole P., Koss, Mary P., and Stone, Mirto. "The Psychological Consequences of Sexual Trauma." *VAWnet*, March 2016, https://vawnet.org/material/psychological-consequences-sexual-trauma. Accessed May 25, 2019.

Yuen, Gene Luen. "Comics belong in the classroom." *YouTube*, uploaded by TED June 15, 2018. https://www.youtube.com/watch?v=xjvTIP7pV2o. Accessed December 31, 2021.

CHAPTER 9

THE GOOD EMPTY

Trauma, Displacement, and Catharsis in *Sabrina*

RUSSELL SAMOLSKY

ANTICIPATORY ANXIETY

Sabrina (2018), by American comics artist Nick Drnaso, begins with a disquieting image that flashes forward to what we will retrospectively come to grasp as the ghastly moment of a murderous attack on a young woman. We are immediately confronted with Sabrina knocked backward, her neck exposed, her mouth caught in a grim rictus, and her hand desperately pushing out beyond the frame of the page to ward off the attack. Just as disquieting as the image itself, however, is the fact that we readers are placed in the same position as the murderer. Beginning with this excerpted image, as it were, *Sabrina* both signals, from the start, that we will not escape traumatic implications in the address of this graphic novel and sets up anticipatory anxiety for what is to come. This is not to say that we know how this story will unfold; what is unsettling, indeed, downright unnerving, about reading *Sabrina* is precisely the dislocating turns that the text takes. But while *Sabrina* is concerned with disclosing the nature of Sabrina's murder, the plot of the text is more concerned with the traumatic consequences of its aftermath and the reverberating effects on Sabrina's sister and her boyfriend, who has fled to Colorado Springs to seek refuge with his childhood friend, Calvin. Rather than deploying the technique of flashback that belatedly reveals blocked or repressed traumatic memories, *Sabrina* engages in a flashing forward or anticipatory anxiety that will come to consume the protagonists.

In order to take account of this anticipatory anxiety, I will analyze the complex economy of traumatic displacement in *Sabrina* that takes place by means of *ironic literalization*—that is, the way in which speech (a remark or conversation) comes to be ironically actualized or embodied as the story progresses. Further, I shall examine the way in which this circulation of trauma takes effect as a performative set of exchanges between the material and media worlds of this graphic text. One possible release from a pullulating and all-consuming trauma that *Sabrina* seems to invoke is nature and the world of animals. Does nature, I ask, offer some respite, or are animals similarly trapped in the traumatic exchanges or economy of this text? What is extraordinary about *Sabrina* is the degree to which its readers are also captivated by anticipatory anxiety, the way in which we readers are inducted into a paranoid mindset that mirrors that of the protagonists. I shall examine, then, whether we and each of the protagonists are unresolvedly caught in its agitated time and space of trauma or if *Sabrina* allows for some way out, some way of working through, and how this equates with catharsis. In literally staging this graphic novel on a knife edge, does *Drnaso* risk a paranoid force taking over this story, replicating itself, leading to a ramifying beyond the author's design, thus becoming, in a bad ironic way, an instance of the very thing it seeks to critique?

The first person to question the ethics behind what he had created was Drnaso himself. In a profile on the artist entitled "American Graphic," D. T. Max discovered how Drnaso came to write *Sabrina* and his struggle with releasing it into the world. *Sabrina*, Drnaso revealed, was born of his profound anxiety over how emotionally dependent he had become on his girlfriend and his fear of something dreadful happening to her. From its inception, then, *Sabrina* emerged from and engaged in an economy of displacement. In an attempt to sublimate those fears, but perhaps also to ward off this horror, Drnaso began working on this graphic novel. As readers of *Sabrina* might suspect, Drnaso drew upon his own viewing of grotesque incidents on video and the internet. He was particularly influenced by videos Elliot Rodger had recorded before committing a massacre near the University of California, Santa Barbara, and was struck by his morbid curiosity at wanting to know more about the life of this perpetrator rather than those who simply fell victim. Rodger would provide one "real life" source for Tim Yancey, Sabrina's murderer. Just as he was prepared to send off the manuscript of "Sabrina," Max tells us, Drnaso bethought himself and decided against publishing. Trump had become president and this colored Drnaso's view of his own comic. He worried about the depraved aspects of his graphic text, and he was particularly troubled by a set of pages in which a men's rights activist raves about wrongs done him and then, in a disassociated manner, stabs Sabrina to death. As Max reports:

> He wondered if reading these pages would be any different from going online and watching an ISIS murder video or, as he had once done, looking at forensic photograph of Jeffrey Dahmer's apartment. As a teen-ager, he had watched "Faces of Death"—a video compilation of beheadings and electrocutions at a friend's house, and he had never forgotten it. Now with "Sabrina," he concluded that he had created a poisonous book out of our poisoned times. (23)

The dilemma Drnaso faced is very much the problem of J. M. Coetzee's fictional author, Elizabeth Costello, who asserts that there are ethical limits to the well of the macabre from which a writer should draw. Plumbing and drawing out such dark depths, she proclaims, is injurious to both the writer's and reader's soul. She has learned this shocking lesson from reading Paul West's graphic account of the gruesome torture of Nazi officers caught in the plot to assassinate Hitler. "To save humanity," she claims, "certain things we may want to see must remain off-stage." She approaches West, who is unexpectedly in the conference audience, to forewarn him of what she is going to accuse him of. As she approaches, we are told that "West glances up from what he is reading, which seems, astonishingly, to be some kind of comic book" (170). What Costello, presumably, finds "astonishingly" incongruent is that this author, who has been touched by evil and by whose art of conduction delivered that "touch of evil" (176) with the force of an electric shock, would be indulging himself in the innocuous genre of the comic.

As we have seen, after finishing *Sabrina*, Drnaso found himself entirely in agreement with Costello—entirely in agreement, that is, except that he had conducted his touch of evil by means of a comic, brought it onto the stage of the world precisely by means of a comic book. Max recounts the crisis propelled by Drnaso's decision not to publish *Sabrina*, at which point he began to reconsider his project and its characters less severely and decided that he could see his way to publishing the book if he cut out the murder scene (23). Perhaps he felt something cathartic in literally "cutting out" a scene of stabbing or cutting of flesh, although, to be sure, the book closes with Calvin's chilling nightmare in which Yancey holds a knife against his throat. In expiation, Drnaso decided to donate his royalties to various charities, including one that helps educate girls in Africa. Despite quick acclaim—Zadie Smith, for example, pronounced *Sabrina* a "masterpiece" in her endorsement of the book—Drnaso expressed lacerating regret at having brought it into the world. "I f*****g hate that book," he told Max, "I don't ever want to look at it again. It was a mistake, and I should never have done it" (24).

And yet, if Sabrina the character does not survive, *Sabrina* itself has been granted a literary life beyond the author's powers of retraction. The question remains: do we concur with Drnaso's bleak judgment and renunciation? Another way of posing this question is to turn to a moment in *Sabrina* that concerns the reading of a book. Sabrina's sister Sandra has lent her a book and asked Sabrina for her opinion. Sabrina answers, "There were some interesting ideas, but I felt empty when it was over" (5). Sabrina seems to judge the book as missing something compelling that left her feeling empty by the end. But either because she misunderstands Sabrina, or because she is countering her judgment, Sandra replies, "Yea. It was a good kind of empty feeling though" (5). Part of what Sandra means by the good kind of empty feeling becomes clearer as we progress through the book. She means a process of emptying out, of the dispelling of bad things, of a kind of catharsis. We might read this exchange in meta-critical terms: Is *Sabrina* fated to leave us feeling empty (or worse) in Sabrina's bad sense, or does some chance remain for the good empty?

TRAUMA AND THE IRONY OF DISPLACEMENT

In *Cruel Optimism*, Lauren Berlant diagnoses the contemporary condition of precarious living in America and Europe as a systemic crisis of the ordinary: "A relation of cruel optimism exists when something you desire is actually an obstacle to your flourishing" (1). Among her primary concerns is an analysis of why it is that people hold to the fantasy of the good life even in the face of accumulating evidence to the contrary, and what happens when this fantasy begins to unravel. One of Berlant's moves in her analysis of our harsh continuous present is to displace trauma theory with its focus on exceptional events that puncture or shock quotidian life in favor of an analysis of an embedded and unyielding structural adversity and the affective response this condition produces. However, in Drnaso's analysis and rendition of our cruel present, trauma as the scene of life-shattering events makes a return, if not of the repressed, then of the displaced. If *Cruel Optimism* displaces trauma in favor of the prevailing "crisis ordinary," *Sabrina* punctures this crisis of the ordinary with the shattering and ramifying force of a traumatic event. Thus, while *Sabrina* certainly depicts the systemic crisis of the ordinary as part of its troubled world, it does not do so by assenting to Berlant's displacement of trauma and trauma theory in favor of an analysis of precarity. This is not to say, however, that Berlant's formulation of cruel optimism will not prove useful in analyzing *Sabrina*; indeed, I shall later take up the question of whether Calvin's desire becomes not only an obstacle to his flourishing but a descent into the underworld of inextricable trauma. But while *Sabrina* returns our focus to a puncturing trauma and its web of consequences as a paradigm of the present, it is with an analysis of traumatic displacement within *Sabrina* that I want to proceed.

In contrast to the excerpted image of a grimacing Sabrina being attacked, the graphic novel opens with a rather quiet, foregrounded image of Sabrina's face. Sabrina is searching for her mother's cat, which she finds, and cuddling the cat in her arms, she says, "Look at that face" (3). Together with the opening images, these words indicate that faces, both human and animal, and the presentation of the face will prove a crucial motif. It is as if *Sabrina* begins by illustrating Emmanuel Levinas' stricture that ethics begins with the face of the other and its insistence that it shall not be harmed (*Ethics*). But if it begins with this stricture, *Sabrina* begins too, not only with its violation but with a foreshadowing of how this violence will become ironically displaced. Sandra proposes that Sabrina join her on a bike trip around the Great Lakes, to which Sabrina replies, "That sounds great. Get out of the city, get away from the internet" (8). However, she voices concern about safety and wonders about the danger of "wild animals." Sandra replies with a story of how she narrowly escaped an attack by sexual predators who were out "hunting" (9) and suggests that Sabrina's worry about riding through the woods is misplaced. "The f*****g wild animals," she warns, "stay in the hotels" (9). The irony, it turns out, is not only that Sabrina would indeed be safer riding through the woods but that the thwarted attack on Sandra seems ultimately destined for Sabrina.

This irony is compounded by the fact that it is not only Sabrina but Calvin who becomes caught in an insidious and shifted violence. Indeed, the economy of the transmission of violence in *Sabrina* appears to be one governed by displacement. Those closest to the epicenter of violence are the ones who slowly make some escape and are afforded some release, while those furthest become more deeply consumed by the aftershock and suffer outsized consequences.

Sandra certainly suffers greatly and grieves deeply about the murder of her sister, but she seems slow to work through her shock and loss, and the last page pictures her cathartic ride around the lakes. In the case of Calvin, however, things seem to be more disturbingly ironic. It is, after all, because Calvin acts as a good person, extending a helping hand to a traumatized Teddy, his school friend whom he now barely knows, that he becomes embroiled in

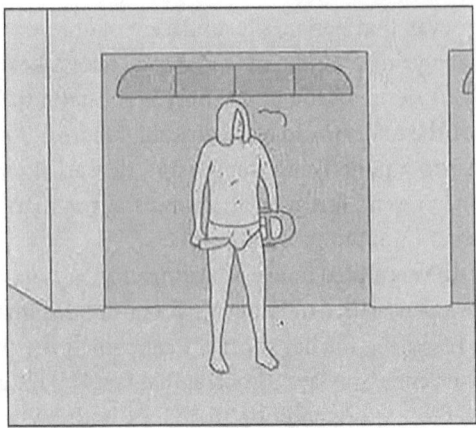

Figure 9.1. *Sabrina,* page 135.

Sabrina's murder and its treacherous aftermath. Teddy is first introduced to us with a closeup panel of his face that parallels the panel introducing Sabrina. He has come to visit Calvin, who works in cybersecurity at Peterson Air Force Base in Colorado Springs. The awkward meeting and Teddy's minimal response to Calvin's overtures quickly alert us to his depleted state. We learn the reason for this is that his girlfriend, Sabrina, has disappeared, and as we progress we see Teddy further reduced. In fact, he becomes so incapable that Calvin has to undress him, and Teddy remains stripped to his underwear throughout the middle portion of the text. Teddy is not only physically naked, however, but psychically bare or nakedly vulnerable to malign influences. These will come in the form of a right-wing radio broadcast and internet conspiracy theories regarding the murder of Sabrina that threaten to engulf him. In a sense, Teddy becomes literally and figuratively stripped to a state of mere life, or even to that state Giorgio Agamben refers to as "bare life," or life that is exposed to death.

True, Teddy is not so much exposed to death in terms of sovereign power, but he does appear driven towards a state of suicide, and we see him at his nadir clutching a large kitchen knife when both the drive towards suicide and an urge to protect himself against his perception of a lethal threat to his life converge. In fact, we are confronted at this violent crossroads, with a panel of an almost naked Teddy holding the radio in one hand and the knife in the other.

Shortly after he undresses Teddy, Calvin himself strips down to his underwear. His almost naked body is juxtaposed against Teddy's. Although he does not quite know it at this point, Calvin, too, has entered into a crossroads. In contrast to Teddy lying prostrate on Calvin's daughter's bed, sitting in his own bed, Calvin joins his fellow airman playing *Call of Duty* (42–3). Like Calvin, we readers are also entered into the game space as panels of Calvin's naked body are juxtaposed with panels of screens displaying scenes of people trying to escape or surrender getting shot. Offering an explanation as to why he is late joining the game, Calvin writes, "Just woke up and can't fall back asleep. Killing people always puts me to sleep" (42). It is not true that Calvin has just woken up, and this little lie is indicative of many that he tells throughout the course of the story. We can't quite be sure if Calvin really means that killing people in the game always puts him to sleep. But the irony is that in his nightmare that closes the novel, Calvin's sleep is interrupted by a masked man holding a knife to his throat. It is as if the knife with which Tim Yancey murders Sabrina, and with which he commits suicide, and the knife that Teddy holds were metaphorically, but also more than metaphorically (if not quite literally) destined ultimately for Calvin himself.

MEDIA AND THE SPACE OF TRAUMA

In a strange sense, *Sabrina* seems to reverse canonical trauma theory, which claims that those closest to severe trauma are least capable of processing the event and get most stuck in the repetition compulsion of its aftermath. For Freud, one of the crucial aspects of trauma is its belatedness; the victim of trauma cannot grasp or fully represent the traumatic event at the time at which it occurs, and the event continues to haunt the victim in a ceaseless repetition that cannot be dispelled. It is only by means of a "deferred action" or *nachträglichkeit* that this trauma might be brought to light and processed.[1] And Dori Laub famously asserts of the Holocaust that it produced "an event without a witness" in that it was the "very circumstance of *being inside the event* that made unthinkable the very notion that a witness could exist" (81). Aspects of classical trauma theory are displayed in *Sabrina* by means of a televised news visit to the 9/11 museum on the sixteenth anniversary of its opening. We are told that those visiting the museum get transported back to that calamitous day and that "Viewers relive the tragedy in painful detail through 23,000 pictures and over 10,000 artifacts, creating an overwhelmingly visceral sensation" (39). It is as if viewers are thrust again into the maw of the tragedy. One visitor whose melancholic face is foregrounded against a red background that is also symbolically associated with Sabrina testifies that "My sister died on flight 1-7-5. The grief stays with me every day" (39). Like Sandra, she is caught in mourning, but unlike Sandra, she seems to be stuck in a state of ever-present melancholia. Another visitor, with a far more distant relation to the tragedy, remarks that while the event is marked in her memory, "It is important to look back and reflect on how far we have come" (39). Addressing the television reporter, a museum official proclaims the duty of the museum to preserve the moment of the event and leave visitors with "an increased sense of the value of a human life, that each one is important and won't be forgotten" (39). Nevertheless, the paradoxical relation of the 9/11 memorial to history and memory is subtly brought out by two panels that record an inscription from Virgil: "NO DAY SHALL ERASE YOU FROM THE MEMORY OF TIME" (39). This inscription, however, is broken by the gutter between the two panels and the repetition of the word "ERASE" is itself cut off (leaving only "SE") or erased. We read a televised caption that says, "Behind this wall is a repository housing some 8000 unidentified remains" (39). Some, sadly, might indeed be erased from the memory of time in this vigil with Virgil.

One important aspect of this televised visit to the museum is that it alerts us that the momentary aftermath of the tragedy in *Sabrina* will be presented on screens. It is by means of this early interlude that we move from the individual trauma of the murder of Sabrina to a national (even global) trauma and back again to Sabrina and the ramifying aspect of the attack on her. Looking attentively at the first mental health survey that Calvin fills out, we see that, portentously, Teddy visits Calvin on the day of 9/11, and from there on out, these surveys act, directly and indirectly, as a device to measure the descent in Calvin's life. I use the word "descent" here not only metaphorically but literally, too. After Teddy's arrival in Colorado Springs, Calvin points out Cheyenne Mountain, which houses NORAD in its deep bunker designed to withstand a nuclear attack. The 9/11 Memorial & Museum is also housed in a bunker of sorts, lying seven stories under the bedrock on which the towers stood. It is as if some small vestige of the attack that the Cheyenne Mountain bunker was designed to withstand is displaced onto the Twin Towers, whose remnants are now housed in a bunker. These bunkers are not, of course, simply holes in the ground but are wired entities replete with screens. At one point early in the novel, Conner, one of Calvin's fellow airmen, pressures Calvin to hold a night session of *Call of Duty* at his house. Teddy has just arrived, so Calvin tries to evade him. To which Conner replies, "Come on, man. Do you know how many hours . . . I put in last night to unlock level 11" (27). We catch an ironic echo of "moving up a level" a page or two later when a Sergeant Smith tries to persuade Calvin to take a position at the Office of Special Investigations. He asks Calvin to consider it carefully, remarking, "It's a chance to move up to the next level. If you are thinking 'career,' this could really open doors for you" (29). The irony is not simply that moving up a level in the game *Call of Duty*, where

Calvin kills people, is conflated with moving up a career level to the Office of Special Investigations, where Calvin may be called on to do the same in life, but that, in committing to this job he may have become trapped in an underworld of black operations for which he is wholly unsuited.

This descent is foreshadowed by a disconcerting confrontation that takes place between Calvin and Conner in an underground room that houses a battery of servers. Calvin is asked to check on a problem with the servers, and we follow him down flights of stairs along a reinforced corridor into a massive room filled with array after array of servers. Tension builds as Conner, appearing as if from nowhere, gives Calvin, as well as the reader, a scare. The situation grows more sinister (Connor's game handle is "sinister") as Connor, who feels Calvin has stolen the job from him, warns Calvin that he has no idea what he has got himself into, including the possibility of extra-judicial killings and operations at black sites: "Once you pass that door," he tells a shaken Calvin, "there is no leaving" (181). This does indeed give a sinister twist to Sergeant Smith's claim for career-opening doors. It is, however, after Conner says, "wait until you find out the truth about nine-eleven or what happened to Sabrina" (182) that Calvin breaks down, screaming, "I can't take it!!" (183). Conner tells him that he is only joking, but Calvin's nightmare at the end of *Sabrina*, in which he desperately wants to take back his choice, reveals that Connor's warning has deeply penetrated Calvin's psyche.

There is a further ironic twist when we consider that Calvin's current job is a "boundary technician" (104), or one who searches for breaches in networks and updates firewalls. Calvin's own psychic and spatial boundaries have been breached. Indeed, it is not only hidden material spaces, or what takes place in bunkers, or behind walls or closed doors, that concerns *Sabrina*, but the way this gets transmitted to the warped media-scape of the internet itself. We recall that Sabrina desires to get away from the internet and, shattered, Teddy utters, "I just want her to come back" (36); it is a bitter-cruel irony that Sabrina comes back in a videotaped scene of her murder that is uploaded to the web. Why does Yancey choose to videotape the murder he commits in this moment of smartphones or internet streaming? Why deploy this retro technology? The videotape is sent to a small newspaper aptly named *The Standard Journal* whose old VCR and television are no longer even connected. Looking carefully, we notice a small red square, like a stylized smudge of blood, on the actual tape. It appears that Yancey is trying to stage his killing of Sabrina with a twisted nostalgia for an older form of the recording and reporting of murder. This strikes me, too, as Drnaso's sardonic commentary on the dangers of appealing to a nostalgic past (that never was) that we hear expressed in the radio show that Teddy is in danger of being captivated by.

Figure 9.2. *Sabrina*, page 72.

Despite Drnaso's cutting out of the actual murder itself, the scene of the murder still presents us with an ethical conundrum. What appears to be Sabrina's body is covered by a sheet, but we are shown Yancey lying in a bathtub in a pool of his own blood after his apparent suicide. The scene is not a ghastly one, however. Although Yancey's head appears to float atop this bath of blood, he seems to be smirking, contented both by murder he has committed (and filmed) and by the staging of his own suicide.

He relishes the envisioned moment of being found and photographed by the police, and we come upon precisely this moment. The detectives are going over this forensic scene that is being photographed, and Yancey gets his wish of having the staged act of his self-slaughter recorded. Drnaso himself stages this ethical dilemma by drawing and presenting exactly this panel. In doing this, he leaves us to decide whether he is simply acceding to Yancey's wishes or undermining them by posing the question of the ethics of this representation itself. In a wry moment, we notice that the bathroom in which Yancy commits suicide is white with blue tile, and Yancy's blood adds red, thereby completing the colors of the American flag. I shall soon comment on the importance of this. A few pages after viewing this scene, we observe an account on the internet devoted to what is known about Yancey. The page juxtaposes the smiling faces of Yancey and Sabrina, but it also juxtaposes Yancey's face with him wearing an executioner's mask. We are also presented with a split image of Yancey's face, half of which shows him

Figure 9.3. *Sabrina*, page 122.

smiling surrounded by a blue background and the other half has him in a mask with a red background. Yancey seems not to have left a suicide note, but he has left a list of his fifty favorite films on a message board, which he signed off, "Bye for now" (81). We come to understand that Yancey views his suicide as the final scene in the film in which he will chillingly reappear. He has removed his executioner's mask to ultimately reveal his contented sneer.

With its focus on the presentation of the face, *Sabrina* asks profound questions about what becomes of Levinas' claim for the ethical primacy of the face, of the naked appearance of the face of the other as carrying with it the primordial commandment, "Thou shall not kill me," in our moment of uploading and streaming of atrocity. Drnaso's twist on the videos of beheadings that he watched is to have the murderer serve up his own smirking head on a platter of blood. It turns out that Yancey has sent out numerous tapes, and despite police attempts to block it, the video of Yancey killing Sabrina has been leaked onto the internet. Calvin also sees a video of Sandra, who, in a gesture that reminds us of Sabrina, holds her hand out to block a video camera and reporters who are hounding her. After he watches the downloaded video, Calvin is sickened and vomits into the toilet, and the panels on the page turn from a background of empty grey to black as the murder in the video literally becomes the space of Calvin's nightmare. We realize, in retrospect, that it is Calvin rather than Teddy who actually witnesses the murder of Sabrina.

If the video of the murder bleeds into Calvin's nightmare, his waking life also becomes incorporated into the nightmare aftermath of the killing. Calvin, too, becomes hounded by reporters, and after innocently mistaking Sandra for Sabrina, he becomes the embroiled subject of conspiracy theories. As with Sandra, we also see a video of Calvin holding his hand out to block the camera. Calvin becomes, in fact, the subject of reports on the internet that are similar to those that popped up for Yancey. He is accused in a blog report entitled "Iron Truth" of being an actor in a hoax that almost worked, but the report continues, "Unfortunately for the conspirators, you can't fool us in the digital age" (119). This would be ludicrous, but for the fact that the hoax theory becomes performative, and Calvin becomes the target of menacing death threats. The irony, of course, is that in this moment of deepfakes and disinformation, we are constantly in grave danger of being fooled, and it is also precisely this possibility and fear of being fooled that fuels contemporary conspiracy theories.[2] In the grimmest of *Sabrina*'s displacements, Calvin is accused of being part of a "False Flag" conspiracy, and he is presented side by side with the masked murderer of Sabrina on a conspiracy website.

An American flag forms the background of this picture, and a caption that reads, "Best Friends" underscores it. Ironically, Calvin now becomes the actor in the scene that Yancey thought would be his final act. The scene of the bathroom suicide is replaced by the image of an American flag. (Subtly, the blue portion of the flag, sans the stars, becomes the blue background with which Calvin is associated.) A photograph of Calvin with his face caught in the scope of a rifle is also featured on the site. Another site subjects Calvin to a comparative facial recognition analysis, asking if Calvin is not himself played by another actor.

What then becomes of Levinas' claim for the ethical primacy of the face in the world of *Sabrina*? We are indeed presented here with a difficult question. On the face of it, *Sabrina* seems to contrast the naked vulnerability of Teddy's body with the possibility of the digital manipulation of Calvin's face. The primordial nakedness of the face of the other, with its immanent demand that it shall not be hurt, is undone by the specter of digital fabrications. But the sight of Calvin's face caught in the crosshairs of a rifle scope also presents his face in all its manifest Levinasian vulnerability. In posing this question, *Sabrina* also subtly poses the question of the relationship between digital screens and the panels of this graphic novel. In other words, do *Sabrina*'s panels act like those digital screens (in the double sense), capturing both its characters as well as its readers in the inescapable space of conspiracy, or are they capable of interrogating and evading this space? It is to this question of escape and the possibility of catharsis that I shall turn in the final section of this piece.

CATHARSIS

What are we to make of the traumatic economy in *Sabrina* whereby Teddy and Sandra, who are closest to the tragic death of Sabrina, seem finally to be the ones offered some release, while Calvin becomes enmeshed in the aftermath of this event? Stating her case for the crisis of the ordinary, Berlant asserts that "The extraordinary always turns out to be an amplification of something in the works, a labile boundary at best, not a slammed door departure. In the impasse induced by crisis being treads water; mainly it does not drown" (10). We have seen, however, that this does not appear to be the case with regard to Calvin. It is not a "labile boundary" that our "boundary technician" faces, and the choice to join Special Investigations does seem a "slammed door departure," or this, at least, is very much what he fears. But this is not to say that ordinary crisis plays no part in pushing Calvin into the predicament he finds himself. It is, after all, because of the failure of his marriage and his wife's rejection of Calvin's efforts to join her and his daughter Cicci in Florida that Calvin resolves to take this position. It is, ironically, he thinks, his way out of his dull, becalmed, and isolated life. What is the justice then in where Calvin winds up? Why should this "good buddy," which is the game handle that Calvin gives himself, be the one to become most ensnared?

Part of the answer to this question is also what makes *Sabrina* such an unnerving read, for as we progress through the graphic novel, we begin to wonder who Calvin really is and what we can actually trust about him. Although Calvin comes across as a good person who unwittingly, and indeed unfairly, becomes caught in the web of a fake conspiracy plot, the situation proves to be more complicated. As we progress through the graphic novel, we become disconcerted by the set of small lies that we see Calvin telling. We are surprised, I think, by the guns he keeps, but we become more disconcerted, even discomposed, to find out that Calvin is a survivalist prepper who has his own "bunker" (it is actually a garage) filled with supplies as well as an emergency kit and gas mask that he keeps hidden in the attic. What sets us on edge is that we discover this through Teddy, who goes searching for the radio that Calvin has hidden from him because he fears that Teddy has become dangerously consumed by conspiracy theories propagated on a right-wing broadcast akin to Alex Jones's Infowars. Teddy goes searching for the radio and finds it hidden behind a trapdoor in the attic. He knows to search there because he has once before startled, even scared, Calvin, who was placing a box in this hiding place. Teddy now opens this box only to find a gas mask, which possibly triggers in his mind a thought of Yancey's mask. It is after his discovery and his recovery of the radio that Teddy picks up a large kitchen knife. The tension comes to a head when Calvin returns later that night. Unbeknownst to him, on the other side of the door, Teddy is holding the knife, poised to strike. As we follow this, we are forced into what I would describe as "suspicious reading." Like Teddy, we become unsure who exactly Calvin is, and we become caught in the paranoid web of this text. What we come to realize is that Calvin is perhaps not so very different from the conspiracy theorist that Teddy has been listening to or that he is at least receptive to such notions. Let me offer a subtle example. When Teddy finds the radio and turns it on, he does not appear to change the station.[3] We are left to wonder why the radio is turned into a conspiracist show. It is odd as the radio appears to belong to Cicci, who would have no understanding of such a broadcast. But we recall that after Cicci left, Calvin moved stuff into her room. Is Calvin, we wonder, a dedicated follower? This may be super-subtle, and perhaps we are meant simply to infer that Teddy has found this station after searching or that the radio just happened to be tuned to this broadcast. But this is exactly the kind of conspiracy thinking that we, as readers, are drawn into. If Calvin then is somewhat responsible, or at least susceptible, to the circumstance he finds himself in, what of the reader? Is there a way out for us? I shall offer some thoughts on this, but first, let me turn to one way in which I think *Sabrina* uses the irony of conspiracy theory to try to counter murderers, or at least to try to counter their message.

Although I have focused on the way in which trauma becomes ironically transferred or displaced in *Sabrina*, it turns out that this irony is also double-edged. When he records his murder of Sabrina, Yancey says, "It has become increasingly difficult for my voice to be heard above the din of the chatter. This is only a means to an end" (114). The irony, of course, is that in some respects, Yancey's voice will not be heard, and the murder of Sabrina, which he thinks will cut through the chatter, will simply become fodder for conspiracy theories. But, even this "ironic justice," if we might call it that, suffers its own displacement as one atrocity broadcast on the web begets another. A man, not unlike Yancey, streams a video on Facebook in which he proclaims, "Where is my parade? I have to express myself somehow. If it can't be positive, it will have to be negative. All that matters is I'm remembered" (143), after which, he commits a massacre in a daycare and then kills himself. This murderer understands what Yancey does not—all that can be counted on is the notoriety that accompanies the act of mass murder. Yet even this will be displaced or replaced by new moments of mass violence.

Although I have now presented the other side of Calvin that is revealed as we move through the book, I do not mean to suggest that Calvin is wholly responsible for the nightmare that awaits him. Like Sandra and Teddy, Calvin gets caught in a web that is not entirely of his making, a concatenation of events that is beyond his agency. One of the elements of the dark side of the web that *Sabrina* is both replicating and critiquing is the way in which it is ironically *machinal*. Jacques Derrida uses the word *machinal* to speak of the way in which something, language, for example, has an automatic, implacable force (81). Indeed, it is not only the internet, but the machine itself that is featured in *Sabrina*. We see a vending machine that is out of order, and this being out of order of the machine finds its way into the dark recess of Calvin's nightmare. Near the beginning of the text, Calvin wishes to play a mixed tape that Teddy made for him for his twelfth birthday. The mixed tape does not get played, but mixed elements, like a mad mixed tape of this graphic novel, get played out in Calvin's nightmare, which includes a masked figure proclaiming, "That machine is still out of order" (199).

While the weight of *Sabrina* is on traumatic descent and entanglement, by the end, the text does gesture to moments of release, perhaps even catharsis. At one point, fairly early in the story, Anna, Sandra's friend, tries to calm Sandra by rubbing her back (something Sabrina does for Sandra at the beginning) and guides her into thinking herself into a place where she feels safe and serene. Sandra finds herself transported into a green natural setting with horses and enters a country house where she lies tranquilly on a bed. Her tranquility is represented by an empty panel of light-colored space over which is inscribed, "You are at peace." This peaceful moment, this good empty, cannot hold, however, and Sandra breaks down, falling into a fetal position that resembles Teddy at his most downfallen. Later in the novel, we are offered a further irony on the difficulty of escaping the web as Sandra stands before a live audience at an event designed to allow people to break out of their isolation and address each other face to face. Sandra chooses to read aloud a series of messages she has received that mostly accuse her of involvement in a conspiracy and even include death threats against her. The reading is met with silence and provides little relief for her, however. But the last page of *Sabrina* ends with Sandra now entering life in that serene green space of nature into which she had previously tried to imagine herself. We follow Sandra on her ride around the Great Lakes during which we are offered both her perspective of vistas of natural space that open before her as well as a view of Sandra cathartically riding into the distance. The good empty that Sandra finds by the end is represented not so much by a peaceful emptiness but rather by the open space of nature itself, or perhaps this itself signifies that she is on the path to a fuller catharsis.

As with Sandra, Teddy's release will also come by way of nature, not so much the nature of fields and forests but of animals—not the wild animals that

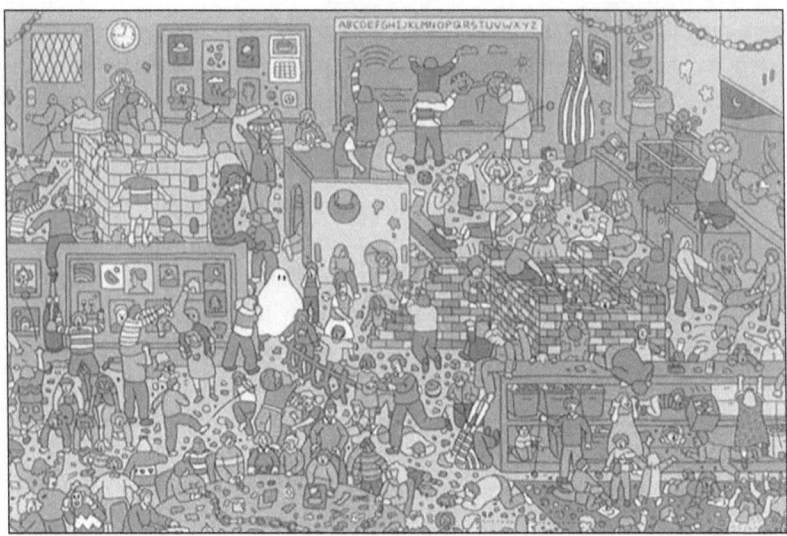

Figure 9.4. *Sabrina*, page 53.

Sabrina feared, but strays and rescues cared for at the animal shelter at which Teddy begins to work. It is not quite with animals, but, rather oddly, with a children's picture book that contains images of animals that we can begin to chart Teddy's path to some form of recovery, to the good empty. After Sandra tells Sabrina that reading her book leaves her with a "good kind of empty feeling," she asks if Teddy read it. Sabrina answers that Teddy isn't really a reader, although he did seem to like a "weird old book about pirates" (5) that she gave him as a present. Early in the story, Calvin finds Teddy sunk in deep psychic despair reading Cicci's favorite book and we are shown a panel that appears to depict a page from it (53). Vividly colorful and densely packed, the image seems to depict children happily playing in a crazy playhouse. One's initial impression is that, reduced as he is, Teddy is seeking a kind of solace or losing of himself in the vitality of this children's book. Looking closely, however, we begin to see how distorted this image really is: a fish tank, for example, in which fish are swimming is also broken and gushing water; a child holds a mask of a skull up to his face, frightening another child; a boy holds his hands to his head in anguish; and children hurl wounding objects at one another.[4] We are left to wonder if this densely packed panel might not be the actual image in Cicci's book, but that image wrenched and distorted by Teddy's grief-stricken mind, made weird, like the old pirate book.

Towards the end of *Sabrina*, we see Teddy turn off the radio show as he breaks free from its perilous hold and turns once more to the children's book. We are again presented with a dense and vivid image of children happily playing, but this image seems to revise the first in that it does not display

Figure 9.5. *Sabrina*, page 191.

the same distortions or violence. Part of the purpose of this book is to teach children to look carefully at pictures, and one of the images presents two side-by-side panels in a 'can you spot the differences' game. In a subtle sense, then, this picture book proves an analog to the graphic novel itself in that *Sabrina* invites us to spot the differences between the two dense images of children playing games. But this difference also bespeaks some form of repair and regenerative vitality that Teddy, perhaps unconsciously, first sought.

The children's book also contains images of animal figures that foreshadow the welcoming face of a dog that Teddy will meet at the shelter. Indeed, this picture of the dog's face could almost fit into the children's book. Levinas was once asked if, like a human, an animal can also have a face. He answered ambiguously that, "One cannot entirely refuse the face of an animal. It is via the face that one understands, for example, a dog. Yet the priority is not found in the animal but in the human face." Levinas continues, "I don't know if a snake has a face... But there is something in our attraction to an animal... In the dog, what we like is perhaps his childlike character. As if he were strong, cheerful, powerful, full of life" ("The Name" 49). It is as if with the panel of the welcoming face of the dog, *Sabrina* picks up on Levinas' analysis and illustrates it, but also answers more affirmatively the question of whether a dog can have a face in Levinas' sense. In fact, this panel seems to reverse Levinas and places the ethical priority of the face of the other in the welcoming face of the dog.

Calvin will come face to face with this dog at the shelter where he goes to see Teddy on his journey to Special Investigations, but he seems to miss the significance of this encounter. The meeting with Teddy, who appears to be working towards some recovery, some repair, is awkward and strained and their paths will diverge even further. We are soon presented with several panels of Calvin on the road with open vistas of natural spaces ahead of him that contrast with those of Sandra as we realize that these are alternate paths that Calvin will probably not take.

It is a rather cruel irony that Sabrina mentions that she would like to be a dog walker, and it is Teddy who winds up becoming a dog worker. Although both Teddy and Sandra find in nature one path of release, one path towards catharsis, *Sabrina* does not, I think, fall into the trap of presenting nature in terms of an innocent sublime. It is, after all, only because Calvin's cat, Randy, goes missing, in contrast with the cat Sabrina finds, that Teddy finds his way to the shelter. Like Sabrina, Randy is probably lost to the world. *Sabrina* is too honest a text to proffer catharsis for all. The economy of ironic displacement is still very much a predisposition of this text. If Drnaso denies himself catharsis in the creation of *Sabrina*, what possibility for catharsis is left to the reader?

One paradoxical possibility that I would like to end with is the overwhelming experience of reading *Sabrina*. Although the panels are minimalist in their composition, with each element attaining added significance, the experience of reading *Sabrina* is one of becoming overwhelmed and drawn into a tightening web of conspiracy thinking and suspicious reading. Yet, it is also precisely this sense of being overwhelmed that compels in us a desire for release, a desire for catharsis. Early in *Sabrina*, Sandra speaks of studying the background actors on the videotapes she watches over and over again during her stay in a hospital (7). She does this because she has nothing else to do. This early emphasis on background offers us a clue, I think, towards the possibility of a cathartic reading. This reading, however, will reverse Sandra's, as we focus not on the actors in the background but on the panels of color, which, if looked at with the right eye, might lead us towards the good empty.

NOTES

1. See Sigmund Freud.
2. "Deepfake" is the term given to synthetic video generated by machine learning techniques.
3. I thank my student, Akira Kane, for pointing out to me that the radio appears already tuned to this station and that Teddy seems simply to turn the radio on. Later, we see Teddy turning to this station, which offers evidence in support of this claim (141).
4. The image strikes me as something like Pieter Bruegel's *Children's Games* (1560), to which it may in fact allude, transmogrified into a contemporary children's picture book.

WORKS CITED

Agamben, Giorgio. *Homo Sacer: Sovereign Power and Bare Life*, trans. Daniel Heller-Roazen. Stanford: Stanford University Press, 1998.
Berlant, Lauren. *Cruel Optimism*. Durham: Duke University Press, 2011.
Derrida, Jacques. *Acts of Religion*, ed. Gil Anidjar. New York: Routledge, 2002.
Drnaso, Nick. *Sabrina*. Montreal: Drawn & Quarterly, 2018.
Felman, Shoshana, and Laub, Dori. *Testimony: Crisis of Witnessing in Literature, Psychoanalysis, and History*. New York: Routledge, 1992.
Freud, Sigmund. "From the History of an Infantile Neurosis (The Wolf Man)." In *Three Case Histories*, ed. Philip Rieff. Collier Books, 1977. 161–280.
Levinas, Emmanuel. *Ethics and Infinity*, trans. Richard A. Cohen. Pittsburgh: Duquesne University Press, 1985. 85–101.
Levinas, Emmanuel. "The Name of a Dog, or Natural Rights." In *Animal Philosophy: Ethics and Identity*, ed. Peter Atterton and Matthew Calarco. London: Continuum, 2004. 47–50.
Max, D. T. "American Graphic." *The New Yorker*, January 21, 2019, 18–24.

V.

CONCLUSION

JORDAN TRONSGARD

Why are comics so good at confronting the bad? It is an (intentionally) simple question, but one that is at the center of where comics studies and trauma studies meet. I believe that part of the answer has to do with the explicit artifice of the medium, as highlighted in the introduction to this volume. By placing the constructed nature of the narrative on full display, comics allow for simultaneous identification with, and separation/distance from, the uncomfortable, the painful, the traumatic, for both creators and audience. And by creating a more comfortable space for thinking about the unthinkable, comics may also allow for catharsis, considering that, as Lear maintained in the introduction, catharsis is not just about emotional release but emotional release in a place of relative security. Therefore, in addition to addressing the question of why comics facilitate representing trauma, we are also asking if there is a role for catharsis in the comics studied in this volume.

For certain contributors, the answer is an explicit yes. Nagtegaal, for example, maintains that there is catharsis in restoring personhood to those who were silenced or forgotten in the post-war Spanish dictatorship, and the film allows for the cathartic release of past and present given the new generations of Spaniards engaging with historical, collective traumas. For Okan, by "voicing and naming" the trauma of sexual violence, the works covered in this chapter provide a space for catharsis for all participants of the narrative exchange: for the writers and readers and for the communities created through the dialogue between the two. In the case of *Sabrina*, a work of fiction, Samolsky notes that the text creates the tension and the conditions for its purgation. Minimalist panels contrast with the building anxiety that overwhelms the reader, compelling in the audience a desire for emotional release, what Samolsky calls "a cathartic reading"—that is a desire for the good empty.

For other contributors, the answer is also yes though in more implicit language. For Pifano, *La herencia del coronel* purges the fear to represent and confront the horrific. The direct depictions of difficult subject matter, such as sexual violence, combined with the distancing of the comics' artifice, gives visibility to the heinous acts of the Argentinian regime in a way that allows for a "speaking out" that is not sanitized. In Ulanowicz's chapter, Igort's comic questions and purges utopic and/or dishonest narratives about Ukraine's past for a foreign audience and presents the nation's history as an "undigested mess," the digestion being an ongoing process. This chapter takes on greater significance and avenues for further study, given the current war between Ukraine and Russia. Finally, Baron acknowledges the release of narrative boundaries regarding how one communicates witnessing trauma by taking advantage of comics' spatial, visual, and textual interplay. This chapter focuses on how the elements specific to graphic memoirs reinforce the notion of text as a witness, in this case to Bechdel's own past in the present, as an avenue for her to explore her relationship with her father and his death.

In the remaining three chapters, the presence of catharsis is questioned and even denied in the works studied. Sohini, for example, maintains that the auto-representation in the comics in question allows these writers to perform their "inbetweenness" as part of an identity process but not as part of a cathartic purge. Nevertheless, in the concluding remarks to this chapter the author does acknowledge the potential for catharsis in the reader's response. For Chau, *A Chinese Life* manifests tension over China's growth and global import as something both celebrated and anxiety-inducing, thus challenging expectations of cathartic healing that one might expect from a graphic narrative of memory that combines individual and collective considerations. In the case of Vij's chapter, real places with real collective histories and concerns are approached via fictional/alternative histories. This complicated dynamic requires nuanced thought, and Vij delivers, maintaining that the "counterfactual narratives" at once provide a space for cathartic repair to the idea of "American exceptionalism" and underline the futility of reparative narratives in this context.

In this volume, we have demonstrated that while the act of creating a comic or reading a comic is not inherently cathartic, catharsis is a potential component of the creation and/or reception of graphic narratives of trauma. And we have only begun to "scratch the surface." One of the objectives of this volume was to give visibility to a varied corpus of texts from different cultural and linguistic backgrounds. With that in mind, the answer to the implied question of "where do we go from here?" is to explore questions of trauma and catharsis in an ever-expanding corpus of comics beyond the usual suspects. Comics is a complex and diverse medium that speaks to who we are, where we have come from, and where we are going in ways that may provoke engagement, reflection, and indeed, catharsis.

LIST OF CONTRIBUTORS

KELLY BARON is a PhD Candidate at the University of Toronto, where she studies representations of intergenerational trauma and memory in contemporary Canadian women's novels. Her work has been published in *English Studies in Canada*, *Studies in Canadian Literature*, *Canadian Literature*, *Literary Review of Canada*, *Modern Language Studies*, *Journal of Latin American Cultural Studies*, and *Philip Roth Studies*. Along with Andrew DuBois, she is the editor of a collected edition on representations in music and literature forthcoming from Lexington Books in 2025.

ANGIE CHAU is assistant professor of Pacific and Asian studies at the University of Victoria, Canada. She has published articles on modern Chinese literature and art, film, and internet culture, and her research interests include contemporary Chinese literature, popular culture, visual art, and translation. Her work has appeared in journals such as *Modern Chinese Literature and Culture (MCLC)*, *Concentric*, and *Chinese Literature Today*, and various edited volumes. Prior to joining the University of Victoria, she taught courses in modern Chinese literature and film at NYU Shanghai, Arizona State University, and UC San Diego.

JENNIFER NAGTEGAAL is a PhD candidate in Hispanic studies at the University of British Columbia in Vancouver, Canada. Her research develops in the areas of comics studies and animation studies, and sometimes at the intersection of both. This is the case of her first monograph, *Politically Animated: Non-fiction Animation from the Hispanic World* (University of Toronto Press, 2023). Jennifer has published a number of essays on Spanish-language comics and animation in high-ranking journals such as the *Bulletin of Spanish Studies*, *Bulletin of Hispanic Studies*, and the *Revista Canadiense de Estudios Hispánicos*, and in the edited volume *The Routledge Companion to Gender and Sexuality in Comic Book Studies*. Jennifer's current doctoral research investigates the influence exerted by comics art on the art world, tracing the development of so-called "expanded comics" within the Spanish-speaking world and, comparatively, beyond its borders.

LEE OKAN is adjunct professor at Simmons University and Northeastern University. As a writer, she explores the intersection of science and literature through the research of Italo Calvino. As an artist, she is interested in how empathy is expressed through visual and narrative aspects in graphic novels and interactive storytelling. She is a PhD candidate in creative writing at Aberystwyth University, and her first novel, *The Lives of Atoms*, was published in spring 2018.

DIANA PIFANO is assistant professor and chair of the Department of Spanish and Latin American Studies at Dalhousie University, Canada. Her research interests include contemporary Latin American literature and the study of humor in Hispanic literature. Her current research explores a methodology that allows for a comprehensive analysis of humor within literary texts. Dr. Pifano teaches courses in Spanish language and Latin American literature.

RUSSELL SAMOLSKY is associate professor of Anglophone literature in the English department at the University of California, Santa Barbara. He is the author of *Apocalyptic Futures: Marked Bodies and the Violence of the Text in Kafka, Conrad, and Coetzee* (Fordham UP), which includes a chapter on Spiegelman's Maus, and he regularly teaches courses on the graphic novel and trauma. His research interests also include South African literature, animal studies, materialisms, and the global humanities.

KAY SOHINI is a Mellon/ACLS Dissertation Completion Fellow and a fifth-year PhD candidate in English at Stony Brook University, where she is currently drawing her doctoral dissertation as a comic. In both her creative and academic work, she focuses on how comics can be utilized by scholars and artists alike in ethnography, in narrative medicine, in public health discourse, in resisting disinformation, and in espousing an equitable future for all. Her work on comics has been published in *The Nib, Graphic Mundi's Covid Chronicles, Assay: A Journal of Non-fiction Studies, Women Write About Comics, Solrad,* and *Inside Higher Ed, Handbook of Comics and Graphic Narratives,* amongst others. She serves on the editorial team of The Comics Grid, in the Executive Committee of the International Comic Arts Forum (ICAF), in Modern Language Association (MLA)'s Committee on the Status of Graduate Students, and is a member of the Feminist Leaders Council at Feminist Press.

JORDAN TRONSGARD is professor of Hispanic studies and chair of the Department of Modern Languages, Literatures, and Cultures at Bishop's University in Sherbrooke, Canada. His field of research and publications deal with the Spanish Civil War and Franco dictatorship in contemporary Spanish film and literature, including comics. Dr. Tronsgard teaches Spanish at all levels and courses on Spanish and Latin American literature and film.

ANASTASIA ULANOWICZ is associate professor of English at the University of Florida, where she researches and teaches children's literature, visual rhetoric/comics, memory studies, and historical fiction. Her first book, *Second-Generation Memory and Contemporary Children's Literature: Ghost Images* (Routledge 2013), received the Children's Literature Association Book Award in 2015. With Dr. Mateusz Świetlicki (University of Wrocław), she is the coeditor of the first Anglophone introduction to Ukrainian children's literature. She is currently writing a book on representations of Eastern Europe in Western comics produced between 1989–2022. She was a Fulbright Specialist at the University of Wrocław, Poland, in 2021 and will return to the university as a Fulbright Scholar in 2025.

AANCHAL VIJ is a doctoral researcher at the University of Sussex funded by the Chancellor's International Research Scholarship. She works on American comics, disability studies, and race studies. As part of a placement funded by CHASE, she is also currently working with Bloomsbury Academic as an editorial intern. In 2020, she organized a three-day symposium on nostalgia called 'Zoom(ing) in on Nostalgia: The Way-Back Weekender' funded by Sussex's Researcher Development Programme.

INDEX

Abraham Lincoln Brigade, 23
abuse, 50, 56, 63–65, 73, 78, 81, 83, 142, 188–92, 194–96, 198, 200–206, 208
active reader, 8, 10, 15, 63, 69, 79
agency, 12, 87, 133, 185–86, 225
allegory, 51–53
Altarriba, Antonio, 3–4, 15n1, 23–26, 44nn11–12
alterity, 63
ambiguity, 36, 62, 76, 89, 227
American exceptionalism, 14, 121–26, 128–30, 132, 134–35, 138–39, 231
animation, 24, 26–28, 31–34, 36–40, 42, 43n9, 59, 79, 113
anxiety, 73, 117, 137, 139, 165–69, 190–91, 193, 199, 211–12, 231
archives, 21–22, 31–33, 36–41, 66n13, 107, 143, 148–49, 155–56
Argentina, 6, 14, 48–68, 231; Buenos Aires, 52, 61; CONADEP (*Comisión Nacional sobre la Desaparición de Personas*), 51; Junta, 14, 48–51, 53–54, 56, 64–65, 65n1, 66nn9–10
Aristotle, 11–12, 128
artifice, 8, 10, 144, 155–56, 165, 230–31
assault. *See* violence
Auschwitz, 55–56, 109
autobiography. *See* memoir
autoethnography, 70, 76–78, 84, 88

Bechdel, Alison, 3–4, 6, 15, 79, 107, 165–84, 231
Becoming Unbecoming, 15, 188, 196–202, 206–7

belatedness, 6, 73, 167, 170, 217
belonging, 13–14, 69–70, 72–73, 75–76, 81–83, 85, 88
Best We Could Do, The, 14, 70–81, 84, 90
birthing, 70, 72, 75
body, 9, 31–35, 37, 39–40, 44n14, 57, 63, 66n10, 84, 89, 91, 133, 150, 161n17, 168, 193, 195, 202, 216–17, 220, 222
borders, 23, 33, 37, 42, 69–71, 75, 89, 101, 114, 161n15
braiding, 72, 74–75, 89, 140n6
Bui, Thi, 14, 70–81, 84, 90
Burrowes, Nina, 15, 188, 204–7
Butler, Judith, 123, 140n2, 154, 155

camera, 27–28, 35–37, 39, 99, 221–22
cannibalism, 145, 150, 156
capitalism, 125–26, 157–58, 161n18
Caruth, Cathy, 6–8, 73, 79, 135, 167–68, 171
catharsis, 4–6, 11–15, 21, 24–26, 39–41, 43n10, 59, 79, 91–92, 99–100, 117, 121–23, 126–28, 130, 132, 137–40, 140n4, 185, 187, 196, 202, 207–8, 211–15, 222–23, 225, 228, 230–32; and comics, 4–6, 10, 12–13, 16n7, 26, 41, 91–92, 109, 121, 185, 191, 195, 230–32; definition of, 4, 11–13, 17n10, 126, 230
Catholicism, 10
child, 17n9, 22, 25, 29, 43nn6–7, 49, 53, 56, 62, 64, 65n1, 66n6, 66n12, 75, 78, 84, 90, 117, 148, 150, 161n16, 173, 181, 182n2, 196–97, 204, 207, 226–27
children, 17n9, 22, 25, 29, 43nn6–7, 49, 53, 56, 62, 64, 65n1, 66n6, 66n12, 75, 78, 84,

237

90, 117, 148, 150, 161n16, 173, 181, 182n2, 196–97, 204, 207, 226–27
childhood, 73, 77–78, 83, 110, 136, 150, 156, 165, 172, 174, 176, 179–80, 196, 201, 211
China, 6, 97–120, 231; Chinese Communist Party (CCP), 99–100, 103, 106, 109, 111, 117; Cultural Revolution, 99–101, 103, 107, 111, 118
Chinese Life, A, 14, 97–120, 231
Chute, Hillary, 4, 8, 16n4, 26–27, 31–33, 36, 41, 55–56, 59, 69–70, 73–74, 79, 84, 86, 89–90, 99–100, 106, 111, 144, 153–55, 157, 166, 169, 176, 178, 183n9
cinema, 3, 8, 11, 14, 21–22, 24–42, 43nn8–9, 44n14, 48, 52, 64, 66n7, 66n12, 178, 221, 230
closure, 12, 85, 137–38, 187
collective identity, 26, 81
collectivization, 145–46, 148–50, 157, 159n2, 160n8
Cold War, 121, 125, 129, 137
colonialism, 16n6, 76–77, 86
Comedian, The, 129, 136
comics, 3–6, 8–15, 16n7, 22–28, 31–33, 36, 38, 41–42, 43n6, 44nn10–11, 48, 50–53, 59, 65nn3–4, 66n13, 69–74, 79, 83–85, 89–92, 97, 99–100, 109, 111, 113–15, 118n2, 121, 128, 132–33, 139, 140n5, 142–43, 148–49, 153, 155, 177, 181, 182n3, 185–88, 205, 207–8, 211–13, 230–32; aesthetic of, 14, 21, 26–28, 33; and catharsis, 4–6, 10, 12–13, 16n7, 26, 41, 91–92, 109, 121, 185, 191, 195, 230–32; taxonomy, 5, 16nn4–5; and trauma, 3–6, 8–10, 12–15, 61, 70, 73, 75, 79, 91–92, 166, 195, 201–2, 205, 208, 230–32; visual medium, 8–9, 69, 71, 77, 79, 106, 185–86, 199, 202, 204, 231
commodification, 135
communism, 77, 80, 99–100, 103, 106, 109, 111, 113, 117, 122, 124–26, 129, 150, 157–58, 159n3, 160n8
community, 11, 15, 16n7, 44n12, 62, 77, 82–83, 87, 91, 147, 187, 190, 196, 199, 207–8
confession, 10, 31, 67n14, 107, 146, 149

counterfactual narratives, 14, 117, 121–23, 126–30, 132–33, 138–40, 140n2, 231
Courage to Be Me, The, 15, 188, 204–7
Cyrillic, 143

death, 3, 24, 41, 51, 59–60, 66n10, 66n12, 67n14, 84, 86, 101, 109, 143–44, 148, 151, 155, 165, 168, 171–73, 175, 179–80, 183n7, 213, 216, 222–23, 225, 231
deepfake, 222, 228n2
dehumanization, 23, 50, 58
democracy, 3, 22–23, 25, 51, 54, 64, 66n10, 81, 161n18
depression, 9, 140n5
Derrida, Jacques, 14, 30–32, 34–35, 38–40, 225
desire, 33, 36, 49, 51, 58–60, 121–23, 126, 134–35, 194, 200, 214–15, 219, 228, 231
dialogue, 6–7, 13–14, 22, 26, 30, 34, 44n12, 44n14, 48–49, 53–54, 62, 64, 87, 89, 98, 103, 106, 108, 121, 128, 139, 204, 209n7, 230
diaspora, 88, 90
dictators/dictatorship, 3, 6, 13–14, 21–22, 25, 27, 30, 34, 36, 48, 50, 52–53, 59, 62, 64, 66n13, 230
disenfranchisement, 80, 83, 87
disinformation, 222
displacement, 15, 70, 90, 108, 211–12, 214–15, 218, 222, 224, 228
documentary, 12–14, 16n8, 21–22, 24, 26–27, 30–35, 38, 40–42, 43n9, 44n14, 48, 100
doll, 49, 57–60, 196–97, 201
Dr. Manhattan, 122, 129–30, 132–34, 136, 138
drawing, 4, 8–10, 13–15, 16n5, 23, 26–27, 31–33, 38, 71, 73–74, 77, 79, 81–82, 84–85, 87, 89–92, 109, 118n2, 143, 148, 153–56, 166, 169, 171, 174, 177, 179, 182n1, 194, 196, 199, 201, 206, 213, 220
Drnaso, Nick, 15, 211–31
Duranty, Walter, 14–15, 142–48, 151–54, 158, 159nn2–4, 159n6, 160n14, 161n16

eating disorder, 193
El arte de volar (*The art of Flying*), 3–4, 15n1, 23–26, 44nn11–12

INDEX

empathy, 13, 77, 89, 185, 187
ethics, 7, 14, 15n3, 100, 122, 130, 139, 142–43, 152, 154, 157, 160n14, 212–13, 215, 220–22, 227
ethnicity, 83, 87, 116, 146, 151–52, 159n6
execution, 34, 42n4, 145, 220–21
exile, 6, 27–28, 80–81

faithful representation, 15, 165–67
famine, 15, 103, 107, 143–44, 146–47, 150–51, 156–58, 158n1, 159n2, 160nn9–10, 160nn14–15, 161nn16–17
fascism, 23, 56, 125–26
fiction, 3, 12–15, 16n4, 16n8, 22–23, 34, 43nn9–10, 80, 121–23, 126, 128, 132, 135–36, 139–40, 186–87, 195, 204, 207–8, 213, 230–31
fidelity, 15, 165–67
film. *See* cinema
flashback, 132, 211
forgetting, 12, 21, 23, 107–9, 111, 118, 123, 187
fragmentation, 7–8, 16n7, 36, 55, 58–59, 61, 66n8, 76, 135, 147, 157, 166, 171–72
frames, 3, 8–9, 13, 22, 27–28, 36–37, 39, 43n6, 58–61, 69, 71–72, 75–76, 78–79, 84, 86–87, 92, 98, 101, 103–4, 106–8, 111, 127, 132, 135–36, 139, 143, 149–51, 154, 156, 166, 169, 172–73, 175–80, 182, 183n7, 187–88, 190, 199, 204, 211, 216–18, 220–22, 225–28, 231
France, 66n9, 97, 113–14, 118n2, 144, 146
Franco, Francisco, 3, 14, 21–23, 27, 34, 36, 38, 42n2, 43n6, 44n14
Freud, Sigmund, 32–33, 36, 121, 128, 132, 134, 136–37, 140n1, 140n7, 167–68, 172, 182n2, 217, 228n1
Fun Home. *See* Bechdel, Alison

generation, 3, 10, 13, 25–26, 30, 41–42, 44n10, 44n12, 48, 53, 69–72, 77, 79, 109, 111, 118, 181, 183n11, 230
genocide, 9, 43n10, 131, 146, 155
ghost, 15, 16n7, 24, 29–35, 38–40, 108, 128, 188–91, 194, 201–2, 207

Ghost Stories, 15, 188–91, 194–95, 199, 201–2, 207
Graphic Medicine, 15, 91–92
graphic narrative, 16n4, 22, 26, 44n11, 50, 55–56, 80, 89, 121, 123, 142–44, 148, 150, 153–55, 157, 160n7, 181, 185–86, 195, 231
graphic novel, 5, 15, 16n4, 22–27, 29–31, 33–34, 36–38, 41, 48, 50, 53, 56, 59, 61, 64, 84, 99–101, 106–7, 110, 112–17, 118n2, 124, 129, 132, 134–36, 157, 166–67, 171, 176–77, 181, 185–88, 191, 194–96, 198–205, 207–8, 208n1, 211–12, 215, 222–23, 225, 227; aesthetic, 14, 21, 26–28, 33
graphic reportage, 14, 142, 148
Green, Katie, 15, 188, 191–95, 201, 205–7
grief, 53, 59, 83–84, 91–92, 179, 194, 217, 226
gutters, 8, 13, 36, 59, 69, 106, 111, 139, 187, 218

hallucination, 49, 58–59, 61
haunting, 14, 16n7, 24, 29–32, 35–38, 40, 42, 44n14, 150, 217
healing, 3–6, 10–12, 15, 16n7, 25, 40, 79, 99–100, 117, 123, 194, 196, 199, 208, 209n7, 231
hero, 22, 122, 125–26, 129, 147, 152, 181; superhero, 122, 124–26, 129–30, 132, 140n5
Hirsch, Marianne, 17n8, 25, 41–42, 72, 109, 181
historiography, 62, 108
Holocaust, 10, 17n9, 108–9, 136, 155, 166, 208n1, 217
Holodomor, 15, 143, 146–48, 150–51, 157, 160n8
human rights, 48–49, 53, 160n14
humor, 44n14, 50, 64, 98, 201
hypersexualization, 57

Igort, 14, 142–62, 231
illustration, 50, 52–53, 56–58, 60–61, 67n14, 103, 149, 151, 154, 156, 186, 196–97, 199, 202, 204
image, 8–10, 13, 15n3, 16n5, 22–25, 27–28, 31–33, 38, 40, 55, 58–60, 63, 69, 72–75, 77,

79, 82, 84, 87–90, 98, 100–101, 107, 111, 132–34, 136–37, 147, 150, 154–56, 159n1, 170–76, 179, 181–82, 182n1, 183nn8–9, 185–87, 190, 195–99, 201–2, 204, 206–8, 211, 215, 220, 222, 226–27
imagination, 8, 16n7, 37, 58, 69, 79, 92, 109, 122–23, 126, 128, 130, 139, 156, 187, 225
incomprehension, 6, 7
India, 6, 14, 80–84
intertextuality, 136
interview, 21, 26, 30, 33, 37, 73, 84, 92, 98–99, 113–16, 118, 134, 143–45, 148–50, 152–55, 166, 169, 176, 178, 187, 195, 202, 204, 208
Iran, 14, 70, 85–89
irony, 31, 33, 35, 44n14, 81, 152, 212, 214–15, 217–19, 222–25, 228
Islamic Fundamentalism, 70, 86–87

justice, 38, 48, 53–54, 59, 62, 64, 129, 168, 200, 203, 223–24

Kashmir, 14, 70, 80–84, 90
Kearney, Richard, 4, 25, 43n10, 99, 122–23
Kim, 3–4, 15n1, 23–26, 44nn11–12
Kirchner, Nestor, 48, 53, 55, 65n1
Kunwu, Li, 14, 97–120, 231

La herencia del coronel (*The Coronel's Inheritance*), 14, 48–68, 231
labor, 70, 72, 75
LaCapra, Dominick, 7, 11–12, 136
layout, 61, 132, 190, 201–2, 204
Levinas, Emmanuel, 154, 215, 221–22, 227
Lex Luthor, 124–28
lieux de mémoire, 10
Lighter Than My Shadow, 15, 188, 191–95, 201, 205–7
liminality, 73, 81, 85, 88
literature, 4, 6–8, 11, 22, 24–25, 29, 34, 43n10, 52, 66n12, 70, 79–80, 91–92, 97–101, 112–17, 118n1, 122, 136, 151, 157, 165–68, 174, 181, 195, 214
Lois Lane, 124, 127–28

Martín, Manuel H., 13–14, 21–47, 230
mass graves, 22, 30, 42n4, 150, 161n17
Maus, 3–4, 10, 41, 56, 81, 99, 107, 109, 155–56, 181, 183n11, 208n1
McCloud, Scott, 5, 16n5, 69, 71, 74–75, 88, 132–33, 177, 186–87, 207
mediation, 75, 89, 143–44, 155–56, 194
memoir, 3–4, 9–10, 12–15, 16n8, 41, 44n11, 69–70, 73, 77, 84–85, 88, 91, 97, 99–100, 102, 106–7, 117, 152, 159n2, 159n4, 161n16, 165, 167–72, 174–76, 178–82, 182nn3–5, 186, 188, 194, 231; autographics, 69–70
memory, 8–10, 17n9, 24–26, 31, 35, 38–40, 44n10, 48–49, 55, 60–63, 70, 72–74, 76–77, 79, 84–85, 88–89, 101, 106–11, 117, 131–32, 136–38, 140n7, 146, 150, 169, 183n9, 183n11, 185, 187, 189–91, 193–95, 201–2, 206, 218, 231; collective, 26, 77, 145, 149–50, 155; historical, 3, 22–23, 25–26, 29–30, 40–42, 42n1, 42nn3–4, 43n5, 44n10, 99
mental health, 201, 208n2, 218
metaphor, 16n7, 22, 29, 35–37, 44n14, 56, 70, 75, 133–34, 205, 217–18
migration, 70, 72–73, 75, 77, 151, 160n14, 185
Millar, Mark, 14, 121–28, 132, 138–40
mise-en-scène, 27, 32, 36
misogyny, 196, 200–201, 208n3
Moore, Alan, 14, 121–23, 126, 128–40
motif, 35, 37, 75–76, 135–36, 215
Munnu: A Boy from Kashmir, 14, 70, 80–85, 90
murder, 15, 56, 67n14, 146, 158, 160n8, 196, 198, 200–202, 208n3, 211–13, 215–22, 224

narrative, 4–8, 10, 12–15, 15n3, 16n6, 23–25, 27–28, 30–32, 35, 38, 40–41, 43n10, 44n12, 49–50, 55–56, 58–59, 62–63, 69–72, 75–79, 83–85, 89–90, 98, 100, 103, 106–9, 111, 113, 117, 121–24, 126, 128–29, 132–36, 139–40, 143, 148–50, 153, 155–58, 160n13, 165–67, 171–77, 179, 181–82, 182n3, 183n7, 185–88, 190,

196–97, 199, 201, 205–8, 230–31. See also graphic narrative
nation, 3, 13–14, 24–25, 30, 54, 56, 77, 80–81, 98, 103, 106, 109–10, 115, 123–26, 128–30, 132, 135, 137–40, 140n5, 143, 146, 148–49, 152, 158, 159n1, 218, 231
Nazis, 23, 131, 149, 213
New York Times, 109, 117–18, 143–44, 146, 175
Nora, Pierre, 10, 62
nostalgia, 100, 111, 113, 121, 129, 134–36, 138–39, 219

Obsessive-Compulsive Disorder (OCD), 9, 165, 169, 172
Oedipal fantasy, 127–28, 140n4
orthodoxy, 7–8
Ôtié, Philippe, 14, 97–120, 231

pain, 3–6, 10, 25, 59, 85, 99, 110, 122, 139, 160n14, 165, 168, 170, 185, 187–88, 190, 194–95, 206, 230
Pakistan, 80–82
pandemic, 91
panels. See frames
paranoia, 124, 126, 129–30, 138–39, 149, 212, 224
paraphilia, 49
patriotism, 104, 106
Persepolis, 3–4, 6, 14, 70, 85–90, 91n2, 99, 107–9, 116, 181
photographs/photography, 8, 22–23, 32, 39–40, 48, 64, 67n14, 133, 149, 154, 156, 158, 161n17, 166, 174–75, 182n1, 183n9, 199, 213, 220, 222
pleasure, 126, 167, 170
postcolonialism, 16n6, 76–77, 86
postmemory, 10, 17n9, 25, 42, 44n11, 72, 109, 181, 183n11
Post-Traumatic Stress Disorder (PTSD), 135–36, 167, 190, 208n2
privacy, 26, 63, 160n12
propaganda, 81, 99, 103, 111–13, 117, 123
Pulitzer Prize, 15, 41, 56, 97, 143, 146–47

purgation, 4, 11–13, 43n10, 91, 148, 160n8, 230–31
purging, 4, 11–13, 43n10, 91, 148, 160n8, 230–31

rape. See under violence, sexual
reader-response, 4–5, 8–10, 15, 27–28, 49–52, 54, 56–65, 69–71, 79, 85, 92, 99–104, 106–7, 111–18, 128, 130, 132, 134, 139, 143–44, 154–57, 173–74, 179, 185–91, 193, 196–97, 199, 202–8, 211–13, 217, 222, 224, 228, 230–31
realism, 8, 24, 31, 33, 56, 58, 204
refugee, 70, 72, 75, 77, 200
release, 11–12, 25, 39–41, 43n10, 73, 87, 99, 123, 128, 188, 190–91, 193–95, 204, 207–8, 212, 215, 223, 225, 228, 230–31
remembrance. See memory
reparation, 65n1, 121, 128
repetition, 6, 12, 17, 121, 123, 132–38, 140n1, 167–68, 171–76, 182, 182n2, 182n5, 217
representation, 5–8, 14–15, 15n3, 16nn6–8, 23–24, 26, 36, 41, 43n9, 48–50, 52–53, 55, 58, 63–64, 66n8, 66n12, 89, 101, 155–56, 166–68, 187, 195, 201, 206, 220, 231
resistance, 43n9, 49, 70, 82, 87, 89, 155
retrospective gaze, 10, 111, 122, 211
Roosevelt, Franklin D., 143–44
Rorschach, 123, 129
Rotoshop, 32
Russia, 6, 122, 125, 130, 142–43, 145–46, 148, 150–53, 158, 158n1, 159n2, 160nn7–8, 160n14, 231

Sabrina, 15, 211–31
Sacco, Joe, 56, 79, 84, 148, 153
Sajad, Malik, 14, 70, 80–85, 90
satire, 50
Satrapi, Marjane, 3–4, 6, 14, 70, 85–90, 91n2, 99, 107–9, 116, 181
Scarry, Elaine, 165–66, 168, 170
Second World War, 23, 98, 147, 150, 157
self-reflexivity, 10, 44n11, 89
sexuality, 170

silence, 3, 5, 9, 21, 29–30, 35, 63, 188, 198, 200–201, 204–5, 230
soundtrack, 27, 29, 35
Soviet Union, 14, 121, 125–26, 142–55, 157–58, 159nn1–6, 160nn8–9, 160n11, 160nn13–14, 161nn15–18
Spain, 3, 6, 14, 21–48; Amnesty Law, 21–22, 30; Historical Memory Law, 22, 42; memory boom, 25, 44n10; moles, 21, 24, 40–41
Spanish Civil War, 3, 14, 21–26, 29–31, 34, 38, 42nn3–4, 43n5, 44nn10–11; Nationalist rebels, 21–23, 42n2, 43n7; Republicans, 21–23, 26–27, 42n2, 43n5, 43n7
Spiegelman, Art, 3–4, 10, 41, 56, 81, 99, 107, 109, 155–56, 181, 183n11, 208n1
Stalin, Joseph, 15, 143–49, 155–58, 159nn3–4, 160n15
Stoian, Maria, 15, 186, 188, 203–5
subversion, 89, 100, 113, 122
suicide, 4, 26, 49, 59, 73, 165–66, 171–73, 176, 179, 216–17, 220–22
superhero, 122, 124–26, 129–30, 132, 140n5
Superman, 14, 121–28, 140, 140n5
Superman Red Son, 14, 121–28, 132, 138–40
survivor, 10, 17n9, 25, 117, 144, 147, 166, 171, 190, 203–4, 207, 209n4, 209n7

taboo, 9, 49, 64
Take It as a Compliment, 15, 186, 188, 203–5
Taylor, Whit, 15, 188–91, 194–95, 199, 201–2, 207
terrorism, 55, 63, 81–82
testimony, 9–10, 12, 15, 21–24, 26, 29–30, 32–34, 36, 38–39, 41–42, 43n10, 44n12, 49, 51, 54, 56, 64–65, 91, 100, 143–45, 149–51, 153–58, 166–68, 170; impossibility of, 15, 165–68, 170–71, 176–77, 182
therapy, 4, 43n10, 79, 187, 190–91, 194–95, 199, 201–2, 206–7
30 años de oscuridad (*30 Years of Darkness*), 13–14, 21–47, 230
Times, The, 109, 117–18, 143–44, 146, 175
Tiananmen Square, 99, 101, 103, 107, 111
torture, 14, 49–51, 54, 56, 59, 63–64, 65n1, 67n14, 213

transcendence, 12–13, 89, 114–15, 123
transcultural identity, 85
translating, 97–99, 103–4, 108, 113, 115, 117–18, 118n1, 142, 158
translation, 97–99, 103–4, 108, 113, 115, 117–18, 118n1, 142, 158
transparency, 56, 170
trauma, 3–15, 15n3, 16nn6–7, 17n9, 21, 24–25, 31, 38, 41–42, 43n10, 44n12, 44n14, 49, 52–56, 61, 63, 70, 72–75, 77–79, 84–85, 87, 90–92, 99–102, 106–11, 123, 126, 130, 132, 135–36, 138–39, 140n2, 143, 148–49, 151, 156, 165–68, 170–72, 175–77, 179, 181–82, 182n2, 185–90, 193–96, 199–202, 206–8, 208nn1–2, 211–12, 214–15, 217–18, 223–25, 230; collective, 3, 5, 13–14, 16n7, 25, 123, 187, 230–32; and comics, 3–6, 8–10, 12–15, 61, 70, 73, 75, 79, 91–92, 166, 195, 201–2, 205, 208, 230–32; narratological, 137; sexual, 15, 185–86, 188, 190–91, 193–94, 196, 199–201, 204–5, 207, 230; studies, 5–8, 11, 13, 16n6, 50, 73, 122–23, 134–36, 165–68, 170–72, 175, 214, 217, 230
Trillo, Carlos, 14, 48–68, 231
Trump, Donald, 23, 142, 212
totalitarianism, 56

Ukraine, 6, 14–15, 122–23, 127–28, 142–62, 231
Ukrainian Notebooks, The, 14, 142–62, 231
Una, 15, 188, 196–202, 206–7
unbelonging, 14, 70, 73, 75–76, 79, 81, 85–87, 89, 90
United States of America, 56, 97, 125–26, 128, 144, 146, 161

Varela, Lucas, 14, 48–68, 231
victim, 15, 15n3, 17n9, 22, 34, 40, 48–49, 51, 53–55, 62–65, 65n1, 66n12, 84, 100, 122, 126, 155, 158n1, 159n2, 161n17, 181, 187–88, 190, 192–96, 198–208, 208n3, 209n4, 212, 217
Vietnam, 6, 14, 70–72, 74, 77, 79–81, 90; war, 14, 77, 80, 122, 129
violence, 14, 42n3, 44n12, 48–50, 53–55, 58–59, 63–65, 82, 84, 89, 103, 118, 131, 147, 149, 151, 155, 189, 196–98, 201, 209n4,

215, 224, 227; sexual, 6, 14–15, 50, 54, 56,
58, 62–63, 190, 193, 196, 199–200, 202–6,
209n5, 209n7, 230–31
voice, 4–5, 9, 88–89, 99, 132–33, 135, 144, 148,
187, 198, 201–2, 204, 206, 208, 224

war, 3, 6, 9, 32, 66n5, 66n13, 70, 73, 75, 77,
88, 98, 117, 129–30, 142, 144–45, 153, 157,
159n7, 160nn14–15, 231; Cold War, 121,
125, 129, 137; Second World War, 23, 98,
147, 150, 157; in Vietnam, 14, 77, 80, 122,
129. *See also* Spanish Civil War
Warsaw Pact, 125
Watchmen, 14, 121–23, 126, 128–40
West, the, 5–6, 15, 86–88, 98–99, 103, 143–44,
147, 151–53, 158, 160n14, 161n16, 208n1
witness, 6, 9–10, 12, 23, 26, 37, 41, 51, 56,
58–59, 62, 65, 69–70, 84, 91–92, 99, 101,
109, 111, 117, 145, 149–51, 154–57, 159n2,
160n13, 168, 174, 181–82, 183n11, 217,
221, 231
witnessing. *See* witness
Wonder Woman, 125
working through, 11–13, 17n10, 121, 134, 137,
139, 212
wounds. *See* trauma
writing, 4, 13–14, 54–55, 65n4, 77, 79, 90–91,
108, 111, 114, 117, 131, 165–66, 202
World War II, 23, 98, 147, 150, 157

YouTube, 34, 182n1